THE SPIRIT

Presence & Power, Sense & Nonsense

DOUGLAS JACOBY

THE SPIRIT
Presence & Power, Sense & Nonsense
Updated Edition. © 1998, 2005, 2010, 2017 by Douglas Jacoby

All Scripture quotations, unless indicated, are taken from the *Holy Bible, New International Version*. Copyright ©1973, 1978, 1984, 2011 by the International Bible Society. Used by permission of Zondervan Publishing House. All rights reserved.

ISBN: 978-1-946800-71-8. Printed in the United States of America.

Interior layout by Toney C. Mulhollan and cover design by Roy Applesamy of Toronto, Canada.

Illumination Publishers titles may be purchased in bulk for classroom instruction, teaching seminars, or sales promotional use. For information, please email paul.ipibooks@me.com.

Illumination Publishers cares deeply about using renewable resources and uses recycled paper whenever possible.

About the author: Since 2003 Dr. Douglas Jacoby has been a freelance teacher and consultant. With degrees from Duke, Harvard, and Drew, he has written over thirty books, recorded over 600 podcasts, and spoken in numerous cities in 120 nations around the world. Douglas is also Adjunct Professor of Bible and Theology at Lincoln Christian University. For more information about his work, speaking schedule, and teaching ministry, view his website at www.DouglasJacoby.com.

There is a free ebook version for all purchases of the hard copy of this book. Go to www.ipibooks.com for details.

www.ipibooks.com

Additional Books by Douglas Jacoby

Answering Skeptics

Life to the Full

A Quick Overview of the Bible

Compelling Evidence for God and the Bible

Jesus and Islam

The Lion Has Roared

Chariots of Fire

Thrive! Using Psalms to Help You Flourish

The Ultimate Bible Quiz Book

What Happens After We Die?

What's the Truth About Heaven and Hell?

Campus Core

Exodus: Night of Redemption

Principle-Centered Parenting

Foundations for Faith: Old Testament Survey

The Faith Unfurled: New Testament Survey

Verdadero Y Razonable

La Aljaba

Contents

Acknowledgments 6

Introduction 7

_____ PART ONE: PRESENCE & POWER _____

INSIDE OUT

1. Am I Filled with the Spirit? 11
   What Controls Me?
2. The Fellowship of the Holy Spirit 16
   It's a Relationship
3. The Spirit of Power 21
   Becoming a Stronger Person—Inside Out!
4. The Spirit of Love 26
   Becoming a More Loving Person—Inside Out!
5. The Spirit of Discipline 34
   Becoming a More Disciplined Person—Inside Out!
6. Am I Stuck with 'Me'? 41
   Character Change—Inside Out!

GIFTS, GRACE, GUIDANCE

7. Open the Toolbox 47
   Gifts of the Spirit
8. The Trillion-Dollar Insurance Policy 55
   Biblical Teaching on Grace and Assurance
9. Led by the Spirit 62
   How the Spirit Guides Disciples

DISTRACTION, INACTION

10. No Nonsense, No Way! 75
    The Superstitious Mind-Set
11. Hot Line to God? 85
    Divine, Psychological or Diabolical?

UPSIDE DOWN

12. A Zeal That's Real 98
    The 'Holy' Spirit
13. 'The Spirit Insists!' 103
    World Evangelism
14. The Spirit of the West 111
    The Curse of Consumerism
15. Free in the Spirit 122
    Freedom False and True

Contents

_____ PART TWO: SENSE & NONSENSE _____

16. Miracles Today? 127
    Pull the Other Leg!

17. Nothing New Under the Sun 136
    Miracles Outside Christianity

18. Miracles in Acts 143
    History, Rhyme and Reason

19. Confirmation of the Word 154
    The Biblical Purposes of Miracles

20. The Hands of an Apostle 162
    How Miraculous Gifts Were Transmitted

21. No Sign Will Be Given! 168
    Jesus: Playing Down the Miraculous

22. Of Angels and Men 175
    Questions About 'Tongues'

23. Correction, Not Direction 185
    Exposition of 1 Corinthians 12-14

24. The 'Warm, Fuzzy Feeling' 206
    Baptism with the Holy Spirit

25. The Unforgivable Sin? 222
    'Who Then Can Be Saved?'

26. Everything You Always Wanted to Know, 1 226
    Difficult Questions About the Spirit

27. Everything You Always Wanted to Know, 2 235
    Problematic Bible Passages

28. Everything You Always Wanted to Know, 3 245
    The Trinity

29. Ghostbusters! 251
    The Spirit and the Occult

APPENDIX

Where Do I Fit In? 258
    Spiritual Gifts Worksheet

Selected Bibliography 259

Glossary 261

Acknowledgments

I begin with the production staff of (formerly) DPI and now IPI, and especially Toney Mulhollan, a tireless worker with whom I had more contact than any other human being, apart from my immediate family, on a daily basis. Second, I confess that I continue to benefit from the flexibility of those who trained me in the Christian ministry. In the twenty years I served as a church worker, they extended me considerable grace, enabling me to engage in many years of study, writing, and creating teaching materials. Third, the feedback of readers and students through the years has also been of enormous help. Fourth, I must acknowledge the nurturing encouragement of fellow writers and friends—a fellowship of minds. I owe a debt to all of them. Above all, I am appreciative of my understanding family and amazingly flexible and supportive wife, Vicki.

Introduction

The Holy Spirit is the most misunderstood and most mysterious member of the godhead. Christians are as intrigued about the workings of the Spirit as we are about the ways of God—for they are one. How the Spirit works in our daily lives has been the subject of thousands of volumes, each with varying mixtures of truth and error. So why another one?

For one, the subject is timeless. We cannot read or write too much about the Spirit. There is a fascination with the Spirit in our day, a thirst which is not easily slaked. Your curiosity—your buying the book—is evidence of the fact. We all want genuine spiritual experience. We want neither to be disappointed nor to be the unwitting victims of religious manipulation or psychological projection. The "genuine article" is in high demand today, as counterfeits proliferate.

There is good news: Your longings will not be left unfulfilled! You can know the truth about the Spirit, and you can know the power of God in your life. And you can experience significant spiritual growth, provided you are willing to pay the price. This will require patience on your part and a willingness to dig deep and often into God's treasure-house of knowledge. Are you prepared for that?

Another reason for this book is the amount of error that saturates the Christian book market! Justifications of unscriptural doctrines and practices, appealing to persons of questionable spiritual stability (2 Peter 3:16), stoke the fires of individuals and groups which have "lost all connection with the Head" (Colossians 2:19). Fortunately, we can know truth from falsehood concerning the Spirit. The only way to confidently divide truth from error is to handle the word of God properly: accurately, reverently, consistently. All temptations to pander to the flesh and feed the soul with spiritual "junk food" must be squarely confronted and vigorously resisted.

At another level, this book needed to be written because of the author's tremendous interest in the Spirit. From initial childhood yearnings to the years "incubating" in the Charismatic Movement to forty years researching and teaching the Scriptures to others, I have probably had more questions of my own than most of my readers—and a determination to find answers. In *The Spirit* I share with you from my own Bible study and from my own experience(s).

Our spiritual appetite is large. May God enable us to "eat" well, shunning the "fast food" and lingering long over first the milk, then the meat, which he has graciously provided us.

Readers, please note that *The Spirit* is a complete revision of my 1987 work, *The Powerful Delusion,* which is no longer in print. The earlier book focused primarily on erroneous views concerning the Holy Spirit, and was rather negative in tone, with little on the actual working of the Spirit in the lives of Christians. Even so, about two-thirds of *The Powerful Delusion* was rewritten and incorporated into *The Spirit,* accounting for about half of the new book. The remainder of *The Spirit* is new material.

Examining the Scriptures Afresh

Sometimes we read and study, not really in order to learn, but to grind our axe, prove our point, or more forcefully defend a preconceived position. As William James astutely put it, "A great many people think they are thinking when they are only rearranging their prejudices." Of course no one, author included, can become fully free of prejudices and preconceptions. But all of us can approach the Spirit of God afresh with humble and eager hearts.

I am asking you (the reader) to try to shed preconceptions as you read this book. There are positions herein which will delight and inform, yet others which may well perplex or even unnerve. All I ask is that you approach the material with an open mind, that you give it a "fair shake."

Please don't read this book if your mind is already set on the subject. Save your time and pass it on to someone who may appreciate it. I do hope, however, that you will make the effort to read, reflect, and as a result, be refreshed.

The Flow

Part One begins with the day-to-day work of the Spirit in our lives, as the first fifteen chapters are devoted principally to the practicals. Then there is a shift. In Part Two you will find material more technical in nature, addressing the modern interest in miracles and preoccupation with them we find in the Neo-pentecostal Movement. That is, there is a lot of nonsense (faulty biblical interpretation) and pretense (posturing as spiritual persons in unbiblical ways), and this needs to be addressed. This material was originally projected as appendixes until its length caused my editors to recommend a change.

This book is certainly not the final word on the Holy Spirit. It does not answer every question that can be asked. We can no more understand everything about the Spirit than we can understand everything about God and his love (Ephesians 3:19). However, God has seen fit to reveal to us much truth that we *can* understand. My prayer is that this book will lead you deeper into that truth. Let's jump straight in!

—Douglas Jacoby
Marietta, Georgia

PART ONE

Presence & Power: The Spirit in Us

God has not left his people without help. He has sent the Holy Spirit into our lives. In Part One you will see how the Holy Spirit is both personal and practical—in particular, how the Spirit brings change, freedom and guidance.

Inside Out

The Holy Spirit is given by God to change us—from the inside out! Behavior modification is not enough. Christianity is not just what we do; it's what we are. When the inside is clean, the outside will be clean as well (Matthew 23:26).

In this section we will highlight the remarkable changes that should be part and parcel of the life of any disciple of Jesus Christ.

1. Am I Filled with the Spirit?
What Controls Me?

We are all familiar with the notion of "control." We have remote controls for everything—garage door openers, stereo systems, televisions and computer games. But at the personal level, we are very afraid of "being controlled." The Morality Revolution of the '60s and '70s taught some of us to fear the awful control (and consequences) of drugs, promiscuity and war. The '80s and '90s brought to our attention the hazards of being controlled by unbridled spending (personal and national), crime, racism, extremist apocalyptic groups and pernicious viruses.

As we launch out into the twenty-first century, we are reaping collectively what we have sown. Perhaps the greatest hindrance to the gospel today is the "integrity gap." Whom can we trust? Everyone has disappointed us: politicians, parents, police, Hollywood idols, sports figures—and we have disappointed ourselves, too. The question is subtly shifting from "What is true?" to "Is it even possible to live something out if it is true?"[1]

How much we as a culture have learned our lesson is debatable, but if the individualism of the "2000s man" and the "2000s woman" is any indication, we fear groups and are having increasing difficulty trusting anyone but ourselves. Yet there is a paradox here. For despite our fear of control, no one can be free of it. As the apostle Peter put it, "A man is a slave to whatever has mastered him" (2 Peter 2:19).[2] Every one of us is controlled by something: fear, family, spouse or girl- or boyfriend, creditors, alcohol, love of money or perhaps the career track. The thing that controls us is that which fills us and defines our life. You are "filled" with something. What is it?

Filled with a Fluid?

The Spirit is not a fluid, although it may be "poured out" (Acts 2:17) and is often compared to water (John 7:38-39). No, the Spirit is not a liquid that "tops up" our reservoirs of faith when we go to church or have a quiet time! It is clear from the Scriptures that the Spirit is personal. Theologians call the Holy Spirit the third person of the trinity. For me the trinity concept is quite hard to grasp, especially when we talk about three separate persons.[3] "Person" is from the Latin *persona*, which means "mask, part, character," as in the characters of a play.[4] The Spirit, though certainly personal, is not a separate person in the modern sense of the word, "an individual human being."[5] And of course this does not mean that God is somehow "pretending," like an actor. Let's check out the Oxford English Dictionary's definition of the Spirit:

Spirit [of God]: The active essence or essential power of the Deity, conceived as a creative, animating, or inspiring influence.

We all desire, deep down, to be filled with the Spirit—the very Spirit of God, because we all want to be creative, animated and inspired! After all, who wants to be dull, dragging, bored and boring?

Jesus was filled with the Spirit. As a man he was more filled with the Spirit than any other individual on the planet. We must aim to live as he lived and aim to live by the power by which he lived—the power of the Spirit.

Alien Invasion?

There have been many "alien" movies over the years. Some concern extraterrestrial invasion, others a more personal invasion, as some multitentacled organism takes over the body of its unwitting host—growing and eventually exploding out of it! It is right to speak of God's power. Yet this is in no way an alien invasion, the creature taking us over, becoming more and more demanding, until we are only incidental to his purposes. No, God wants to dwell in us as an invited and welcomed guest.

Yes, God is powerful, but he[6] is also intimately personal. He resides in the hearts of his children (John 14), not as some alien creature, but as love incarnate.

'Spirit Filled'?

Here is a dilemma: When many of us hear the words "Spirit filled," images of hooting, hollering and rolling on the floor may come to mind. Would we possibly lose control, make a scene and disgrace ourselves if we were to become "Spirit-filled Christians"? We are turned off by the very words. Yet despite some modern-day excesses, we want to follow the Bible—and being filled with the Spirit[7] is "Bible." Don't be afraid of the terminology; in fact we have no right to dispense with it. Unless we allow the Spirit of God to dwell in us richly, we will never know Christ as we were meant to know him or reach our potential as disciples of Jesus Christ.

Be very careful, then, how you live—not as unwise but as wise, making the most of every opportunity, because the days are evil. Therefore do not be foolish, but understand what the Lord's will is. Do not get drunk on wine, which leads to debauchery. Instead, be filled with the Spirit (Ephesians 5:15-18).

If someone is "filled" with wine, that person has come "under the influence" (or control) of it. Paul charges the disciples in Ephesus to "be filled with the Spirit." As he also points out, our decision to be filled with the Spirit has an effect on how we use our time—precious and limited commodity that it is.

When I was writing this chapter, my wife was away at a conference in London. So who was taking care of the kids and doing all the cooking? I cook more (much more) in one week when I "have to" than in all the rest of the year when Vicki is here. Fortunately, she enjoys cooking and is very good at it. When Vicki prepares the meal, the house is filled with the smell of Indian, Thai, Chinese or perhaps Malaysian cooking (our favorite). When I cook, on the other hand, the house is "filled" with the smell of frozen dinners thawing in the oven, or maybe the sticky vapors of eggs and blackened bacon!

What does this have to do with the Spirit? A lot. When Vicki is in the kitchen, we know it: Our home is filled with the sweet smell of hot curry, and we are filled with anticipation thinking of the feast to come. When you are filled with something, that something characterizes you. Being filled with the Spirit of God means we are filled with God, and we make people think about God. They smell the aroma of life (2 Corinthians 2: 14-16). When we are Spirit-filled, people will know it.

Quite simply, being "filled with the Spirit" means being spiritual. Spiritual, Christlike, godly—thus all "persons" of the trinity are present in our lives.

How to Become Spirit Filled

As soon as we are born again, we are filled with the Spirit. Repentance and baptism bring not only forgiveness of sin, but the gift of the Spirit. God "moves in" to our heart (John 14:23). We are cleansed of an old life and filled up with the source of a new life.[8] As an example, Acts 9:17 shows us that Paul (Saul) was to be filled with the Spirit the moment he became a Christian.

However, the phrase "filled with the Spirit" in Scripture refers not to conversion but to (a) spirituality—see Ephesians 5, above—or (b) increased holiness in response to prayer or an urgent situation. In Ephesians the verb Paul used helps us: (1) It is an imperative. That means it is a command. Being filled with the Spirit is not an option. (2) It is in the "present/progressive" tense, which in Greek carries the idea of continuous action. Thus, we are to keep on being filled with the Spirit again and again. It is not a one-time thing.

We find the second idea about being filled with the Spirit in Acts 4. Peter and John have been released from the Sanhedrin as persecution is mounting in the early days of the Christian faith.

> When they heard this, they raised their voices together in prayer to God…. "Now, Lord, consider their threats and enable your servants to speak your word with great boldness. Stretch out your hand to heal and perform miraculous signs and wonders through the name of your holy servant Jesus." After they prayed, the place where they were meeting was shaken. And they were all filled with the Holy Spirit and spoke the word of God boldly (Acts 4:24-31).

The group did not become Christians after the prayer; they already were. But they were filled with the Holy Spirit. God took firmer, deeper, more life-changing control because they were not afraid to let him. The outcome: fervent evangelism.[9] Are you willing to let God take control? Can you trust that much? Lord, increase our faith! (Luke 17:5).

False Ideas

Many people teach that "Spirit-filled" means you have miraculous abilities, speak in "tongues" or have a "hot line" to God. They think that through "Spirit baptism" you ascend to a higher level, becoming a more serious follower of Jesus. There are serious problems with this view, however. For one, the Bible says John the Baptist was Spirit-filled before birth (Luke 1:15), and yet he never performed a miracle (John 10:41).

In considering the second idea, two tiers of commitment is hardly the New Testament way. The ground is level at the foot of the Cross, and those who want to come after Jesus must each deny themselves and surrender the controls (Luke 9:23-26). There are more mature and less mature disciples, but never two levels of commitment.[10]

Being Spirit-filled is not a higher level of awareness for advanced Christians but the natural result of following the Spirit in our lives instead of the flesh. It is not so much the ultimate experience as it is the challenge of every new day. In my experience, the more I have let God control my life, the more order, peace and success I have known. When I have resisted God's control, my life has gone out of control!

I Surrender All

Inside-out change is attainable with the Holy Spirit. The Spirit never forces us; it's up to you and me to trust the Lord, let him fill us and control us, and surrender all we have and are (Luke 14:33).

In chapters 3 through 5 we will explore three areas of our lives that can begin to change immediately once we have decided to allow God's Spirit to fill us. At the end of each chapter you will find a few thought-provoking questions. After all, as Socrates said, "The unexamined life is not worth living."[11]

QUESTIONS FOR THOUGHT

- *What influences are controlling me?*
- *Am I filled with the Spirit? Is that how others would describe me?*
- *Are there parts of my life over which I am consciously refusing to let the Spirit gain control?*
- *Am I willing to pray, "God in heaven, fill me with your Spirit; take control and use me as you will"?*

_____ NOTES _____

1. See Kevin Graham Ford, *Jesus for a New Generation* (Downers Grove: InterVarsity Press, 1995); also Robert Wuthnow, *Christianity in the 21st Century: Reflections on the Challenges Ahead,* (New York: Oxford University Press, 1993).

2. See also Romans 6:15-22.

3. Early Christianity was, not surprisingly, misunderstood by some as being "tritheism": three gods! This is all the more understandable when we realize that many ancient religions had "trinities" among their pagan gods and goddesses.

4. Theatergoers, think about the term *Dramatis personae.*

5. You will find a somewhat more technical discussion of the Spirit in Chapter 26.

6. Throughout the book God is referred to by the masculine pronoun, for that is appropriate. Feminism decries this, yet its objections are neither biblical nor consistent. Where is the movement campaigning for the "femininity" of Satan? No one seems to mind that we consistently conceive of the devil as a "he"!

7. The terminology appears some ten times in the New Testament alone.

8. Luke 11:24-26 shows us that after the "housecleaning" we need to guard ourselves against the hollow, empty faith which is an invitation to Satan to "repossess" our lives! Being filled with the Spirit will give the adversary no opportunity.

9. More to come in Chapter 13.

10. Commitment is one thing, maturity another altogether. The transition from worldliness to spirituality, from being carnal to spiritual (1 Corinthians 3:1-4), comes with Christian growth. Yet there were never two options with Christ: more committed and less committed. Of course we take it higher as our roots grow deeper. The option, however, is to follow or not to follow! (John 6:60-69).

11. The words of Socrates (469-399 BC), as reported in Plato, *Apology*, 38a.

2. The Fellowship of the Holy Spirit
It's a Relationship

Before we are finished with this examination of the Spirit's work in the lives of disciples, we will address many unbiblical teachings that have arisen over the years. We will particularly be concerned with a tendency for subjectivism to run amuck when people start talking about how the Spirit moves. But we must be careful here not to overreact. A relationship with the Spirit is just that—a relationship. Allowing the Spirit to work in our lives is not solely a matter of careful thinking and the following of certain propositions. While not excluding either of those, we are still involved here with something that is warm, personal, close and reassuring.

Divine Intimacy

In my marriage I am committed to certain principles. They are from the Scriptures, and I have seen again and again that they are powerful. I also have to think and reason to keep my marriage growing. Being unreasonable and illogical are the sources of much frustration in marriages. But there is still something in my marriage that goes beyond principles and clear thinking. The best word to describe it is "intimacy." There is a shared life. There is deep awareness that Vicki is with me, and I am with her. There is confidence that she is for me and will be with me through whatever comes.

As we examine the Scriptures, we see that many of them describe our relationship with the Spirit in terms very much like these. It is not surprising. To know the Spirit is to know God. To know the Spirit is to know Christ. And our relationship with God and Christ are described in the most familiar and personal terms. God is King but to us he is also Father, or *Abba*, to be more specific.[1] Jesus is Lord, but he also wants us to know him as a friend.

We are describing in this section of the book an inside-out change—the only kind God is interested in. But most of us know that nothing helps people change from the inside like a heart-to-heart relationship. Take an adolescent who is surly, rebellious and heartless. Put him in a strict structure, and you may change some of his behavior, but nothing will help him change from the inside out like a relationship with someone who can become his friend and his hero— someone who finally gets to his heart.

The primary way, then, that the Spirit changes us is through this relationship with us. Like all relationships, there is an element in it that defies description (a bit frustrating to us logical types). Perhaps only the poets and songwriters can really do it justice.

Profound Mystery

While our relationship with the Spirit is certainly not some vague, undefined thing that you can just make to be whatever you want it to be, it is one that humbles and awes us (or should). We cannot totally analyze and understand how he is in us, how he gives us power, how he reshapes our characters; nor can we predict how he is going to move and where he is going to lead us next. To be sure, our relationship with the Spirit is not all mystery and enigma. He has revealed much to us that our minds can grasp quite well, but when all is said and done, there is still an element of mystery that we will not—and need not—remove. In the midst of his discussion of the husband-wife relationship, which he parallels to Christ and the church, Paul concludes by saying:

> "For this reason a man will leave his father and mother and be united to his wife, and the two will become one flesh." This is a profound mystery—but I am talking about Christ and the church (Ephesians 5:31-32).

The most intimate relationships are a profound mystery. They have a depth to them that is beyond description. They have an impact on us that is beyond logic and rationality. The most intimate relationship of all is that between God and his people, between the disciple and his Lord, between the Spirit and the Christian. When you deeply love someone and are deeply committed to them, and when they deeply love you and are committed to you, *and when they have the power that called the world into being,* good things happen. Some of these things may be hardly recognizable, but some will be "immeasurably more than all we ask or imagine" (Ephesians 3:20).

It is from this relationship that will come the changes described in the next few chapters. Without this relationship we are just into behavior modification.

Father and Son—and More

Perhaps no passage in the New Testament describes this intimate relationship any more than Romans 8:15-17. In this key chapter on life in the Spirit, Paul writes:

> For you did not receive a spirit that makes you a slave again to fear, but you received the Spirit of sonship. And by him we cry, "Abba, Father." The Spirit himself testifies with our spirit that we are God's children.
>
> Now if we are children, then we are heirs—heirs of God and co-heirs with Christ, if indeed we share in his sufferings in order that we may also share in his glory.

The short passage literally overflows with the language of intimate relationship. (1) You received the Spirit of sonship. The Spirit that enters into you adopts you into the family. You are no longer a slave or a hired servant; you are a child (and as we see later, an heir). (2) By him (the Spirit) we cry, "Abba, Father." It's pronounced Abbá (stress on second syllable). The Spirit within us cries out to God using the most intimate word that could be used.[2] (3) The Spirit testifies with our spirits that we are the children of God. In some fashion beyond scientific examination, the Spirit unites himself with our spirit and produces conviction that we are the children of God and with that comes the confidence that we are co-heirs with Christ himself. It is also possible that the testimony referred to is the evidence of Christ in our personal lifestyles.

Who among us can completely understand or grasp all of this? But what we can grasp is that God is committed to being in us, with us and available to us. And who among us is not refreshed, encouraged, inspired and compelled by this knowledge?

Glimpses from the Word

We have a book (The Bible), and we must still read it and obey it. Without it we will wander off into the murky shadows of subjectivism and self-deception. But we have something more now than a book. Now we serve, Paul says, "in the new way of the Spirit, and not in the old way of the written code" (Romans 7:6). We have the book, but we also have the relationship that empowers us to follow the book.

A host of passages describe the refreshing, empowering, supportive relationship we can enjoy with the Spirit. Here are just a few:

> "Whoever believes in me, as the Scripture has said, streams of living water will flow from within him." By this he meant the Spirit, whom those who believed in him were later to receive (John 7:38-39a).

> And hope does not disappoint us, because God has poured out his love

into our hearts by the Holy Spirit, whom he has given us (Romans 5:5). May the God of hope fill you with all joy and peace as you trust in him, so that you may overflow with hope by the power of the Holy Spirit (Romans 15:13).

You show that you are a letter from Christ, the result of our ministry, written not with ink but with the Spirit of the living God, not on tablets of stone but on tablets of human hearts (2 Corinthians 3:3).

If you are insulted because of the name of Christ, you are blessed, for the Spirit of glory and of God rests on you (1 Peter 4:14).

But you, dear friends, build yourselves up in your most holy faith and pray in the Holy Spirit (Jude 20).

Each of these passages communicates how closely connected the disciple is to the Spirit, and each communicates that the Spirit is at work in our lives. As we go on in succeeding chapters to talk about those things that the Spirit seeks to produce in us, we must keep in mind that it all springs from this relationship. Without the relationship, we are right back to the old way of the written code (exactly what Paul was concerned was going to happen to the Galatians).

In the same way, the Spirit helps us in our weakness. We do not know what we ought to pray for, but the Spirit himself intercedes for us with groans that words cannot express. And he who searches our hearts knows the mind of the Spirit, because the Spirit intercedes for the saints in accordance with God's will (Romans 8:26-27).

This passage is particularly noteworthy. (1) It reminds us that in our weakness the Spirit does not condemn us but helps us. (2) It shows that a primary work of the Spirit is to help us pray (and have an intimate connection with God). (3) The passage also shows us what the Spirit's primary objective always is: to get us to the will of God. His work is not to do something very showy or grandiose, but to help us do God's will (which the Spirit has revealed through the Word).

This is what it means to have fellowship with the Holy Spirit. This is why the apostle Paul ends one of his most personal letters by saying:

May the grace of the Lord Jesus Christ, and the love of God, and the fellowship of the Holy Spirit be with you all (2 Corinthians 13:14).

QUESTIONS FOR THOUGHT

- *How is your intimacy in relationships generally? Do you see how this affects your relationship with God and his Spirit?*

- *A neglect of the Spirit is really a neglect of God himself. Is the verse "God is spirit" (John 4:24) taking on fresh meaning in your life?*

- *What are you doing to nourish your intimacy with God and his Spirit?*

_____ NOTES _____

1. See Mark 14:36, Romans 8:15, Galatians 4:6.

2. William Barclay adds much insight to this discussion with these comments from his book *The Mind of Jesus:* "When we come finally to examine Jesus' conception of the fatherhood of God, we meet with two most significant and illuminating facts.

"(a) There is the *extraordinary rarity* with which Jesus uses the name 'Father,' as applied to God, at all. In Mark, the earliest of the Gospels, Jesus calls God 'Father' four times (Mark 8:38; 11.25; 13.32; 14.36). Further, in Mark Jesus does not call God 'Father' at all until after Peter's confession at Caesarea Philippi, and then he only does so within the circle of the disciples. There is only one conclusion to be drawn from this. To Jesus, to call God Father was no theological commonplace; it was something so sacred that he could hardly speak of it at all in public; and, when he did speak of it, it was only in the presence of those who, at least to some extent, understood.

"(b) There is the *extraordinary intimacy* which Jesus put into the term. Jesus called God *'Abba,* Father' (Mark 14.36). As Jeremias points out, there is not even the remotest parallel to this in all Jewish literature. *Abba,* like the modern Arabic *jaba,* is the word used by a young child to his father. It is completely untranslatable. Any attempt to put it into English ends in bathos or grotesqueness. It is a word which no one has ever ventured to use in addressing.

"For Jesus the fatherhood of God was something of almost inexpressible sacredness, and it was something that he came to say about God in his relationship with men" (William Barclay, *The Mind of Jesus* [New York: Harper & Row, 1960], 117).

3. The Spirit of Power
Becoming a Stronger Person—Inside Out!

We have clearly seen that every one of us needs to be filled with the Spirit. God calls for it. Now let's get practical. We saw in the last chapter that the Spirit is intensely personal. Now we want to see how he is intensely practical. As Paul wrote to Timothy,

> For God did not give us a spirit of timidity, but a spirit of power, of love and of self-discipline. So do not be ashamed to testify about our Lord, or ashamed of me his prisoner. But join with me in suffering for the gospel, by the power of God, who has saved us and called us to a holy life—not because of anything we have done but because of his own purpose and grace. This grace was given us in Christ Jesus before the beginning of time (2 Timothy 1:7-9).

The presence of the Spirit in our lives means we will be different people: different from the world around us, but also different from our "old selves." If we never change, it can only mean that the Spirit is being grieved (Ephesians 4:30).[1] This chapter and the next two explore three essential attributes of the Holy Spirit: power, love and self-discipline. Let us give our attention to each attribute in turn. Power is the first.

Power Check!

Let's do a power check (just in case you are powerful enough to be a "lone ranger" who is already sufficiently strong to carry out the will of God in this world).

- To start with, how is your physical strength? Can you run a marathon?
- Would you survive the Iron Man competition? (I wouldn't!)
- How's your political clout? Are you a senator or a mayor? Do the powers that be sit up and listen when you speak? Chances are, you have a little more political power than the power of one vote.
- How about your intellectual power? Think you might be in line to receive a Nobel prize in recognition of your brilliant contributions to mankind?
- Or shall we discuss your economic power? No?
- Well, how's your emotional strength? Do you crack under pressure?

- Next, check your stamina, your focus: How many plates can you spin at the same time without dropping any? How hard can you work without complaining about it or calling attention to the difficulty?

If you passed all these tests, what kind of relationship power do you have: Do you have the power to make your marriage work, the power to have great relationships with your children, the power to build great friendships?

Hopefully somewhere along the line, you got the point. You are weak; we are all weak. Not many of us are powerful, influential, noble or mighty (1 Corinthians 1:26).[2] Even those who have worldly power have great weakness at the same time. But with the Holy Spirit, we are equipped to accomplish something significant and lasting. That's because the power we have at our disposal—really, when we are at God's disposal—is resurrection power.

Resurrection Power

You have heard of electric power, solar power, gas power, geothermal power and nuclear power. But power of the Spirit leaves its competitors in the dust. The power of the Spirit is the power that raised Jesus from the dead (Romans 8:11). Resurrection power is incomparable! It is the greatest power on earth, and it blows away any power form or source you may have heard of before. Paul's prayer for the Ephesians can be our own prayer—that God give us the strength to keep going:

> I pray also that the eyes of your heart may be enlightened in order that you may know the hope to which he has called you, the riches of his glorious inheritance in the saints, and his incomparably great power for us who believe. That power is like the working of his mighty strength, which he exerted in Christ when he raised him from the dead and seated him at his right hand in the heavenly realms (Ephesians 1:18-20).

Resurrection power not only empowers us to change from the inside out; it enables us to share our faith unashamedly (2 Timothy 1:8). This is the power that can animate, refresh and motivate you to walk in the steps of Jesus without tiring, run the race without faltering, and soar on wings like eagles.

Powerless Christianity

In 2 Timothy 3 Paul describes the godlessness that characterizes our society. He is talking about people who profess to be religious. Religion may have a bad name, but true religion, which matches up to the Scriptures, is a good thing. Those who "have a form of godliness but deny its power" are false believers (2 Timothy 3:5). They are not led by the Spirit, since they find the flesh and the material world more appealing (Romans 8:12-14, 1 John 2:15-17).

Imagine trying to vacuum a whole house without the unit being plugged in! You'd be exhausted and dripping sweat from all that pushing and pulling of the vacuum cleaner. I suppose there would be some results—it will have swept up some dust. But is that the way to clean house? Or, men, picture yourself trying to shave with an electric razor and no power! Your face would probably look like Legion's before he met the Lord! (Mark 5:5). No, no, no—this is not God's plan for us! "Plug in" and let the Spirit—God's power—energize you!

Christianity was never meant to be futile and frustrating. His commands are not burdensome, but relatively "light" (1 John 5:3, Matthew 11:30). That's true not because they are easy, but because we are given the power to fulfill them. It is miserable to go through the motions of godliness while denying the power.

Interior Power

The real power of Christianity comes from deep within us. This is not some inner psychic power—as some Eastern religions teach—which we need only tap into. We do not share in God's divine nature by virtue of being alive, but only when we become Christians (2 Peter 1:3-4 [below]). Most religions vainly look to a power either "beyond" or innately "within." You are supposed to "summon it up" or "coax it out." Not so with the Holy Spirit! We are not compelled to wrest power from God—he gives it to us whenever we require it.

> His divine power has given us everything we need for life and godliness through our knowledge of him who called us by his own glory and goodness. Through these he has given us his very great and precious promises, so that through them you may participate in the divine nature and escape the corruption in the world caused by evil desires (2 Peter 1:3-4).

The power source is actually external—from God, not ourselves. It becomes internal insofar as God's Spirit dwells in our hearts (the "indwelling"). For example, our sun is far hotter at the core than on the exterior. Did you know that, at its surface, the sun is normally "only" a few thousand degrees centigrade? But the interior is millions of degrees hot. In the case of the sun, the power is within, at the center of this enormous ball of gas. Think about the sun as you read this passage about the indwelling of the Holy Spirit within disciples:

I pray that out of his glorious riches he may strengthen you with power through his Spirit in your inner being, so that Christ may dwell in your hearts through faith. And I pray that you, being rooted and established in love, may have power, together with all the saints, to grasp how wide and long and high and deep is the love of Christ, and to know this love that surpasses knowledge—that you may be filled to the measure of all the fullness of God. Now to him who is able to do immeasurably more than all we ask or imagine, according to his power that is at work within us, to him be glory in the church and in Christ Jesus throughout all generations, for ever and ever! Amen (Ephesians 3:16-21).

This powerful passage teaches us a lot about the power of the Spirit:

- The strengthening takes place in our "inner being." While he does not miraculously build up our muscle tissue, we do receive actual strength through the Spirit. Naturally, this extra energy spills over into our physical dynamism and stamina. Are you experiencing this measure of vim and vigor?
- As the Spirit dwells in us, Christ dwells in us. (No, we aren't indwelled by four spirits—ours, the Father's, and the Son's, in addition to the Holy Spirit. See Romans 8:9-11 for another example of how interchangeable references to God, Christ and the Spirit are.)
- We receive power to know (experience) the love of Christ. That really keeps you going!
- With the incomparable power of his Spirit, God can do immeasurably more than we even dream of. Let's put an end to small thinking. In context, Paul was probably referring to the Spirit bringing Jews and Gentiles together (Ephesians 2:14-22). That was amazing, but also was a sign of other great things that can be done.
- The power is at work within us, through the church, in Christ. We are not meant to "fly solo." We are to be "together with all the saints." Christianity is a team sport.
- This is God's plan for every generation of disciples: for you, your children and even your grandchildren! And there's no need to improve the plan; why try to improve on perfection?

Power Outage?

God wants all of us to lead dynamic Christian lives, for that is the only way we will persevere in our mission and evangelize the world. Moreover, lives that are not dynamic stagnate, and those who lead them tend to fall away from the faith. Are you suffering from power outages? Don't blame God! Plug into the power source; stop trying to do it alone.

In your heart, do you really desire a powerful Christian life? As we have seen, that is one of the main activities of the Spirit. It is always much easier to say an enthusiastic (but unrepentant) "Amen!" than it is to truly change. Here are just three of the areas where God will bless us with extra energy and motivation when we utilize the power of the Spirit:

- Energy to get up in the morning—the first time! See the snooze button for what it is: an electronically sanctioned excuse—straight from Satan—to get your day off course as early as possible!
- Energy to maintain balance and perspective through the hardships the day is sure to bring. Reactionary people are not spiritually strong people. Jesus was not reactionary.
- Energy to remain outward focused. You will definitely need the Spirit to keep on loving! (But then, that's the subject of the next chapter.)

StrongerThan Ever

It is time to take it higher, to become spiritually stronger than you have ever been before. Decide today to become a stronger person, from the inside out!

QUESTIONS FOR THOUGHT

- *Can it be said that I have a powerful, evangelistic lifestyle? Am I spiritually anemic, or energetic?*

- *Do others view me as dynamic? Am I an upward call to other disciples of Jesus? To outsiders?*

- *Do I fear that if I totally trust God to work in me powerfully, I won't have enough time, resources or energy for the rest of my life?*

_____ NOTES _____

1. The context of Ephesians 4:30 is our relationships with others. If we are not living in harmony with others, we are grieving the Spirit, who desires our unity, cooperation and mutual success. (Not to say that there are no other ways to grieve the Spirit; but that is the context of the passage.)

2. Hopefully you don't go around expecting everyone to call you "the Great Power!" (Acts 8:10).

4. The Spirit of Love
Becoming a More Loving Person—Inside Out!

Returning to the text at hand, 2 Timothy 1:7, we read that God gave us "a spirit of power, of love and of self-discipline." Second in the series is the quality of love. Love is vital because without love, power is harsh, noisy and unattractive. Without the love of the Spirit working in our lives, power easily degenerates, making us hard, careless, domineering—like resounding gongs or clanging cymbals (1 Corinthians 13:1). The spirit of love is definitely not a feeling. Feelings are usually part of love, but love is much more than a feeling; it is a commitment. The Bible shows us that the essence of love is sacrifice. When you love someone, you are willing to sacrifice for that person.

Are you a loving person? (Not your answer to the question—but what would others say at home, or on the job, or even the strangers you reach out to?) We need the Spirit of Christ in our hearts if we are going to last long in the kingdom of God. The Bible tells us that God has "poured" his love into our hearts:

> Not only so, but we also rejoice in our sufferings, because we know that suffering produces perseverance; perseverance, character; and character, hope. And hope does not disappoint us, because God has poured out his love into our hearts by the Holy Spirit, whom he has given us (Romans 5:3-5).[1]

God didn't just sprinkle a little love on us when we were saved; he poured it on through the Holy Spirit! Did you know that? You see, our hearts can be as full of his love as we are willing. Jesus Christ's heart was filled to overflowing, wasn't it? That's why, as we follow in his steps, our own peace and happiness increase—more and more every year we are Christians.

Our most important relationships as disciples are summed up by the acronym JOY. That stands for Jesus first; Others second; Yourself last. This is an excellent mnemonic for keeping our priorities straight. In this chapter, however, we will break it down and become more specific still.

God is Love

God is love, but he is also invisible.[2] It can be hard to give your heart to invisible beings, to abstract powers. (I find it hard enough to love those whom I can see!) Since God is a spiritual being, we definitely need spiritual help to love him. As with all relationships, there are times when it is easier to love God than others. One thing is certain: How we may be feeling at the moment toward God tells us a great deal about our hearts, but nothing about his. As someone said, "When God seems distant, guess who moved?"

The Spirit of God is in our hearts moving us to love God more deeply. When we wake up in the morning, how determined are we to refresh our hearts and minds in life-changing Bible study and prayer? Can we truly say, with the man after God's own heart,[3] "I love you, O Lord, my strength"? (Psalm 18:1). If our relationship with God is drudgery, if the sense of wonder has departed and the flames of love have died down, watch out! They can certainly be rekindled: Fan them into flame (2 Timothy 1:6).

Loving Spouse and Children

We need to work at love. "Spontaneity" is a catchword these days, but the greater part of love has little to do with spontaneity and everything to do with commitment through thick and thin.

I remember well standing next to my bride-to-be. The minister stated that one day hard times would come, and then I would need to sacrifice in order to put my wife's needs first. In my head I knew he was right, but in my heart I refused to believe that staying in love would ever cease to be anything but easy. Maybe others would struggle, but not me. (Surely, I was an exception!) But he was right. A day was coming and did come when my own pigheadedness prevented me from appreciating that beautiful bride I stood beside and vowed always to love, honor and cherish. Love is work![4] Remember: It is a decision to put the other person first, not a feeling of euphoria.

> Likewise, teach the older women to be reverent in the way they live, not to be slanderers or addicted to much wine, but to teach what is good. Then they can train the younger women to love their husbands and children (Titus 2:3-4).

This makes sense of the mysterious Titus 2:4. As a younger Christian, I wondered why anyone would need "training" to love her (or his) spouse and children. But then it dawned on me: Love is work. The nature of love is sacrifice. Since when did self-sacrifice come easy to anyone? If even Jesus had to forfeit his own preferences to lay down his life for us (Matthew 26: 36-46), how much more are we going to struggle from time to time?

Wives, have you been married long enough that you see your need for training to love your husband? How about the kids? Do they get on your nerves sometimes? (It's okay to say yes; it could be therapeutic!) Men, are you receiving training from an older couple so you can love your wife and children in a Christlike way? Or are you neglecting them? (Are you constantly forgetting family devotionals and discipling times with the kids? Is your wife an upward call because you are not as spiritual as she?)

How spiritual is your home? If you cannot honestly say that it is, then to that extent the Spirit is not in control. Don't give up on God; his Spirit will transform all your relationships, most importantly those at home. The next topic is closely related: loving those we grew up with.

Loving Close Relations

We need the Spirit's help in loving our relations (parents, grandparents, etc.). Often when we become Christians we fail to see all the positive things that we have received from our families. We tend to "reinterpret" the past in a negative light, remembering the things that happened to us when we were younger which hurt us or led to our not becoming disciples sooner. We become fixated on "baggage." But we forget all the blessings—material and otherwise—that God has given us through our families (e.g. the countless times mother or father stayed up with a sick child; their teaching us just about everything we knew in the earlier years; their support through tough times). This is not right!

Honoring, respecting, and caring for our families of origin is incredibly important in God's will (Exodus 20:12, 1 Timothy 5:4). The Scriptures do not distinguish between "good" and "bad" parenting where honor and respect are due. In fact, they give the benefit of the doubt (Hebrews 12:9–10). If you feel you have been wronged—by a parent, uncle, older brother, whoever—the Spirit will, in time, allow you to work it through and totally "let go." If you do not let go and you harbor bitterness, your heart will harden, and you will not make it to heaven (Hebrews 12:15).[5] This is not my opinion—Jesus said so himself (Matthew 6:1–15). And besides, if you are not willing to forgive, do you really think your children will forgive you for the mistakes you make in raising them? Your heart and actions are the example they are watching and, in all likelihood, preparing to imitate![6]

Loving the Lost

Love is godly and Christlike, since "God is love" (1 John 4:8).[7] He so loves us, and values his relationship with each of us, that he "lays down his life" for us

(John 3:16, 1 John 3:16, John 10:11, 15:13). Jesus' whole life—his cares, prayers, affection, schedule, his life and his death—was all about people. We are called to live the same life of love (Ephesians 5:1–2). Could "For God so loved the world… that he gave…" be rewritten: "For Richard so loved the world…"? (Or Rachel, or Michelle, or Brendan—plug in your name!) Evangelism is a hallmark of a true Christian. How can we claim to have the love of God in our hearts if we harden our hearts toward those around us? As Paul wrote to the Thessalonians:

> We loved you so much that we were delighted to share with you not only the gospel of God but our lives as well, because you had become so dear to us (1 Thessalonians 2:8).

Notice that in our relationships with outsiders it is not just preaching the gospel that God values. It is sharing our lives as well. Don't expect that most men and women will become Christians through your efforts if you share only the gospel. People are seeking friendship, and Christianity is spread by relationships! But they also need to see what you are talking about modeled in your life: your drive, patience, conscientiousness, sense of family, commitment to excellence and willingness to sacrifice.

Incidentally, do you think reaching out to the lost is more important than bonding with your fellow Christians? As urgent as the mission is, the Bible teaches otherwise (Galatians 6:10, Luke 15:3–7). Evangelism will prove an exercise in futility if the spiritual family into which we are inviting outsiders is not truly "family." Consider this qualification about the difference between mission and purpose: Your purpose is to have a relationship with God and go to heaven; your mission is to bring good news into the lives of others. Evangelism is not your entire purpose! When we confuse mission and purpose, our joy is very likely to depend on how many people are listening to us.

Is "evangelism" difficult for you? Don't worry! The Spirit lives in you—not a "spirit of timidity," but a spirit of love (2 Timothy 1:7). As you yield to it, you will eventually overcome your timidity. You will learn not to be ashamed! (2 Timothy 1:8).

Loving Roommates

If you are single, chances are good that you live with a roommate or housemates. Obviously, here is another area where the Spirit rejoices in doing his work. Love means two things: calling one another higher (Colossians 1:28) and bearing with one another (Ephesians 4:2–3).[8]

The first is a command of God. There is only one standard for a Christian: discipleship. That means commitment, not compromise. But the second is equally a command of God. We must bear with one another, because even good-hearted disciples—and I am of the opinion that nearly all disciples are fundamentally good-hearted—will rub one another the wrong way occasionally. Things like not doing your part to keep the apartment clean, financial irresponsibility,[9] failing to relay messages, missing meals and prayer times together, relating to one another like "ships passing in the night"—all these things take their toll on relationships.

Are you impatient and moody around your roommates? What are you really like first thing in the morning? Are you too hard on them? Or maybe you "look the other way" when they are not putting God first (the "I'm okay, you're okay"approach to Christian relationships)? Neither extreme is love. How spiritual is your apartment or place of residence?

One last consideration: Unless you are content to remain single, excelling in your single household is superb preparation for marriage.

Loving Partners in Discipleship

How are your relationships with those who are making a special effort to help you to mature in Christ? Are you easy to teach, or do you drag your feet, or manage to remain hard to contact? Sometimes disciples confuse the messenger with the message. Let us not be like the "mocker" of Proverbs 9:7-9. Remember, even if no one were discipling you, the truth is still the truth, and we all have many things to change. Here is obviously another area in which the Spirit can lead us and teach us many things.

'Colorblind' Love

In mainline Christendom, Sunday is "the most segregated day of the week." This is a travesty! Jesus would not have stood for it (John 17:22–23).

One of the most striking evidences of the Holy Spirit is the genuine love existing in churches of disciples. In the large metropolitan areas of the United States, for example, churches of disciples are highly mixed. Interracial marriage is not uncommon, and when Christians choose to form households, racial homogeneity is the exception, not the rule.

It may well be that you were brought up with a certain degree of prejudice (White against Black, Black against Oriental, Hispanic against White, etc.). One African-American disciple shared with me how she was treated atop the Statue of Liberty. Shockingly, one hateful individual spat in her face, saying, "What are you doing up here? Get out of here! You don't belong." Sadly, racism and bigotry are all around us. Let's make sure we are not playing by the world's rules. By the way, from what race are your friends? And from which social class? (The same as your own?) Love does not look down on others or associate only with its "own kind." The Spirit transcends all borders.

Bigots, racists and prejudiced people in general are amazed by the love among Jesus Christ's people and in his church. The Spirit binds us all together (Ephesians 4:4) and prepares us for heaven, where there will be no racial distinctions (Revelation 7:9). But if we still struggle with lingering prejudice, we need to read what the apostle John wrote to the first-century disciples:

> We love because he first loved us. If anyone says, "I love God," yet hates his brother, he is a liar. For anyone who does not love his brother, whom he has seen, cannot love God, whom he has not seen. And he has given us this command: Whoever loves God must also love his brother (1 John 4:19–21).

It is much harder to love God (whom you cannot see) than to love your brother (who is worshiping the Lord right beside you). Any brother or sister we "just cannot love" potentially brings our entire relationship with God into question. Someone has said that we only love God as much as we love the person we love the least. Only by the Spirit can we love one another deeply, from the heart, despite our differences (1 Peter 1:22).

Together or Separately?

It cannot be stated emphatically enough that the church of God must be unified. Not only racially and socially, but in terms of communication, doctrine and theology. Ephesians 4:3 says we should "make every effort to keep the unity of the Spirit through the bond of peace." Not that the Spirit can become disunified; it is our unity that is in question. Here are seven marks of a unified church:

1. Unified in leadership: "From the top down," friendship, honesty, frankness and integrity must typify church leaders, their relationships with each other and with others.
2. Unified ethnically and socioeconomically: The Spirit of God redeems people across all classes.
3. Unified in marriages: Our most key relationship is that with our spouse.
4. Unified in prayer: The church that prays together, stays together.
5. Unified doctrinally: on the first principles of the faith (not necessarily

opinion matters).

6. Unified in love for the poor: every disciple caring for the needy.
7. Unified in the mission: every disciple sharing the Word.

The goal of world evangelism is but a pipe dream if we cannot maintain our unity as the people of God. As Franklin wisely quipped at the beginning of the American struggle for independence, "We must indeed all hang together, or, most assuredly, we shall surely hang separately."[10] Only when we allow God to meld us together will we truly go forth in the power of the Spirit to take the light to this dark world.

QUESTIONS FOR THOUGHT

- *Are there specific people whom (I now admit) I have a hard time loving? What can I do about my lack of love for him/her/them?*

- *Do I share my faith out of duty, or do others sense the love of Christ in me?*

- *Is there any lingering racial prejudice in my heart?*

- *Is there anyone I am hesitant to phone, or feel uneasy around? It may be that I am holding something against him/her. Am I not forgiving? What sorts of communication do I think God would want me to be engaging in to resolve things? How much longer am I going to wait before taking action?*

- *What does the statement "God is love" (1 John 4:7) mean to me?*

_____ NOTES _____

1. More on the outpouring of the Spirit may be found in Titus 3:6 and in Chapter 16.
2. Proof text: 1 Timothy 1:17—in case you think you have visibly seen him!
3. David—see Acts 13:22.
4. For an excellent treatment of love, see C. S. Lewis, *The Four Loves* (London: HarperCollins, 1977). Lewis masterfully discusses the nature of *agape, philia, eros* and *storge*.
5. An interesting introduction to Systems Theory—a fresh angle on relationships—is Roberta M. Gilbert's *Extraordinary Relationships: A New Way of Thinking About Human Interactions* (Minneapolis: Chronimed, 1992). Also helpful is Edwin H. Friedman's *Generation to Generation: Family Process in Church and Synagogue* (New York: The Guilford Press, 1985).

6. Highly recommended: two books by Sam and Geri Laing, *Raising Awesome Kids* (Spring, Texas: Illumination Publishers, 2017) and *Friends and Lovers: Marriage as God Designed It* (Spring, Texas: Illumination Publishers, 2016).

7. That does not mean "love" and "God" are somehow interchangeable or synonymous, or that if you are a caring person, God is somehow living in your heart. It means love is one of the—if not the—basic characteristics of the Lord.

8. Single Christians will appreciate Adam and Bethany Smith (ed.), *Singlehood Redefined* (Billerica, Mass.: DPI, 2012).

9. Mark Twain commented, "The holy passion of friendship is of so sweet and steady and loyal and enduring a nature that it will last through a whole lifetime, if not asked to lend money"(!). Actually, disciples should keep the Proverbs 19:17 principle in mind. In the Scriptures prudence is advised as much as tightfistedness is condemned.

10. Benjamin Franklin (1706-1790), in a remark to John Hancock, at the signing of the Declaration of Independence, July 4, 1776.

5. The Spirit of Discipline
Becoming a More Disciplined Person—Inside Out!

Power is dynamic; love is caring; but without discipline we will fritter away the precious hours God has given us to accomplish his will and love those he has placed in our lives. We now examine the third result of the Spirit's work: self-discipline.

It's time for an armor-piercing question: *Is your life disciplined enough to back up the message of surrender to God that you preach?* In the final analysis, we will be ineffective in our outreach and discredited by our lives if we are unable to control ourselves. The good news is that no matter how disorganized, lazy or unproductive we have been, we can change! That's because God's Spirit empowers us.

Discipline Is Godly

God is a God of order (1 Corinthians 14:33). Do we reflect that order in our lives? It's time for a Greek lesson: The word for order is *cosmos*. The opposite is *chaos*! Which describes your life? Your thought world? How about the place where you live, your relationships, your personal finances? Discipline is not a "fine point." It is the work of the Spirit, and it is godly.[1] The person who mocks at discipline—especially the one who claims to be Spirit-led—stands in contempt of God and his Spirit.

This chapter aims to be very, very practical. We have to get specific; good intentions do a poor job of paving the road we have decided to travel.

Shortcuts to Discipline

If this subtitle excites you, you already know what your problem is! Character, like muscle, is built through much strain and repetition. But culturally we are growing weaker and weaker in the character department. A terrible softness has crept in.[2] We are always looking for a quicker way, an "easier road" (Matthew 7:13). The whole idea of a "shortcut to discipline" is a contradiction in terms. There are no shortcuts.

Are we listening to the Spirit of God? The Word, inspired by the Holy Spirit, has clearly revealed God's will about discipline. We can, by God's power, become more disciplined persons, from the inside out.[3] None of the following seven areas allows shortcuts. So read carefully, digest fully and allow the Spirit of discipline to be your spirit. That's spiritual, that's godly, that's Christlike—and that's Bible!

1. Disciplined in Sleep Habits

The first sixteen seconds of your day may well determine the quality of the following sixteen hours. How long does it take you to respond to your alarm clock—or to convince yourself that you do not have to?

Yet it is not just getting up on time that God wills; we also need to show the discretion to go to bed on time. Not that disciples will not "burn the candle at both ends" (2 Corinthians 6:5). When we are called on to sacrifice sleep, we certainly need to do that with a cheerful attitude. The lack of discipline in the area of sleep is closely connected with other areas.[4] My advice: Make your bed as soon as the alarm sounds. This is an excellent deterrent against returning to the horizontal position.

In short, it is highly unlikely that we will be in tune with the Spirit when we are not even in tune with the decisions we ourselves have made (just hours earlier) about when to rise. Spirituality requires a certain measure of integrity and maturity.[5]

2. Disciplined in Punctuality

How we honor time tags is usually symptomatic of our entire lives. Perennial latecomers usually have many other areas of life not under the control of the Spirit—finances, house cleaning and scheduling being three common companion areas. Problems in the area of punctuality stem from the tendency to procrastinate. "Procrastination is the thief of time."[6] Are you being robbed in this area?[7]

Some people were just "born five minutes too late"! These people lower productivity in companies, raise tension levels in marriages, sap the spirit of church services and show disrespect for others—inconveniencing everyone but themselves. Since God is a God of order, his Spirit wants us to show integrity in our use of time. When we say we will be somewhere at a certain time, our "Yes" needs to be "Yes." (Matthew 5:37, James 5: 12).

Of course, it isn't spiritual to behave rudely or huffily to someone who is late—there may have been good reasons. (We're all late sometimes!) Be gracious and prepared to be flexible![8] Yet realize this: Those who are responsive to the Spirit will be responsible.

3. Disciplined in Body Shape

The Bible gives little specific counsel on the ideal size or shape for the human body, which vary to some extent from culture to culture and generation to generation. Yet there is one very clear principle we are bound to respect: The body is "a temple of the Holy Spirit" (1 Corinthians 6:19[9]).

Do you respect that reality? Do you exercise regularly? Eat properly? (If not, you may well experience general sluggishness.) Can you imagine a sluggish, overweight Jesus? Since we are trying to walk in his steps, let's stay in good enough shape that we don't get out of breath as we follow him! Keep in step with the Spirit (Galatians 5:22–25).

Your effectiveness and confidence will be greatly enhanced when you feel great about how you look. How is the "temple" looking?

4. Disciplined in Personal Finances

The Spirit has revealed many things about financial management which are beyond the scope of this book. Let's address just one issue, an issue that robs many a disciple of his or her joy: debt. Romans 13:8 instructs us that no debt is to remain outstanding. Are you borrowing from one credit card (Peter) to pay off the other (Paul)? My advice: If you struggle to spend wisely, get rid of all your credit cards but one. Resist the temptation to incur fresh debt before the old ones are retired. Are you in debt to other disciples? This is, in the long term, neither good spiritually for you nor for them. It is time for a good "retirement plan." Know also for sure that "impulse spending" is definitely not at the impulse of the Holy Spirit! And beware the spirit of materialism—which the Bible simply calls "greed" (Ephesians 5:3, Colossians 3:5). There will be much more about this in Chapter 14.

5. Disciplined in Speech

The area of what we say and how we say it is the subject of hundreds of verses in the Bible. The most copious source of passages on the tongue is Proverbs. Perhaps the most colorful chapter on the tongue is James 3. The most comprehensive verse probably is Ephesians 4:29; the most convicting verse, Matthew 12:36. Here are some areas of speech the Bible covers:

Lies and deceit	*Exaggeration*	*Gossip and slander*
Oaths and vows	*Flattery*	*False teaching*
Longwindedness	*Boasting*	*Careless words, rash words*
Promises and reliability	*Insensitivity*	*Honesty and frankness*
Arguing and quarreling	*Mocking*	*Whining and complaining*
Testifying before authorities	*Praising God*	*Evangelism*

Bearing false witness	*Confession*	*Flippancy and immaturity*
Counseling	*Singing*	*Encouraging words*

Chances are high that the Spirit is working on you *somewhere* in the broad area of speech. Where do you need to change?

6. Disciplined in Purity

The covenant of Job 31:1 is easier said than done. The radical dealing with sin described by Jesus (Matthew 5:29–30) leaves few disciples unscathed. God demands purity in thought, word and deed! (Psalm 19:14). The Spirit is very sensitive to sexual impurity. Because our consciences are so easily sullied by unclean thinking and actions, remaining open to the leading of the Spirit requires constant cleansing.[10] Let us pray with David,

> Create in me a pure heart, O God,
>> and renew a steadfast spirit within me.
> Do not cast me from your presence
>> or take your Holy Spirit from me.
> Restore to me the joy of your salvation
>> and grant me a willing spirit, to sustain me.
> Then I will teach transgressors your ways,
>> and sinners will turn back to you (Psalm 51:10–13).

What happens when we are disciplined in purity?
- We are steadfast, consistent.
- We are filled with joy; our light shines.
- We are willing, seldom requiring coaxing to do what is right.
- We are outward focused.
- Others are converted to God.

What happens when we resist the Spirit in this area?
- We are inconsistent and unstable.
- We are not enthusiastic. "The lights are out."
- We are reluctant, critical disciples.
- We spend much time thinking about ourselves.
- The mission is not on our mind.

Not allowing the Spirit to keep us pure can have terrible consequences. We read in 1 Timothy about those who have left the narrow road:

The goal of this command is love, which comes from a pure heart and a good conscience and a sincere faith.... Some have rejected [faith and a good conscience] and so have shipwrecked their faith (I Timothy 1:5, 19).

Without purity, our consciences, and soon our faith, become shipwrecked. If you are "playing with fire" (Proverbs 6:27), you already know how your conscience and conviction have been affected. Do the waves seem higher and higher? Is the sea growing rougher by the week? The good news is that the shipwreck can be avoided, if we remain sensitive to the leading of the Spirit through the Word and we open up to others about what is going on.

7. Disciplined in Prayer and Study

Since power in all other areas of our lives flows from our relationship with God, why cut ourselves off from our source of power to implement all these changes? Through a close walk with God we will be "more than conquerors" (Romans 8:37) over our areas of "indiscipline" that cry out for change.

Whatever time of the day you decide to read and pray, let me encourage you to be diligent. Open the Word and speak with the Lord at a time and place where you can remain alert and self-controlled (1 Peter 4:7). The payoffs for consistent devotional times are immense![11]

Discipline Overdose?

Is it possible to "o.d." on discipline? Sure! We have all met people who are in abject slavery to their watches, calendars, planners, and rigidly inflexible plans. They do not know how to stop and smell the flowers. If you are like that, someone will tell you! (Let it be someone else who tells you that you have gone far enough, or too far—not you yourself! Especially if you confess that you struggle with discipline.) But most of us err more on the liberal side. Let's make sure we are vanquishing laziness before we start "fine tuning."

Persevere!

The Christian life demands discipline. Those who fail to train (1 Timothy 4:8, Hebrews 5:11–14) seldom survive in the long term. God has truly given us a spirit of discipline. Let's commit our spirits into his hands and pray for the spirit of discipline to change us from the inside out.

On to the Heights

I close this chapter with one of my favorite poems, by the English poet

Longfellow. Like Psalm 18:33, Habakkuk 3:19, and many other biblical passages, it calls us to go on to the heights:

> The heights by great men reached and kept
> Were not attained by sudden flight
> But they, while their companions slept,
> Were toiling upward in the night.[12]

QUESTIONS FOR THOUGHT

- *Has the Spirit been trying to teach me how to be a more disciplined person lately?*

- *Do the words "hard work" (1 Corinthians 15:9–10) describe my life?*

- *Am I frequently late for church? If I am, do I realize the disrespect this shows not only to the church, but also to God?*

- *What's the biggest area of weakness in my discipline? Through the Spirit, what can I do to master it?*

NOTES

1. As William Blake (1757-1827) aptly said, "He who would do good to another must do it in the minute particulars. General good is the plea of the scoundrel, hypocrite, and flatterer; for art and science cannot exist but in minutely organized particulars" (*Jerusalem*, p l.55, l.60).

2. Voltaire (1694-1778) urged, "Shun idleness. It is a rust that attaches itself to the most brilliant of metals." Moving from the personal level to the societal, hear Mahatma Gandhi's diagnosis of our social malaise, "The Seven Deadly Social Sins":
   1. Politics without principle
   2. Wealth without work
   3. Commerce without morality
   4. Pleasure without conscience
   5. Education without character
   6. Science without humanity
   7. Worship without sacrifice

3. Not to say that nothing has been written which can simplify the process. In addition to the book of Proverbs, I highly recommend Stephen Covey, *The Seven Habits of Highly Effective People* (New York: Simon & Schuster, 1989) and Richard Taylor, *The*

Disciplined Life (Minneapolis, Minn: Beacon Hill Press, 1962).

4. Incidentally, Psalm 3:5 has nothing to do with "the Spirit waking me every morning when he wants me to get up"! It has more to do with not dying in the night! And Psalm 127:2, in context, speaks about relying on God; it does not sanction the attitude, "I'm no good if I don't get my twelve hours a night"! (Of course there are some legitimate, medically diagnosed, situations in which one will require more sleep.)

5. Proverbs provides several other verses on sleep: 6:9–11, 19:15, 24:30–34, 26:14.

6. Edward Young (1683-1765), *The Complaint: Night Thoughts* (Night i, 1.393). Or, in the pithy words of the Earl of Chesterfield (1694-1773), "Know the true value of time; snatch, seize, and enjoy every moment of it. No idleness, no delay, no procrastination, never put off till tomorrow what you can do today."

7. "Morgen, morgen—nur nicht heute!" sagen alle faule Leute! ["Tomorrow, tomorrow, only not today," say all wicked people!]

8. In all fairness, neither 1 Timothy 3:15 nor 2 Timothy 4:9 offers comfort to the chronically late. These verses do not justify the kind of lateness under discussion since they have more to do with long range planning (matters of weeks and months) than with being on time (minutes and hours).

9. 1 Corinthians 3:16, several chapters earlier, is speaking not of the body of the disciple, but of the body of disciples (the church).

10. Recommended: Roy and Revel Hession, *The Calvary Road* (Fort Washington, Pennsylvania: Christian Literature Crusade, 1950).

11. I highly recommend *Be Still My Soul: A Practical Guide to a Deeper Relationship With God* (Spring, Texas: Illumination Publishers, 2015) by Sam Laing.

12. Henry Wadsworth Longfellow (1807-1882), *The Ladder of Saint Augustine.*

6. Am I Stuck with 'Me'?
Character Change—Inside Out!

"Speeding snails." That may sound like a contradiction in terms—which it is, of course—but the meaning will be clarified soon enough. The question this chapter addresses, "Am I stuck with me?" is one we all ask at some time. The good news: No! You're not stuck with "you"; none of us has to stay the same. The Spirit will change us deeper and faster than any worldly resolution, program, injection, philosophy or religion ever could. I believe the point was summed up well in a Christmas present I received in 1995. The necktie is covered with snails. All the snails are moving in the same direction, but one is "speeding" past the others—as best a snail can do![1] Deep character change takes time. It is a slow process, and the slowness of this changing can be frustrating. But take heart: Some of us "snails"—those with the Spirit "speeding" them along—will absolutely grow in character and personality far, far faster than our friends in the world. If we are patient, keeping in step with what the Spirit is showing us in the Word, our "velocity" will place us leagues ahead of the rest.[2] Rapid change is seldom God's method. It simply is not God's way of doing things, of bringing things to be.[3] Farmers know that crops take months to mature. Babies require a full nine months. Getting into shape physically takes consistency over an extended period of time. No amount of prayer is likely to accelerate these processes. It is the same with character change. Don't be like the young Christian who prayed, "Lord, I want you to make me a more patient person—and I want you to do it *now*!"

Transformation

Transformation is defined as "change in character or discipline."[4] To be transformed, we need to have a spiritual, sacrificial attitude. Paul put it well in his letter to the Romans:

> Therefore, I urge you, brothers, in view of God's mercy, to offer your bodies as living sacrifices, holy and pleasing to God—this is your spiritual act of worship. Do not conform any longer to the pattern of this world, but be transformed by the renewing of your mind. Then you will be able to test and approve what God's will is—his good, pleasing and perfect will (Romans 12:1–2).

We have a choice: to conform to the pattern of the world or to let the Spirit transform us by the renewing of our minds. Change occurs not from the outside in—by osmosis or going through the motions—but from the inside out! Character change is wrought by the Spirit.

Fruit Cocktail

Fruit cocktail was one of my favorite desserts as I was growing up. My favorite part was the cherry! The Holy Spirit is also in the fruit business. Galatians specifies nine fruits—more than enough for a cocktail, though there are plenty of other "fruits" or virtues extolled in the Bible. The fruits of the Spirit are nothing other than the basic personality traits of Jesus Christ. The Spirit creates or develops these fruits in our lives, transforming our personalities to be Christlike.

> For the sinful nature desires what is contrary to the Spirit, and the Spirit what is contrary to the sinful nature. They are in conflict with each other, so that you do not do what you want. But if you are led by the Spirit, you are not under law...The acts of the sinful nature are obvious... But the fruit of the Spirit is love, joy, peace, patience, kindness, goodness, faithfulness, gentleness and self-control. Against such things there is no law. Those who belong to Christ Jesus have crucified the sinful nature with its passions and desires. Since we live by the Spirit, let us keep in step with the Spirit (Galatians 5:17–18, 22–25).

However, this does not mean that non-Christians necessarily lack these fruits. I often come across nonbelievers with amazing levels of self-control, or patience, or joy. In the New Testament, the word "spirit" often refers to our own spirit—that part of us (from God) that wants to do good. Note: even when the word is capitalized, it may not be referring to the Holy Spirit, as there were no upper/lower case distinctions in the original manuscripts. The translator makes assumptions.

Flesh (sarx in Greek, translated "sinful nature" in the NIV) and Spirit (pneuma) are opposites. There is a struggle going on in your inner being. There is a way to vanquish the flesh and grow in the fruit of the Spirit, and Galatians 5:18 says it clearly: We must be led by the Spirit! (See more about that in Chapter 9.)

When I was a young Christian (during my first five years or so) my attitude was, "The fruits of the Spirit aren't really that important. They're good, but there are more important things in life, like winning souls. That's real fruit bearing." Not surprisingly, I was often condescending, if not outright abrasive toward others. Now I see that the two go together; we can hardly be effective if we are nervous, depressed, impatient or lacking in self-control! Moreover, most people who say that in John 15:8 the fruit of the Spirit is *all* Jesus had in mind usually lack the fruit of producing disciples. The Spirit gives us love (Galatians 5:22, 2 Timothy 1:7). He also gives us joy (Galatians 5:22). One way in which the Spirit gives us joy is through the growth of those we are striving to mature in Christ (Luke 10:21, 1 Thessalonians 3:8). Joy as a fruit of the Spirit must not be confused with the human joy (happiness) God gives to all men through the positive circumstances of life (Acts 14:17). Personal peace (Galatians 5:22, Romans 14:17) is yet another tremendous blessing and one which we must attain if we are to make Christ real to our fellow man. Peace at a church level is linked with numerical growth in Acts 9:31.

The Spirit also gives us hope (Galatians 5:5, Romans 15:13, 5:5). Many other qualities could be added to the list. In short, the Spirit is helping us to become more and more Christlike.

Winning the Battle

How can we become more Christlike? We must understand the battle between flesh and Spirit that rages in each of us as we struggle to pray, "Not my will, but yours be done." There is a real battle going on (Galatians 5:16–17). The lifestyle of the flesh is lazy, selfish, undisciplined and inward focused. But the lifestyle of the Spirit is hard working, giving, disciplined and evangelistic. Indeed, there is a real war being waged. If we yield our wills to the Spirit, the transformation is liberating!

> Now the Lord is the Spirit, and where the Spirit of the Lord is, there is freedom. And we, who with unveiled faces all reflect the Lord's glory, are being transformed into his likeness with ever-increasing glory, which comes from the Lord, who is the Spirit (2 Corinthians 3:17–18).

The freedom the Spirit brings (more on this in Chapter 15) is awesome! Every new year we are disciples, we taste greater freedom, for we are being transformed—if we are being led by the Spirit. If we are not more Christlike now than we were six months ago, we may have stopped growing. If this is the case, be assured of one thing: The Spirit is being grieved, for he desperately desires our spiritual maturity in Christ. How are we doing in these areas?

- Diligently using the opportunities God gives us to act as his ambassadors?
- Concentrating during sermons, classes, teaching days? (Note taking usually proves helpful.)

- Seeking advice from mature disciples before important decisions?
- Systematically reading the Bible and other spiritual literature?
- Keeping a humble and grateful spirit? (Lord forbid we should be complainers—Philippians 2:14!)
- Staying sincere and transparent? (No "faking" character change or zeal. This will damage you more than you realize; no one will know who you are any more, nor be able to help you.)
- Praying for character change to take place in our areas of weakness?

Personality Versus Character

Like it or not, your basic personality type will probably never change. You are who you are, even *after* becoming a Christian. There are certain aspects of your personality that will never change—and need not change! This is part of the wonder of the remarkable "unity in diversity" we have in the church. So watch out for false guilt when you compare yourself to someone totally different from you (physically, emotionally or in terms of intellect, or family background). Of course sin is sin, and the commands of God are the commands of God. (Neither genetics nor personality type provides a license for sin or an exemption from obeying the commands.) But *character* is different from *personality*.

The Spirit will build character in our lives as we persevere faithfully. Notice how neither of the following passages promises a shortcut to character:

> Consider it pure joy, my brothers, whenever you face trials of many kinds, because you know that the testing of your faith develops perseverance. Perseverance must finish its work so that you may be mature and complete, not lacking anything (James 1:2–4).

> Not only so, but we also rejoice in our sufferings, because we know that suffering produces perseverance; perseverance, character; and character, hope. And hope does not disappoint us, because God has poured out his love into our hearts by the Holy Spirit, whom he has given us (Romans 5:3–5).

As mentioned in the last chapter, character, like muscle, is built up rather slowly, over time. As someone said, "Experience is a hard teacher; because she gives the test first, the lesson afterwards." How many people become disciples, yet quit after only a few months, disappointed that they were not seeing change occur fast enough? Not to sanction laziness, yet in one sense we need to "go easy on ourselves." But in another sense, we unquestionably need to push ourselves!

Be patient with yourself? Push yourself? Yes, it can be confusing at times. Regardless, these twin truths must be held in tension. May we never lose our radical edge! Jesus Christ was perfectly "balanced."

So What's the Mystery?

It may sound as though we are effecting all these changes on our own, without the Spirit. After all, even unbelievers can quit smoking if they are determined enough. Surely if we just wait long enough, we are sure to change, right? No way!

If you think time alone will cause you to mature—like a bottle of wine—just try to mature without the Spirit. You will tread water at best, be carried downstream in all likelihood, and quite possibly go under. The Bible makes it patently clear that real change demands we surrender ourselves to the Spirit of Christ.

You don't believe me? You still think change is accomplished by human effort? (Galatians 3:3). Ignore these scriptural principles. Try to change without the Spirit. (Good luck—you'll need a lot of it!)

We change from the inside out. No, you are not "stuck with you." Because of the Spirit of God, we can see genuine character change, from the inside out.[5]

QUESTIONS FOR THOUGHT

- *Have I felt a sense of futility about changing certain aspects of my life?*
- *Am I "going through the motions"? Or am I changing, by the power of the Spirit of God, from the inside out?*
- *Which of the nine fruits of the Spirit in Galatians 5 is most present in my life? Most absent?*
- *Am I the same as I was six months ago, or has my character changed?*
- *Am I willing to make every effort to be Christlike?*

_____ NOTES _____

1. Thank you, Ben. And, yes, I still sport the tie on occasion!

2. Some Christians regularly observe "spiritual birthdays." In the course of human biological growth, everyone pretty much knows what turning two, ten, twenty-one or fifty means. As far as years in the Lord, many brothers and sisters "at two" are doing things some "ten-year-olds" are yet to attempt. Spiritually, we all grow at different rates. I am not sure that the Lord wants us in the comparison game.

3. For a technical work on cosmology see Keith Ward's *God, Chance and Necessity* (Oxford: Oneworld, 1996).

4. Adapted from the Oxford English Dictionary.

5. "Sow an act, and you reap a habit. Sow a habit, and you reap a character. Sow a character, and you reap a destiny." Charles Reade (1814-1884).

Gifts, Grace, Guidance

As we have seen, God's Spirit changes us from the inside out. This does not exhaust the discussion of how the Spirit works in our lives, however! Much needs to be said about God's gifts, grace and guidance.

These three areas are usually "undertaught"— usually out of reactionary fear. We are afraid that if we emphasize the gifts, we might float off into the Pentecostal ether. We fear that an emphasis on grace may slow down the work of the kingdom. And we hesitate to talk about the leading of the Spirit—despite the fact that the Bible teaches it—for similar reasons.

In this second section we will see how God's gifts, grace and guidance bring immeasurable blessings not only to us, but to the church as well—and through the church to the world.

7. Open the Toolbox
Gifts of the Spirit

Whether it is our birthday or some other special occasion, we all appreciate gifts. Speaking for my fellow men, we especially appreciate gifts that help us "get the job done": power tools, office organizers, assorted gadgets. My favorite tool is a knife. (No, not a weapon!) It's the Swiss Army Knife my friend Mike gave me. It can open bottles, scale fish, punch holes, remove corks, magnify print, saw, cut, snip, write, screw, file, measure—and much, much more! I take it with me when I travel; no matter what comes up, there is always some feature on this device that will get the job done. What a great gift!

Teamwork

God has given disciples something even more versatile than a Swiss Army Knife: His spiritual gifts are spread throughout the church. Some people "write" or "file." Others "scale fish." A rare few seem to have multiple gifts. Everyone has at least one skill. Unlike the knife, where every tool is found in one place, in the church the various functions are diffused throughout the fellowship. This arrangement makes us come together and work as a team, since, as John Donne put it, "no man [or woman] is an island."[1]

> For by the grace given me I say to every one of you: Do not think of yourself more highly than you ought, but rather think of yourself with sober judgment, in accordance with the measure of faith God has given you. Just as each of us has one body with many members, and these members do not all have the same function, so in Christ we who are many form one body, and each member belongs to all the others. We have different gifts, according to the grace given us (Romans 12:3–6).

God works through the church, equipping it with various gifts. The gifts are equated with different functions. One member of the body can easily have more than one function; for example a human hand can grasp, signal and bring food to the mouth. Do you have any idea what your spiritual gifts are? When every member is using his or her "tools," the work the Father has given us will get the job done (John 17:4).

Wait a Minute!

What do you mean, "my" spiritual gifts? I thought all the gifts expired when the generation of the apostles passed away. Weren't they just for the early church?

Well, to begin with, the New Testament never said that all the gifts of the Spirit would pass away—only a few of the more sensational ones, like apostleship and miraculous languages did.[2] Should we shy away from the gifts just because of modern-day excesses (such as those of the Charismatic Movement)? Are we to deprive ourselves of the divine assistance we need just because some have seemingly abused it?

Let's calmly examine the evidence. There are five lists of spiritual gifts in the New Testament: Romans 12:6-8, 1 Corinthians 12:28, 1 Peter 4:10-11, 1 Corinthians 12:8-10 and Ephesians 4:11. The total number of gifts represented is at least twenty! And this excludes several other spiritual gifts mentioned in the Old Testament (e.g. Exodus 31:3-5).

Spiritual Versus 'Miraculous' Gifts

You may be thinking, "But aren't all spiritual gifts miraculous?" Not necessarily. The phrase "miraculous gifts" appears nowhere in the New Testament. It is a modern term, not a biblical one. Generally, we realize that God is active among us (and we need to have a sense of his ceaseless working), but we do not refer to this as miraculous. "Miraculous" is when God does something that is not "normal" but is out of the ordinary. For example, if God gives a person the ability to learn a new language, that may be a divine gift, but we would not call it a miracle. But if the person suddenly begins to speak in a new language without having learned it, we would say that it was a miracle. Some of the spiritual gifts in the New Testament were clearly miraculous gifts, such as healing, prophecy and speaking in languages. But it is just as clear that others are not miraculous at all: giving money, showing mercy, service.[3] The problems occur when we equate the miraculous gifts with all the spiritual gifts.

The New Testament Greek word for gift, *charisma*, does not necessarily denote anything miraculous. Paul uses *charisma* when discussing his gift of celibacy (1 Corinthians 7:7). It is the word in connection with eternal life in Romans 6:23. It is also the word in Romans 12:6 referring to a host of things that are not miraculous. Is encouraging "miraculous"? How about giving generously? Leadership? (How many of you in the working world would say that you have been "miraculously" suited for your vocation?) Putting it all together, we see that spiritual gifts include both miraculous and nonmiraculous gifts. The distinction between the two is useful for any analytical study.

It is possible that all of the gifts mentioned in 1 Corinthians 12:8–10 are miraculous, but it is unlikely that all of the gifts in 1 Corinthians 12: 28 are miraculous. (Look at them yourself.) As for Romans 12:6–8, with the possible exception of prophesying, all of the gifts mentioned there are nonmiraculous—but they are gifts all the same. Ephesians 4:11 is a different sort of passage, since all the gifts there are teaching gifts. 1 Peter 4:10 is a passage for all Christians: "Each one should use whatever gift he has received to serve others, faithfully administering God's grace in its various forms."

It is the assumption of these texts that every Christian possesses one or more gifts (Romans 12:6, 1 Corinthians 1:7, Ephesians 4:7, 1 Peter 4:10). I do not believe every first-century Christian possessed a miraculous gift, but I do believe that every Christian in any century has received some spiritual gift. It is obvious, as we look at our local congregations, that some people are better suited for some things than for others. We all have different talents and abilities; this is a fact, whether or not we choose to give God the credit for the various gifts. Again, every disciple has at least one *charisma*. In the words of John Stott, "God works primarily in nature, not in supernature—in history, not in miracle."[4]

We thank God for our food. (Oral prayers of thanks are returned to God before every single meal in the New Testament.) Now, if God is the Provider, then he is the one we thank for the food. Who would say, "We obtained our lasagna miraculously; it is from God"? No one—not unless Jesus himself came down and prepared it! (John 21:9).

All Gifts Are from God

In fact, we all acknowledge the presence of the gifts when we speak of a person as being "gifted" or say that God has given him a special ability in a particular area. As James said,

> Don't be deceived, my dear brothers. Every good and perfect gift is from above, coming down from the Father of the heavenly lights (James 1:16–17).

The Bible teaches that God sends his gifts and blessings on Christians and non-Christians alike (Matthew 5:45). And since God has given liberally to us, we are to share our gifts liberally with others. As Jesus said, "Freely you have received, freely give!" (Matthew 10:8).

When Do We Receive Our Gifts?

Does God give some of us special gifts at baptism? Does he begin to give others gifts even before they are in a right relationship with him? I believe that we begin to receive gifts *well in advance* of our becoming Christians. Then, after our conversion, God continues to work with the gifts with which he has been equipping us in our lives up to that point. The insight of John R. W. Stott is to the point:

> ...Is it not *a priori* unlikely that God will give a spiritual gift of teaching to a believer who in pre-conversion days could not teach for toffee, or a spiritual gift of encouragement to a brother or sister who by temperament is unsympathetic and unfriendly? It would not be impossible to God. But would it not be more in harmony with the God of the Bible, whose plans are eternal, to suppose that his spiritual gifts dovetail with his natural endowments? And that (for example) a "son of encouragement" such as Barnabas (Acts 4:36), who exercised his particular ministry both by generous giving (verse 37) and by personal friendship (e.g. Acts 9:26, 27; 11:25, 26), was already that kind of person, at least potentially, by creation?
>
> In this case we must look for the peculiarities of the spiritual gifts of teaching and encouragement in the heightening, the intensification, the "Christianizing" of a natural endowment already present, or at least latent. Thus, a man may be a gifted teacher before his conversion, and may after it be given the charisma of teaching to enable him to expound with insight, clarity and relevance. Or he may have a sympathetic disposition by nature, but after conversion be given the spiritual gift of "encouragement" to enable him to exercise a specifically Christian ministry of "encouragement in Christ" (Phil. 2:1).[5]

Looking at things from the eternal perspective, we see that it is no less a gift of God just because it is not bestowed at conversion. In fact, like Jeremiah (Jeremiah 1:5), Paul was prepared by God for his ministry from birth (Galatians 1:15–16). In the final analysis, it would be difficult to prove that someone received a particular gift at conversion, since undiscovered talents may be discovered at almost any time. A gift is no less from God just because it is not miraculous!

This view of the spiritual gifts puts 1 Corinthians 12:12–26 in its proper context. Each member has a different gift (function). This is not to say that evangelism is a gift; Ephesians 4:11 says that God gave some evangelists as gifts to the church. Not all are evangelists, but all are to be evangelistic. No disobedience to a command of God can be excused with a "that's not my gift" attitude.

An Exception

There is one exception to the above analysis. In the first century a few individuals received gifts—miraculous ones—through a miraculous outpouring of the Spirit or, more often, through the laying on of the apostles' hands.[6] In each case there was an historical purpose for these exceptional events, and there is no reason to believe that our generation is such an "exception." (See Chapters 16, 17, 18, 20 and 26 in Part Two for a full discussion.)

Are You a 'Natural'?

If you are a good athlete, for example a great basketball player, consider where all your talent came from. Maybe you think, "I'm just a 'natural.' God didn't need to give me anything; I already had the ability. I did it all myself." If that is what you think, your ignorance is matched only by your arrogance. Where do you think your ability ultimately came from? Are you the one who determined your genetic make-up? Did you make the arrangements for your up-bringing? Were you the one who worked it out to be born in a nation where you would have plenty of opportunities to train, instead of having to work fifteen hours a day from an early age? Did you provide the food to strengthen you in childhood and the nutrients and immunizations to fend off the disease which could have crippled you?

How many of these advantages are you taking credit for? Are you so sure you want to eliminate the Lord from your analysis? Even a "natural" has been well endowed and endued by God. Of course, no one says, "Michael Jordan [even though he is a 'superhero'] plays supernaturally. He shouldn't be allowed to compete—he has God helping him." But there is some truth in that last statement: Every good thing "M.J." has, God has given him—directly or indirectly. And the same applies to you and me! There's no such thing as a "self-made man." As Paul said, "For who makes you different from anyone else? What do you have that you did not receive? And if you did receive it, why do you boast as though you did not?" (1 Corinthians 4:7).

Pitch In

For the church to be all that God intends it to be, we must all humbly utilize our gifts. God has left no one empty-handed, and there are ways in which all of us can contribute to the kingdom. Determining your gift(s) should not be terribly difficult; most of our gifts God has made obvious, and other people will be able to help you identify those that are hidden.

To sum up, my position is that the spiritual gifts are still with us, even though the miraculous ones, having fulfilled their purpose, have run their course.[7] Let's all do our part.

A Short List of Gifts in the Bible

There are many gifts mentioned in the Bible, and these may well be taken as representing broad classes of gifts, sometimes in combination with other gifts. In other words, this list is nowhere close to exhaustive. (Could one not also add the gifts of athletic talent, cooking, mechanical skill and so forth?)

Artistic gifts	Exodus 31:3, 35:31
Contentment	Ecclesiastes 3:13, 5:19
Prophecy	Romans 12:6
Serving	Romans 12:7
Teaching	Romans 12:7
Encouraging	Romans 12:8
Contributing	Romans 12:8
Leadership	Romans 12:8
Showing mercy	Romans 12:8
Celibacy	1 Corinthians 7:7
Message of wisdom	1 Corinthians 12:8
Message of knowledge	1 Corinthians 12:8
Faith	1 Corinthians 12:9
Healing	1 Corinthians 12:9
Miraculous powers	1 Corinthians 12:10
Distinguishing spirits	1 Corinthians 12:10
Languages	1 Corinthians 12:10
Translation	1 Corinthians 12:10
Apostleship	1 Corinthians 12:28
Administration	1 Corinthians 12:28
Evangelist gift	Ephesians 4:11
Shepherding gift	Ephesians 4:11
Hospitality	1 Peter 4:9
"Whatever"	1 Peter 4:10

The Charismatic Church

As we have seen, a true church is a "charismatic" church. We acknowledge that God is the source of our gifts and that we have an obligation to use these gifts to change the world. We in the kingdom of God need to change how we do ministry. By all means we need to talk about the spiritual gifts. As disciples, we are charismatic (gifted)!

Any philosophy of ministry that fails to recognize God's equipping of the members to do the work of ministry in the church is not only unbiblical; it is not, in the long run, going to enable us to evangelize the world. So let's open up the toolbox and get to work!

QUESTIONS FOR THOUGHT

- *What are my most obvious gifts for the Kingdom of God?*

- *Are the leaders in my church aware of my talents? Have I made myself available to contribute to the fellowship?*

- *Am I kidding myself by pretending to be gifted in an area in which the Spirit has not blessed me?*

- *Am I willing to be a "team player," or do I insist on using my special gifts and talents on my terms only?*

Follow-up:

Go through the Spiritual Gifts Worksheet, and carry out a self-inventory. The form is found in the Appendix (page 258).

NOTES

1. John Donne's (1571 or 1572-1631) famous lines "No man is an island, entire of itself... And therefore never send to know for whom the bell tolls; it tolls for thee" are from his *Meditation XVII*.

2. There are three positions on the gifts. All the gifts have passed away—none remain; or none of gifts have passed away—all remain; or some of the gifts have passed away—others remain. The first position is that of many "non-charismatics." The second is that of most "charismatics." The third possibility is the one I believe is true, and for which I present a rationale in this book.

3. John R. W. Stott, *Baptism and Fullness*, (London: InterVarsity Press, 1975), p. 96. Excerpted with permission from IVP. This book provides an excellent grasp on the distinction between God's miraculous and nonmiraculous modes of working.

4. *Ibid*, 93ff, excerpted with permission from IVP.

5. *Ibid*.

6. The outpouring of the Spirit, prophesied in Joel 2, occurred in Acts 2 at Pentecost.

See Chapter 20 for the discussion on the apostolic laying on of hands. Here is provided just one example: that of Stephen and Philip. In Acts 6:6 the apostles lay hands on both Stephen and Philip. In Acts 6:8 we see Stephen now has the ability to perform miracles, and in Acts 8:6 we see that Philip, too, has the ability to perform miracles. Yet evidently Philip (not the Apostle Philip, but Philip the Evangelist) cannot lay his hands on others to transmit the miraculous gifts. In Acts 8:14ff he does not lay his hands on the Samaritans; the apostles must be called in. When they arrive, Simon the Sorcerer is astounded that the miraculous gifts were passed on through the laying on of apostolic hands (Acts 8:18).

    7. Notice that 1 Corinthians 13:8 refers only to the miraculous gifts. For a more extensive discussion of 1 Corinthians 12–14, see Chapter 23.

8. The Trillion-Dollar Insurance Policy
Biblical Teaching on Grace and Assurance

My father, Charles Jacoby, was vice president of a large American insurance company. After finishing his mathematics degree, he served in the Pacific (World War II), and then completed grueling actuarial exams which are essential in the insurance industry. Insurance policies have many benefits. The other day I heard about a policy that costs only $1.50 a day. If you die at age 30, someone gets one million dollars. Sounds good—if you think you might die young. But the "policy" God offers is infinitely superior! Everyone can afford the premiums and, even better, when you die, you move on to a resurrection. (You are the beneficiary of your own "life insurance" policy!)

Considering the "win/win" plan God has given us, why would anybody struggle with grace, confidence and feeling saved? Why should we have to look any further than the pages of our Bible for assurance?

The aim of this chapter is to make sure all of us feel great as disciples and understand the secure position we enjoy as God's highly loved sons and daughters. Our "policy" is infinitely precious. (Even a million times a million dollars, which is one trillion dollars, pales in significance!) As we will see, all this has a great deal to do with the Spirit's work in our lives.

Grace Versus Obedience?

One reason many of us struggle with grace is the false teaching to which we have been exposed. Status quo religion often unwittingly, through what it emphasizes and what it neglects, pits grace against obedience, the Spirit against the Law, the Old Testament against the New, even the Son against the Father. In actual fact, grace is no more opposed to obedience than God's love is to his wrath. Any perceived contradiction is purely in the eye of the beholder (Romans 11:22, Deuteronomy 7: 9–10).

If anything is clear from the thousand plus chapters of the Bible, it's that God is forgiving and delights in giving us a fresh start. Do you need a fresh start? Perhaps you are not experiencing God's grace as he intends you to. Don't stop doing the will of God to navel-gaze. Never pit grace against obedience. It's not "either/or"—it's "both/and" in biblical Christianity.

The GSAT

High school juniors in the United States take the Standard Aptitude Test (SAT). Test scores tell college admissions officials how strong applicants are in verbal and mathematical skills. Prospective medical students take an exam called the MCAT. Law students need the LSAT. Before I began my Masters in Theology, I had to take the GRE. What we need as disciples is the GSAT. That stands for "Grace SAT." This test can show you whether you are one who accepts the grace of God or if you prefer trying to do things on your own (a crucial question according to Galatians 3:3).

Those who struggle to comprehend the depth, height, length and breadth of the love of God exhibit similar patterns of behavior, emotions and growth. Are you one of these persons? Ask yourself the questions below and answer honestly.

GSAT

1.	Am I consumed with my feelings?	Yes	No
	Do I try to be my own psychoanalyst?		
2..	Do I suffer from inner turmoil?	Yes	No
	Do I struggle with depression or guilt feelings?		
3.	Am I slipping back into "old ways"?	Yes	No
4.	Do I struggle to have heartfelt gratitude for the myriad ways God has blessed me?	Yes	No
5.	Do I struggle with worldly desires?	Yes	No
	Do others comment on my worldliness?		
6.	Am I less evangelistic than usual?	Yes	No
7.	Do I feel "more saved" when things are going well than in bumpier circumstances?	Yes	No
8.	Am I uptight, stressed or stiff, rather than spontaneous?	Yes	No
9.	Are other priorities than God receiving the bulk of my energy/devotion (Jonah 2:8)?	Yes	No
10.	Do I doubt my salvation from time to time?	Yes	No

Scoring: Give yourself one hundred points for each NO answer.
YES answers earn no points.

000-200 = Will this chapter ever help you!

300-600 = Sounds like you could use a theology "upgrade."

700-900 = This will be a great refresher.

1000 (!) = Your name must be "Grace."

How did you do on your GSAT? How is your "grace aptitude"? If you find yourself answering "yes" to a number of these questions, chances are your understanding of grace is shallow.

"Works motivation" in the long run is encouraging to no one. Not only that, it severely inhibits the process of spiritual maturation. Just as a disapproving father hurts his child's development and a critical wife can damage her husband's confidence (and *vice versa*), so laboring under the burden of wrong theology on grace will mess us up spiritually.[1]

The Spirit of Grace

Did you know that the Holy Spirit is a "spirit of grace"? Consider the following two passages, one from the Old Testament, one from the New (italics mine).

> "And I will pour out on the house of David and the inhabitants of Jerusalem a *spirit of grace* and supplication. They will look on me, the one they have pierced, and they will mourn for him as one mourns for an only child, and grieve bitterly for him as one grieves for a firstborn son" (Zechariah 12:10).

> How much more severely do you think a man deserves to be punished who has trampled the Son of God under foot, who has treated as an unholy thing the blood of the covenant that sanctified him, and who has insulted the *Spirit of grace*? (Hebrews 10:29)

Since the Holy Spirit is a Spirit of grace, it follows that our struggling to accept God's grace might well hinder the Spirit from acting in our lives, changing us from the inside out, and giving us his fruit, such as joy and peace.

Overcoming Sin; Being Zealous

When someone is not changing, you know God's grace is being stymied—grace that should teach us to say "No" to sin and live a "fired up" life for Jesus every day. As Paul told Titus, the evangelist on the Mediterranean island of Crete:

> For the grace of God that brings salvation has appeared to all men. It teaches us to say "No" to ungodliness and worldly passions, and to live self-controlled, upright and godly lives in this present age, while we wait for the blessed hope—the glorious appearing of our great God and

Savior, Jesus Christ, who gave himself for us to redeem us from all wickedness and to purify for himself a people that are his very own, eager to do what is good (Titus 2:11–14).

The spiritual electricity practically jumps off Paul's pen! When we are doing well spiritually, the Spirit of grace changes us from the inside out—what excitement! What a great feeling!

Grace Makes Us Hard Workers

How hard of a worker are you? Do you ever get challenged on laziness? Laziness is a sin, according to the word of God (Proverbs 6:6–11, Ecclesiastes 10:18, Matthew 25:26, Hebrews 6:12). (Qualification: workaholics have their own special challenges; God is not calling us to neurosis!) Paul deeply appreciated God's grace, as is evident from his comments to the Corinthian Christians:

> For I am the least of the apostles and do not even deserve to be called an apostle, because I persecuted the church of God. But by the grace of God I am what I am, and his grace to me was not without effect. No, I worked harder than all of them—yet not I, but the grace of God that was with me (1 Corinthians 15:9–10).

As we saw in Titus 2:11–14, commitment to Jesus Christ is the natural result of the heart that appreciates grace. No one worked harder than Paul! Nor was anyone more confident that when he died, he would be meeting the Lord (Philippians 1:21–23, 2 Timothy 4:6-8). Many have pointed out a progression in Paul's appreciation of grace and in his humility:

Year	Verse	Self-description	Comparison group
56 AD	1 Corinthians 15:9	"Least of the apostles"	Apostles
60 AD	Ephesians 3:8	"Less than the least of God's people"	All disciples
65 AD	1 Timothy 1:15	"The worst of sinners"	All human beings

Notice the deepening awareness of his own unworthiness, the appreciation of grace. Notice also that the "comparison group" grows broader and broader. Who are you comparing yourself to? Are you growing in humility? (Dare any of us answer in the affirmative?) If we are not growing in our appreciation of God's grace—and becoming harder workers in the process—what are we becoming?

Grace Gives Assurance

Assurance is the confidence that we are saved. Although the Bible assures us that we can be totally confident in Christ, still we can struggle to really believe that God's Spirit actually lives in us—that we are not still just the "same old me" as ever. Some people even "doubt their conversion," so shallow is their understanding of God's grace. The Bible assures us we can know we have eternal life.[2]

Recently I was talking with a young man I was studying the Bible with. He was holding back from making a commitment to Jesus as Lord, and said, "I don't want to know whether I'm saved or not. I try not to think about that. I really don't want to know."

My reply was simple: "You *do* want to know! That's like saying, 'I don't want to know whether my house is burning down or not. I'll just stay here in my bedroom—either way's okay with me. I'm happy as I am.'" Nonsensical, right? *Of course you want to know!* And you can.

> And this is the testimony: God has given us eternal life, and this life is in his Son. He who has the Son has life; he who does not have the Son of God does not have life. I write these things to you who believe in the name of the Son of God so that you may know that you have eternal life (1 John 5:11–13).

Do you believe in the Son of God? Are you walking in the light (1 John 1: 7)? If you are, you have a promise that your sins are forgiven continually![3]

Grace Gives Reassurance

We all get great assurance when our sins are washed away (Acts 22:16). Still, it is nice to have reassurance as we go along! Here are some perspectives to help you to better understand God's grace:

1. We may confuse *feelings* of darkness with actual lostness. Whenever we knowingly sin, we "taste" the darkness to some extent. It is as though the act of sin attempts to reconnect us with the old self. Of course it cannot, since the old self has died (Romans 6:6, Galatians 2:20, 5:24, 6:14). The natural feelings of guilt that accompany sin are one thing; damning guilt is another thing altogether.

2. When we are playing a sport and miss a shot, we may say, "My bad." That means that we messed up—we acknowledge our responsibility and quickly move on. We realize that there is no use dwelling on it! There is a huge difference between "My bad" and "I'm bad." Why drag yourself through the mud every time you make a mistake? That is not spiritual! No verse in the Bible tells you to do

that. Pick yourself up and keep on walking (Jeremiah 8:4). Go—be free!

3. As one wise man said, "It's always easier to doubt your conversion than to trust in the grace of God." Many people doubt their conversion every time they go through a "bad patch." That is the easy way out! It's as if we are blaming God: "If he had really forgiven me and given me his Spirit, I wouldn't be here again!" Tell yourself what Jesus told Thomas: "Stop doubting and believe!" (John 20:27).

4. It is possible to be scripturally converted and then slip backwards. How about the Corinthian church? The entire congregation was plagued with petty squabbles, doctrinal confusion, scandalous sin, and yet nowhere in 1 Corinthians does Paul suggest that they are not real Christians or that they should be baptized again. What about Simon the Sorcerer, whose conversion seems highly suspect to many? Not even he was told to go and become a Christian (Acts 8:9–24). He was told to get his heart right, however.

Yes, it is possible to repent and then "renege." In Jeremiah 34:8–17 the people repent and free their slaves. Later they reneged, taking back their slaves. Bad move! What does God say? "Recently you repented..." (34:15). Relapse after repentance does not invalidate the repentance! They did repent, but later they changed their minds. When you made Jesus Lord, you were exercising your free will. From that point on you still have your freedom of choice; you can choose to do right or to slip back.

5. Preachers tend to "camp" on the "do's and don'ts," commitment and the programs of the church. (And I say, "Amen!") In some of our churches too little is said about the biblical teaching on grace and assurance—sometimes out of a fear that it will "backfire" and encourage the church to be complacent. To the preachers I say that this must change. The gospel is first and foremost the gospel of God's grace (Acts 20:24). You are not preaching the gospel if you are not preaching grace. However, to the rest I say, whether your local preacher(s) invigorate you by their sermons or "refrigerate" you—as a preacher, I am not without sin!—it is still up to you to ensure your own grasp of God's grace and to keep your "balance." Keep studying the whole Bible and deepen that walk with God!

6. The more active we are in the Lord's work—and I didn't say "hyperactive"—the more we will appreciate God's grace. Once I asked a group of young people in a church where biblical discipleship was not emphasized how confident they were they were saved. I said "Close your eyes. Now raise your hand if you think you are saved." Not even half the hands went up. A few years later I asked the same question to a church where every member was expected to be active and was held accountable, not just by the leaders, but by one another. Nearly

one hundred percent of the hands went up! (And it wasn't because these people thought they were earning their way to heaven.)

Conclusion

Disciples should be the most secure and confident people on the planet! After all, we have a "trillion-dollar insurance policy"! We should never wonder whether we have the Spirit or not.

The real question isn't whether we have the Spirit, anyway, but whether the Spirit has us! Through the grace of God, his Spirit will reform and re-form our lives. We will never be perfect in this life. So let's set our minds at ease, be thankful for his grace, and let the Spirit do his work.

QUESTIONS FOR THOUGHT

*   *Am I confident in my salvation, or uncertain?*

*   *Have I been influenced by incorrect theology, pitting "grace" against obedience?*

*   *Are there specific areas in my life which are robbing me of confidence? How can I overcome in these areas?*

NOTES

1. Highly recommended: Gordon Ferguson, *The Victory of Surrender* (Spring, Texas: Illumination Publishers, 2014).

2. I have more extensively expounded on this subject in *Life to the Full: The Powerful and Practical Writings of James, Peter, John & Jude* (Spring, Texas: Illumination Publishers, 2006), Chapter 18.

3. Sometimes it is incorrectly taught that we are forgiven of our past sins at baptism. But that is only half the picture; it covers future ones as well.

9. Led by the Spirit
How the Spirit Guides Disciples

Now that we are feeling secure in the gifts and grace of God, let's turn our attention to how God guides us. How can we be sure we know God's will? As we will come to see, being led by the Spirit is no different than being led by God or being led by Jesus. They are one and the same.

Spiritual Gyroscopes?

The notion that if we follow our own inner light we will stay on the path has been popular through the ages and remains so today. Richard Carlson, author of best-seller *Don't Sweat the Small Stuff*, states (in a book with some otherwise sound advice):

> You have at your disposal a foolproof guidance system to navigate you through life. This system, which consists solely of your feelings, lets you know whether you are off track and headed toward unhappiness and conflict—or on track, headed toward peace of mind. Your feelings act as a barometer, letting you know what your internal weather is like.[1]

Sadly, this sounds remarkably like much literature found in the Christian bookstores. Some may wonder if this is the meaning of being led by the Spirit. Are some people so holy that Proverbs 14:12 and Jeremiah 17:9 (below) don't apply to them?

> There is a way that seems right to a man,
>> but in the end it leads to death (Proverbs 14:12).

> The heart is deceitful above all things and beyond cure.
>> Who can understand it? (Jeremiah 17:9).

If anything is certain, it is the fact that it is dangerous to follow our feelings. Feelings have little to do with being led by the Spirit, and they certainly will not keep you "upright." And anyway, the gyroscope rights itself only because of another force: gravity. Without spin (our daily decision to follow Christ) and gravity (the force of the Word in our lives), the gyroscope soon topples.[2]

Led into All Truth?

Most Neopentecostals[3] cite John 14:26 and 16:13 in their claim that the Spirit is leading them. Just to clear up the confusion, we had better quote these texts in full:

> "All this I have spoken while still with you. But the Counselor, the Holy Spirit, whom the Father will send in my name, will teach you all things and will remind you of everything I have said to you" (John 14:25–26).

> "I have much more to say to you, more than you can now bear. But when he, the Spirit of truth, comes, he will guide you into all truth. He will not speak on his own; he will speak only what he hears, and he will tell you what is yet to come" (John 16:12–13).

First of all, who is being addressed in these passages? These are among Jesus' final words to his apostles before his arrest. They, not we, are the ones guaranteed (a) to be reminded of what Jesus had been teaching, and (b) to be guided into all truth. The first promise applies to those who heard him teach, but whose human memories might, without divine assistance, forget some of the things he taught. The second pertains to the future, the equipping of the church. These twin promises are fulfilled in the New Testament: The Gospels record what Jesus said and how he lived; Acts, the letters and Revelation apply the teaching of Jesus to the church. There is no support for the notion that all Christians are on the same level with the apostles or that the Spirit has special revelation for us![4]

The Bible Says…

Being "led by the Spirit" is biblical terminology. The problem is that it has been twisted and rather creatively reinterpreted by millions into a thoroughly unbiblical concept! The popular teaching about being led by the Spirit is that, once the Spirit comes into our hearts, we have an automatic guidance system that enables God to lead us through life and its maze of decisions, like having "a spiritual gyroscope" in our nose cone. What does the Bible say? The two clearest passages on the Spirit's leading are found in Romans and Galatians:

> Therefore, brothers, we have an obligation—but it is not to the sinful nature, to live according to it. For if you live according to the sinful nature, you will die; but if by the Spirit you put to death the misdeeds of the body, you will live, because those who are led by the Spirit of God

are sons of God. For you did not receive a spirit that makes you a slave again to fear, but you received the Spirit of sonship. And by him we cry, "Abba, Father" (Romans 8:12–15).

So I say, live by the Spirit, and you will not gratify the desires of the sinful nature. For the sinful nature desires what is contrary to the Spirit, and the Spirit what is contrary to the sinful nature. They are in conflict with each other, so that you do not do what you want. But if you are led by the Spirit, you are not under law (Galatians 5:16–18).

In each passage the Bible teaches us that being led by the Spirit is putting to death the sinful nature (literally, "the flesh"). The Spirit leads us in God's moral will, not his mystical will for every detail of our lives. Most of the decisions in our lives we will need to make ourselves, without divine direction. Of course this does not in any way rule out prayer, seeking advice and careful weighing of biblical principles.

Old Testament Background

As we see in Romans 8 and Galatians 5, being led by the Spirit is putting the flesh to death. That is the most common New Testament meaning of the term. What is the Old Testament background?

Ezekiel 36:27 shows that the Spirit will move us to obey God—assuming, of course, that this is our desire (see Psalm 40:8, 25:5). The Spirit does not override our free will. My favorite verse on the subject is Psalm 143:10:

Teach me to do your will,
    for you are my God;
may your good Spirit
    lead me on level ground.

We see that being led by the Spirit is a matter of discipline. There are no shortcuts. (How different this is from the charismatic view, where being "led" often means taking the path of least resistance.) Because we are becoming obedient, being led by the Spirit is a learning process, not just following hunches and impulses.

An historical illustration is found in Numbers 10, especially verse 31. The Israelites were led in the desert by a pillar of cloud (or fire, at night). You'd think the direction in which God was trying to lead them would be hard to miss, with that huge cloud out in front, showing the way! So why is Moses so intent on obtaining a good guide? "You can be our eyes," he says to Hobab. Most likely, because even with God's guidance, there are still numerous decisions on a lower level that we will have to make.

The application: God leads us through the cloud (the general principles of his word, the inexplicable turn of events, his providence, etc.), but also through people, logic, common sense and the specific application of the Bible. We must strike a balance between the two, neither relying wholly on man's strength (especially our own) nor floating off into the spiritual ether.

Yes, guidance comes through the Word, but in a broader sense the Spirit leads us through the entire obedience process, as we see in Psalm 143:10 and Ezekiel 36:27. The Spirit is at work in our lives, in God's providence, in ways we do not understand. The analogy of the guiding cloud is a good one to keep in mind as you consider the human and divine side to God's leading of his people.

Conviction of Sin

It is not biblical terminology to say, "The Spirit led me to skip church today" or "The Spirit prompted me to go to McDonald's for lunch." Yet this is the way it is used in Neopentecostal circles: in the sense of influencing someone to take a particular course of action. Interestingly, I have heard few in the Charismatic Movement claim, "The Spirit convicted me to repent of overeating" or "The Spirit is leading me to repent of prejudice and love people of all races." And yet the Bible is clear that the activity of the Spirit is to *convict of sin*.

> When [the Spirit] comes, he will convict the world of guilt in regard to sin and righteousness and judgment: in regard to sin, because men do not believe in me; in regard to righteousness, because I am going to the Father, where you can see me no longer; and in regard to judgment, because the prince of this world now stands condemned (John 16:8–11).

At first glance it might appear that the Spirit convicts whether or not the Word has been preached. But this is not so! The word of God is what is said to convict men (Jeremiah 23:22) and lead them to faith (Romans 10:17). Nehemiah 9:20-30 shows that the Spirit spoke to people in the Old Testament—through the prophets. The chief shortcoming of the false prophets was that they did not convict people of their sin (Lamentations 2:14). So we see that when we are convicted about our need to change things, the Spirit has been working on our hearts through the word of God. I praise God for the powerful sermons and direct challenges from men and women who love me. I need the challenge! And when we change, God is glorified.[5]

Once again, the Spirit leads us into God's moral will ("level paths"[6]) by convicting us of sin. Not that this is all the Spirit does. (If it were, this book would be much shorter!) This is the aspect of the Spirit's work most often neglected in contemporary Christendom, in favor of the more showy kind of religion—which is, more often than not, first cousin to the Psychic Friends Network.

Led Through Men and Women of Faith

The Scriptures teach over and over again that we are likelier to follow the right path when we make plans by seeking advice (Proverbs 12:5, 12:15, 13:10, 15:22, 19:20, 20:18). Receiving advice helps, not because our adviser is somehow inspired, but because we are able to obtain a more objective perspective on the issue with which we need help. With multiple advisers, we are more likely to find wisdom than we are with only one.

Naturally, there are some things about which we can receive perfectly good advice from a nonbeliever. You hardly need a strong disciple to advise you on how best to maintain your car or tie your shoes! Yet it would be foolhardy to rely entirely on outsiders for dating and marriage advice or suggestions on prayer and Bible study! (Proverbs 13:20, Isaiah 19:11, Ezekiel 11:2).

God works through the counsel of others, but do not mistake these persons as inspired! Some people seem to think that, because they are in some position of leadership, whatever advice they give is thereby "God's will." This is not only illogical and unbiblical, but has the potential for great abuse. Unless there are biblical grounds for it, it is quite possible that advice is no more than the opinion of man.

While it is nice to have a special friend, or discipler, who is able to give you guidance through your Christian life, often God's will becomes clear only after consulting a number of men or women of faith. This is certainly a way the Spirit leads God's people.

We can also come to a clearer understanding of God's will by observing the lives of men and women of faith (1 Corinthians 4:15–17, 11: 1, Philippians 4:9, Hebrews 6:11–12, 13:7).

Excursus: The Spirit and Romance

One of the most difficult areas in which to discern God's will is the domain of romance. How can you distinguish actual love from *feelings of love* for a person? Being in love—the euphoria, the emotional power surge—is not the same thing as loving. In general, it would be wise not to attribute to the Spirit certain events or feelings that occur in connection with romance.

Many a person has rationalized an unspiritual marriage on religious grounds (e.g. "The Spirit is telling me she's the one."). The Bible is clear: If we are disciples, we are to marry only another disciple (1 Corinthians 7:39, 2 Corinthians 6:14ff; Ezra 9–10).

In Genesis 29 is the admirable example of Jacob, who served seven years for Rachel, all the while maintaining sexual purity. The rather long period of courtship passes quickly, because of his love for her. (Had he not loved Rachel,would the time have dragged on at an agonizingly slow pace?)

Finally, here are a few pitfalls to avoid in romantic relationships:

- Rushing too quickly into a relationship.
- Becoming emotionally invested in a man or woman outside the faith.
- Sign-seeking in selection of a mate. ("If she looks at me when I look at her, I'll know she's the one.") There is simply no way to be sure that God is "playing your game."
- Discarding biblical principles. Dating an unspiritual brother or sister will cost you in the end.
- Being too picky. Perfectionism may well prolong your "bachelor" years!
- In the event of breaking up, a spiritual nose dive can take place when you have been propping up your Christian walk with euphoric feelings. A false sense of security and well-being can give way to deep discouragement.

Led Through the Word

Spiritual guidance comes through the Word, since all Scripture is inspired by the Spirit of God. Thus when we resist the plain teaching of the Bible, we are resisting the Spirit. Many say the Spirit convicts people apart from the Word. Often this is said in self-justification: "When the Spirit shows me that what you say is right, then I'll change." But the Scriptures teach that the Spirit convicts us through the Word (2 Timothy 3:16–17, John 16:8).

Once the Word is in our hearts (Jeremiah 31:33) through conditioning ourselves to follow its principles habitually, the Spirit will naturally be more able to lead us without our needing to look up verses or consult with others. It becomes second nature. Yet even then, "second nature" is never foolproof. The ultimate authority is the word of God.

Summary: Spirit Led

Before we begin an introductory exploration of the superstitious mind-set (to be continued in Chapters 10 and 11), let's sum up our findings:

- The Spirit does not lead us through feelings. All talk of "promptings," inner feelings, and mystical revelation is little more than "psychobabble."
- The only persons guaranteed to be "led into all truth" were the apostles.
- The central activity of the Spirit is convicting us of sin and enabling us to overcome it. The two fullest passages on this in the New Testament, Romans 8 and Galatians 5, are clear.
- Being led by the Spirit does not mean we no longer make our own decisions.
- The deeper the word of God is in our hearts, the more we may be able to go with our hunches. Yet this is never infallible.
- The Old Testament connects following the Spirit with obedience to God and his word.
- The Spirit convicts of sin. A spiritual person is thus an upward call to others; a spiritual sermon is a message that deeply convicts the listeners of biblical truths.
- God's Spirit leads through the principles of the Word.
- Be extremely cautious about attributing events to the Spirit of God where romantic forces are in play.
- The Spirit also leads us through men and women who are mature in the Word.

'I Feel Good!'

The religion of many is bound up in "feeling good." There's nothing wrong with feeling good, yet this is a confused spirituality. The basic fallacy: Spirituality means *feeling* God, as opposed to *following* his word. Rather than understanding what God's word is saying and then obeying it, emphasis is placed on tuning in to the divine wavelength. In short, subjectivity rules.

Feelings are the means by which many people make decisions. They seek God's will by looking into their hearts, for that is where they believe the Spirit speaks. They must be alert to the prompting of God, interpreting the signs in events, words, scriptures, dreams, the weather and so forth. If they do this, they are "led by the Spirit." Sadly, they are not aware of what the Bible really says.

Bliss?

The following excerpt from *The Pilgrim's Progress*, by John Bunyan (1628-88), captures the spirit of the discussion perfectly. It is a dialogue between Christian (Chr), the main character, and Ignorance (Ign), the blissful religious person. If you can wade through the Elizabethan English, I believe you will find it an enjoyable piece. As we will see, "Ignorance" is still alive and well!

Chr: Come, how do you? How stands it between God and your soul now?

Ign: I hope well, for I am always full of good motions that come into my mind to comfort me as I walk.

Chr: What good motions? Pray tell us.

Ign: Why, I think of God and heaven.

Chr: So do the devils and damned souls.

Ign: But I think of them, and desire them.

Chr: So do many that are never like to come there; the soul of the sluggard desires, and hath nothing (Proverbs 13:4).

Ign: But I think of them, and leave all for them.

Chr: That I doubt, for leaving of all is a hard matter; yea, a harder matter than many are aware of. But why, or by what, art thou persuaded that thou hast left all for God and heaven?

Ign: My heart tells me so.

Chr: The wise man says, "He that trusts his own heart is a fool" (Proverbs 28:26).

Ign: This is spoken of an evil heart; but mine is a good one.

Chr: But how dost thou prove that?

Ign: It comforts me in the hopes of heaven.

Chr: That may be through its deceitfulness; man's heart may minister comfort to him in the hopes of that thing for which he yet has no ground to hope.

Ign: But my heart and my life agree together; and therefore my hope is well grounded.

Chr: Who told thee that thy heart and life agree together?

Ign: My heart tells me so.

Chr: "Ask my fellow if I be a thief." Thy heart tells thee so! Except the Word of God beareth witness in this matter, other testimony is of no value.

Ign: But is it not a good heart that has good thoughts? And is not that a good life that is according to God's commandments?

Chr: Yes, that is a good heart that hath good thoughts; and that is a good
          life that is according to God's commandments: but it is one thing
          indeed to have these, and another thing only to think so.[7]

   Christian put it well: It is one thing to follow God's commandments and
quite another only to imagine that you are living as a Christian.

Jesus Visits Texas

   In his book *You Can be Led by the Spirit of God*, Kenneth Hagin, an influential charismatic author-speaker, reveals some of the secrets of the trade. In the
preface he shares his "open vision" of Jesus in an El Paso, Texas, hotel room,
followed by a thirty-minute conversation with the Lord himself. Jesus was 5 feet
11 inches tall and weighed 180 pounds—a real giant by the standards of first-century Palestine.

   I believe we should weigh very carefully any statement made by a person
convinced he is so important that Jesus has paid him a personal call. All the more
so when Hagin introduces us to his premise: "God's Spirit leads us through our
spirits."[8]

   Hagin goes on to state that the primary means by which God leads his children is the "inward witness." Claims Hagin, "If you renew your mind by the
Word, whatever your spirit tells you to do will be right."[9] One of his chapters is
even entitled "Listen to Your Heart"![10]

   In his conclusion Hagin states: "If you will follow these points...after a
while you can know the will of God the Father even in the minor details of life.
You will receive guidance and will always instantly get either a yes or a no. You
will know in your spirit what you should do."[11]

   This is erroneous for two reasons: (1) It assumes there is a will of God for
every minor detail of our lives. It is undeniable that God works in all our lives,
that "in him we live and move and have our being" (Acts 17:28), that he has
"predestined [us] to be conformed to the likeness of his Son" (Romans 8:29), that
his providence works even through our mistakes (Romans 8:28) and that he cares
about our lives on a personal level. But where is the proof God has a "plan" for
every detail of our lives?

   Ecclesiastes 9:11 says "time and chance" happen to us all. The scriptural
evidence is slim indeed, and the passages normally enlisted to support the traditional view are ambiguous at best.[12]

   (2) The superstitious position assumes we can trust our feelings and thus
allows complete confusion between God's will and our desires. One corollary of

this approach is that, as long as you go by your feelings, you can never be wrong (after all, it was the "leading" of the Spirit that made you do what you did). Ultimate responsibility for your actions thus falls upon God; you are cleared of personal responsibility. Not surprisingly, such a philosophy encourages a superstitious approach to life, as the question is always asked, "I wonder what this means?"

'You're Judging Me!'

We must show love toward those caught in the tangled web of superstitious spirituality. To bring the subject to life, let me share with you the story of Neil and the story of Darin.

When I first lived in London (1982), I met a friendly Australian chap who lived downstairs from me. Neil was quite religious, and very soon we began studying the Bible together. We had a particularly challenging study from Revelation 3:14-22, a passage which calls us to live a holy life (see Chapter 12 of this book). I then asked him whether he thought he was right with God. When he smugly replied he thought he was, I said, "How do you know?"

He said, "Oh, I just *know* I'm saved."

"Okay, but how do you 'just know'?" I asked.

"I know in my heart," he exclaimed.

"But Neil, what about the things we just saw in God's word?"

"Now you're judging me! I don't want to talk about it any more."

Needless to say, this young man's attitude cooled considerably. When such a person stakes eternity on feelings and when you point him to the word of God and he is still unwilling to give an inch, there is little you can do. Back up; try again. If he is still adamant, move on (Matthew 10:14). Pray that God may give him a change of heart at a later time (2 Timothy 2:26).

What a contrast we see in Darin! When our family first lived in the state of Maryland, a fiery fellow named Darin came to the church where I preached. Afterwards he said he was eager to spend some time together in fellowship, but would have to do so quickly, as he was going to "preaching school" in five days' time.

We arranged to meet, and it soon became apparent that Darin, as evangelistic and committed to the truth as he was, was staking his salvation on his feelings and experiences. Because he believed he had the power to "speak in tongues," he wrongly assumed he had understood the gospel (Acts 19:1-5). After three days of intensive Bible study—including his confronting some of his old friends on their confused doctrine—Darin took the step of becoming a disciple. Although he experienced considerable opposition, he decided not to go to preaching school, but rather to remain in the DC area as a part of a discipling ministry. Soon he was enrolled in a local university and is a happy, fulfilled and confident Christian to this day. Darin is thrilled that his new friends were willing to tell him where he stood according to the Scriptures (Ephesians 4:25) and point him in the right direction. (What a contrast to Neil!)

Judgment is the Lord's—the judging of motives as well as final, executive judgment. Yet the Scriptures teach that we are to judge, help, counsel, teach and admonish one another in Christ (Matthew 7:1–6, 1 Corinthians 5:12–13, 6:1–5, John 7:24, Colossians 1:28–29). As all disciples experience, some people are open to correction, others are not (Proverbs 9:7–9, 12:1).

Do not underestimate the effects of false doctrine on a person's spirituality, and even on his or her salvation. Let's have the heart to speak the truth in love (Ephesians 4:15) where important doctrinal matters are at stake.

Conclusion

Certainly the Holy Spirit can work any way he chooses to work, and at times he may lead us in ways we do not understand. The Spirit is not limited by our thoughts about him. Those who try to reduce the Spirit's work to human formulas will not succeed in keeping him in their man-made boxes. However, the Spirit leads the people of God primarily through the word of God, and the Spirit would never lead anyone to act contrary to the Word. Popular religion, contrary to Scripture, teaches, in effect, that *feeling* God is more important than *following* him.

We need to point people to the word of God. Feelings change, but the word of the Lord is a constant in the equation of life (1 Peter 1:25). Encourage people to read the Bible, obey it and allow the Spirit to lead them.

QUESTIONS FOR THOUGHT

- Is the Holy Spirit truly leading me through the Word? Am I aware of that fact?

- Is the Spirit triumphing over the flesh in my life?

- Am I superstitious or gullible? Have I had misconceptions about how the Spirit leads me?

NOTES

1. Richard Carlson, *Don't Sweat the Small Stuff* (New York: Hyperion, 1997), 217.

2. A word about 1 John 2:18-29. It is quite in fashion these days to speak of God's anointing on a person or a speaker. This "anointing" confers an inspiration from God, with special access to his will and guidance. Here the "anointing" we received from the Spirit—referring most likely to our instruction and induction in the ABCs of the faith—means that false teachers do not have to lead us astray. Although we will not discuss the passage beyond this one observation, ask yourself a question. "Does this even remotely sound like the 'anointing' many preachers are claiming today?" The answer is obviously "No." Anointing is not inspiration, nor does it have anything to do with having an inside track on the will of God.

3. Neopentecostalism is different from Pentecostalism, which is the doctrine of the Pentecostal denomination. Neopentecostalism refers to contemporary charismatic religion, pentecostal in theology, which is prevalent in nearly all major denominations. In other words, it is the movement in which Pentecostal teachings and practices have spilled over into non-Pentecostal churches.

In consideration of the variety within the Charismatic Movement, and the divergence, at times, of Neopentecostalism from classical Pentecostal denominational doctrines, the term "Neopentecostalism" will be used from this point forward.

4. Furthermore, the apostolic and prophetic fulfillment of these promises constituted the foundation of the church (Ephesians 2:20). Since the foundation is already laid, there can be no prophets or apostles today.

5. That we must hear the word in order to come to faith is clearly spelled out in Romans 10:13-17, where we discover the sequence: Hear the Word ⋯→ believe the Word ⋯→ call on name of the Lord ⋯→ receive salvation. This is important because many believe you can be saved without hearing or really understanding the gospel. For a living illustration of the sequence in action, see Acts 22:1-16.

6. For the biblical background, see Proverbs 2:13, 4:11, 4:25–27, Hebrews 12:13, Mark 1:3 (cp Isaiah 40:3).

7. John Bunyan, *The Pilgrim's Progress* (Grand Rapids, Mich.: Zondervan Publishing House, 1961). Used by permission.

8. Kenneth Hagin, *You Can Be Led by the Spirit of God* (Tulsa: Faith Library Publications, 1981), 15.

9. Ibid, 31, 98.

10. This is reminiscent of the apocryphal Ecclesiasticus 37:13, where we are told, "Stick to the advice your own heart gives you; no one could be truer to you than that."

11. Hagin, *You Can Be Led By the Spirit of God*, 137.

12. Recommended: Garry Friesen, *Decision Making and the Will of God* (Portland, Oregon: Multnomah Press, 1980).

Distraction, Inaction

Do not let anyone who delights in false humility and the worship of angels disqualify you for the prize. Such a person goes into great detail about what he has seen, and his unspiritual mind puffs him up with idle notions. He has lost connection with the Head (Colossians 2:18–19a).

Incorrect theology is bound to lead to either inactivity or the wrong sort of activity. These days, much weirdness is being taught in the name of the Spirit of Christ, to which we were briefly introduced in Chapter 9. Undue emphasis on feelings and experiences leads not only to a form of spiritual narcissism, but also to distraction. The inevitable result: inactivity.

When people are caught in this web of pseudo-spirituality, the vicious cycle feeds itself: distraction—inaction—distraction—inaction….

The following two chapters scrutinize the claims of superstitious forms of Christianity.

10. No Nonsense, No Way!
The Superstitious Mind-Set

Is this a chapter about black cats, stepping on sidewalk cracks or the number 13? Not at all. This is a chapter about the superstitious mind-set that permeates much of Christendom. Understanding this confused concept of spirituality is essential if we are going to avoid the pitfalls of its theology and help out those who have fallen into them.

A familiarity with the dictionary definition of "superstition" will prove helpful in identifying this misguided theology:

1. An irrational religious belief or practice; a tenet, scruple, habit, etc. founded on fear or ignorance. 2. Credulity regarding the supernatural, irrational fear of the unknown or mysterious; misdirected reverence. 3. Religion or practice or particular opinion based on such tendencies.[1]

The basic fallacy is that spirituality has to do with *feeling* the will of God, as opposed to *following* it. Once again some people think they have a corner on true Christianity! Many thoroughly superstitious people consider themselves to be "radicals." In this case, we must agree with Franklin D. Roosevelt's definition: "A radical is a man with both feet firmly planted in the air."[2]

In this chapter we examine three components of the superstitious mind-set: experience seeking, feelings orientation and irrationality. As we shall see, such pettiness in faith leads us away from Christ, not toward him. Distraction reinforces inaction.

Experience Seeking

For the superstitious person, spirituality—and even salvation—is based on the experiences one has had. The more experiences, or the more spectacular the experiences are, the more esteem (esteem within the group, as well as self-esteem). There is nothing wrong with experiences in themselves; their interpretation is what can reinforce doctrinal and moral error.

Once again, most people like fun and interesting experiences.[3] Take me, for instance. One afternoon, deep in the woods of the Boy Scout camp where I was working, I was thinking about God. I took out my pocket knife and carved a cross into a tree. Then I stabbed it with my knife, seven times! Immediately I heard a thunderbolt, saw a flash of lightning, the darkening of the sky and a sudden downpour of rain, followed by a howling wind. My heart was pounding, and as I moved away from the tree I looked back and saw a trail of light—created by the sunrays directly behind the tree, reflecting off the glistening leaves wet from the thundershower—from the cross to me. What an eerie feeling! I felt exhilarated, uplifted, as though God had revealed himself to me.

What is the interpretation of this wonderful experience? I have no idea. Yet many would stake their entire salvation on such an experience. It is edifying to exchange stories of experiences or "testimonies." The more wonderful things that have happened to you, some seem to think, the more evidence that you are saved! You may recall Paul's words about the superspiritual Colossian angel-worshipers, who, psychologically at least, operated on a similar basis:

> Do not let anyone who delights in false humility and the worship of angels disqualify you for the prize. Such a person goes into great detail about what he has seen, and his unspiritual mind puffs him up with idle notions. He has lost connection with the Head... (Colossians 2:18–19a).

Those who were troubling the Colossians[4] went into great detail about what they had seen. They mistakenly assumed that the more experiences they had, the more spiritual they were. But they had lost all connection with the Head (Christ); as for the depth of their spiritual insight, they were in theological "deep space." As with these "superspiritual" people, many today seek experiences. In their version of the gospel, spiritual experience takes the place of spiritual obedience. The free-floating "Spirit" is exalted at the expense of the crucified Christ.

Feelings Orientation

In Chapter 9 we explored the feelings mind-set of Neopentecostalism. We learned that feelings alone are the means by which many people make decisions. They seek God's will by looking into their heart, for that is where they believe the Spirit speaks. They strive to stay sensitive to the "prompting" of the Spirit, seeking signs and portents in current events, words, weather, dreams and so on. This position is erroneous for two reasons. First, it assumes that there is a "will of God" for each minor detail of our lives. This is far from proven. Second, it assumes that we can trust our feelings. Thus there is a complete blending, or confusion, between "God's will" and our desires.

Still, we all have something in common. The Neopentecostals are protesting against the cold rationalism and formalism of the traditional church—a criticism widely shared among Bible believers.[5] Can you really blame people for seeking a more feelings-based spirituality, when this traditionalism has been their experience?[6]

- "God just doesn't seem real here—all these meaningless ceremonies...."
- "How do they expect my kids to believe in Christianity when this is what it's like?"
- "There's a lot of talk, but no power here—the church is dead."
- "The fellowship just isn't warm. Newcomers are ignored. I'm a member, but I feel like an outsider."
- "The preacher puts me to sleep. I get the feeling the pastor doesn't really believe what he's saying."
- "I feel like something is missing in my life, but whatever it is, I know I won't find it here."

Considering the spiritual poverty of much of Christendom (Amos 8: 11–12), it is easy to see why people are drawn into feelings-based spirituality. When we begin to empathize with those feelings, we are on our way to making progress in helping people. Do not be aloof, intimidated or disdainful when you meet people who want to share their frustration with mainline Christianity.[7]

Irrationality

There is a palpable antirational strain in much modern religion. Reason, logic, even education, are to be mistrusted, since they may lead you to wrong conclusions about spiritual reality or the interpretation of the Bible. Instead of the sciences, research and the quest for understanding of our world providing evidence of the wisdom, majesty, creativity and intelligence of God, they are all suspect. All too often rationality is a challenge to the Neopentecostal mind-set.

This antirational strain is apparent in much of the literature. Take, for example, *The Fourth Dimension,* authored by Paul Cho, pastor of a 480,000 member Yoido Fellowship (Assemblies of God) church in Seoul, South Korea.[8] In the preface, Robert Schuller, former pastor of the Crystal Cathedral in Garden Grove, California, said simply, "Don't try to understand it, just start to enjoy it!"[9]

"Don't try to understand it"? Here is the crux of the problem. Cho is certainly a man of vision, but publishing such an introduction to his book will hardly make the thinking person more receptive to his message! Granted, there are some things we need not weary ourselves trying to fathom (Psalm 131:1), but the most effective way to win someone to your position is not to beg him to take what you say on blind faith. Christianity is in fact hailed as "true and reasonable" (Acts 26:25) in the Scriptures.

Another example of this anti-intellectual trend is found in the words of Mel Tari, who advises his readers to "take out that small computer which is your brain and put it in a little box and shoot it to the moon. Then let God use your heart." Incredible! He then generalizes: "The main difference between science and Christianity is this: science we must experience to believe; Christianity we must believe to experience."[10] In other words, for Tari, if one will just believe—and please don't ask too many questions—everything will become clear. But this is the opposite of the biblical approach to faith: We believe on the basis of evidence and testimony. (The gospel of John brings out the importance of this most clearly: 14:11, 5:31–40, etc.)

For one final example of the irrational bent in superstitious faith, I recall being dumfounded as I listened to a do-it-yourself cassette tape on how to learn to "speak in tongues." The instructions said: "Put your brain in neutral; put your tongue in high gear; and step on the gas!" Brain in neutral? No thank you! That is quite different from the admonition of Jesus (Matthew 22:37), Paul (Colossians 3:2) and Peter (1 Peter 1:13).

Neutral to First

Well, there you have the superstitious mind-set. How are we to communicate effectively with people who think this way and bring them to a more rational position? How can we help them move from "neutral" to "first gear"?

The truth that sets us free (John 8:32) is not an interpretive free-for-all, arrived at emotionally. The truth, though more than just a list of correct doctrines, is objective in nature: facts revealed by God, assented to by men, which bring us into the glorious freedom of the family of God. In order to bring a superstitious person to a knowledge of the truth, we must effect a fundamental change in the way he thinks.

No Nonsense! (But Do Be Sensitive!)

Following are some faux pas we should be wary of committing as we help our friends come to a "no-nonsense" spirituality.

Arguing Against Experience

It is not only insulting, but also illogical, to argue against experience. There is no way to prove that people have not really had the experience they claim. The interpretation of the experience may be open to debate but never the experience itself. If someone says she saw an angel, well, she saw something! Whether it was an angel or not, a good one or a bad one, or just an hallucination, may be determined later. But she did experience something. People sometimes exaggerate unwittingly; usually they are trying to be honest.

Someone tells you, "I was healed. They prayed for me, and my ulcers all went away!" How thoughtless, how insensitive it would be to say: "No, you were not healed! You still have those ulcers, and I think you are just pretending the pain isn't there." How discourteous! You may disagree with a position or find fault with an argument, but you cannot argue against an experience. (That is not to say that we may not suggest alternative explanations.)

Maybe his illness did go away, maybe she did feel a warm, exhilarating glow on that walk through the woods. Arguing against experience is fruitless, because you cannot prove logically that a person did not experience what he says he experienced. Furthermore, such an approach leads to sidetracked discussions and many headaches. Brothers and sisters, never argue against experience!

Many non-Christians have had religious experiences at some point in their lives; these cannot all be discounted. For instance, consider the promise "Seek and you will find" (Matthew 7:7). If a non-Christian begins to seek God, prays for God's guidance, and God begins to work in that person's life in a special way in answer to his prayers, who are we to say that those strange coincidences, those answered prayers, those occasional glimpses of the light that made more and more sense, are nothing more than psychological phenomena or the work of Satan?[11]

Rather than dispute experiences, it is more effective to challenge lifestyles; discuss discipleship. In the summer of 1980 I had just graduated from college and was traveling in Scandinavia. I met a Finnish fellow who noticed my Bible as I walked down the street and invited me to coffee. He said "I feel that the Lord has brought you into my life, Douglas." After we had finished our coffee and a long discussion, he bowed down and started "speaking in tongues."

"Well," I said, "what is that supposed to prove?" "I'm speaking in tongues!" he replied.

"I know," I said, "but there are lots of people who speak in tongues who aren't right with God. Tell me something: How often do you read your Bible? Every day?"

"No, I'm afraid not." "Then every other day?" "Well, no."

"Once a week?"

"I try to make time to read, but...." (I could see his lack of commitment to the Word).

"I think you're right. The Lord did lead me to you, and I have a message for you: Read your Bible. Stop basing your salvation on your feelings and read God's word every day!"

He needed that challenge, rather than an argument on the psychological explanation of tongue-speaking! We must learn to show people that we can have confidence in our salvation because of God's word (1 John 2:3-6, 5:13).

Mockery

Comments like, "If you believe in faith healing, why do you still wear glasses?" are not likely to win points. Moreover, there were a number of people God did not heal through men who definitely had the gift of healing. For example, Paul left Trophimus sick in Miletus (2 Timothy 4:20), told Timothy to drink wine for his stomach illnesses (1 Timothy 5:23) and himself had a thorn in the flesh which God would not remove even after three prayers for healing (2 Corinthians 12:8).

Sarcasm also falls into this category.

Denying the Working of God

God works in the lives of everyone, whether or not they are following the Bible. One of the worst errors we can commit is to ascribe good deeds and sincere religious experience to the devil. Sometimes it is erroneously taught that, since "God does not listen to sinners" (John 9:31—We must keep in mind that this is the Pharisees speaking and that in the context Jesus said they were wrong), he does not have anything to do with the lives of unbelievers. This is false.

God can and does work in everyone's life—certainly in those seeking him (Matthew 7:7, Acts 14:17, 2 Kings 5:1-15).

The Bottom Line

The bottom line is that spiritual experience does not authenticate salvation. Miraculous activity is no guarantee of a right relationship with the Lord. Men who prophesy or perform awesome signs are not necessarily to be trusted. For example, in 1 Samuel 19:23 we read about the Spirit falling on Saul. He even prophesied. Does this mean that he was saved? No; the Lord had already left Saul (1 Samuel 16:14), who demonstrated the wickedness of his heart through disobedience to the clear instructions of God. Furthermore, he gave vent to his insane jealousy of David (who was fast rising up to eclipse him), repeatedly attempting to take his life. Even though God had rejected him as king over Israel, he caused the Spirit to fall on Saul (for God's own purposes), as well as on the three companies of men Saul had sent before him to capture David.

In 1 Kings 13 the young prophet forfeited his life because he chose to treat another man's word as of higher authority than the revealed word of God. And in Deuteronomy 13:1–5 we find, I believe, the clearest Old Testament passage on the danger of following people merely on the basis of their miraculous activity:

> If a prophet, or one who foretells by dreams, appears among you and announces to you a miraculous sign or wonder, and if the sign or wonder of which he has spoken takes place, and he says, " Let us follow other gods" (gods you have not known) "and let us worship them," you must not listen to the words of that prophet or dreamer.
>
> The LORD your God is testing you to find out whether you love him with all your heart and with all your soul. It is the LORD your God you must follow, and him you must revere. Keep his commands and obey him; serve him and hold fast to him. That prophet or dreamer must be put to death, because he preached rebellion against the LORD your God, who brought you out of Egypt and redeemed you from the land of slavery; he has tried to turn you from the way the LORD your God commanded you to follow. You must purge the evil from among you (Deuteronomy 13:1–5).

The Lord may be testing the purity of our hearts and our devotion to him through the seemingly "miraculous" event![12]

About Counterfeits

Many times I have had people tell me, "This definitely happened—I know it wasn't counterfeit." When I question them further about how they can be so sure, they usually say, "I just know." There's a problem with that response. What kind of person has the experience required to distinguish between a counterfeit and the genuine article?

Many years ago in England I had an encounter with the police, for allegedly using counterfeit money—in a video game machine! The fifty-pence piece looked perfectly normal to me. But when the coin jammed the machine, the proprietors of the establishment called the constable. After a short time of questioning (no jail time), I was released with the warning, "There are quite a few of these coins circulating around, mate. Watch out for counterfeits!"

How can you tell the difference between a clever counterfeit and the original? Unless the counterfeit specimen is shoddily produced, or unless you are an "expert" in miracles, you cannot! We simply do not have the expertise to say with certainty, "This is genuine; that is phony."

Here are a few handy passages in which miracles clearly do not prove someone is saved:

- Deuteronomy 13:1–11: God may be testing us to see if we will hold closely to his word. Don't be sentimental; even close friends and relations may be deceived.

- 1 Samuel 19:18–24: The Spirit may fall even on people who are not right with God. Miracles have a purpose, but they say nothing about the salvation of the one God is working through.

- 1 Kings 13:1–26: One prophet is duped by another prophet to question the word of God and dies for his mistake.

- Mark 13:22: False messiahs perform "miracles." Many religious groups spring up around "wonder-workers."

- Acts 19:13: Some Jews were casting out demons. Exorcisms (none occur in the Old Testament) are done in some cases by those who are not even following Jesus Christ (Mark 9:38–40).

- 2 Thessalonians 2:9–11: We must really love the truth to see the truth. God becomes an active agent in hardening our hearts, in "turning us over" to what we want to believe.

- Revelation 13:13, 16:14, 19:20: These are examples of more false miracles. (These highly figurative passages, as in the Thessalonians reference above, are no proof that Satan possesses power to work miracles. Scripturally, he can only counterfeit them.)

Doing the will of God, not miracles, is what authenticates salvation! As Jesus said emphatically,

> "Not everyone who says to me, 'Lord, Lord,' will enter the kingdom of heaven, but only he who does the will of my Father who is in heaven. Many will say to me on that day, 'Lord, Lord, did we not prophesy in your name, and in your name drive out demons and perform many miracles?' Then I will tell them plainly, 'I never knew you. Away from me, you evildoers!'" (Matthew 7:21–23).

Conclusion

Let's remain level-headed, renouncing superstition. Distraction brings inaction. Let's teach people how the Spirit really works.

QUESTIONS FOR THOUGHT

- *Am I superstitious? Am I someone who looks for "signs," or am I content to accept God's will as revealed in the Word and strive to implement it through responsible decision making?*

- *Am I willing to have the patience it will take to instruct a superstitious person in the principles of the Word?*

_____ NOTES _____

1. Adapted from the Oxford English Dictionary.

2. Broadcast address to Forum on Current Problems, 26 October 1939.

3. In May 1997, Scripps' Howard News Service profiled former lawyer James Kelley of Washington, D.C., one of a small group at his local church who are enthusiastic Episcopalians but who do not believe in God. Said Kelley, "We all love the incense, the stained glass windows, the organ music, the vestments, and all of that. It's drama. It's aesthetics. It's the ritual. That's neat stuff. I don't want to give all that up, just because I don't believe in God" ("News of the Weird," 9/12/97).

We all have an inner longing for spiritual experiences—atheists included! This is not bad in itself; but it may be misdirected, as in the case above. The bottom line is truth, not fulfillment.

4. Technically, Judaizing Gnostic ascetics.

5. This dissatisfaction accounts for the rise of the monastic movement (third century), a reaction against the lack of spirituality in the Catholic Church of the day. Men left the church and banded together in separate communities, often becoming mystics, seeking fresh revelations from God and intimate experiences of fellowship with him. In fact, such reactions against worldliness have been chronicled countless times in the annals of the major religions of the world. So it is with those who, disillusioned with traditional Christianity, strike out to join Neopentecostalism.

6. Much research has been conducted into the Charismatic Movement, or Neopentecostalism. In the following survey, some eighty-two percent of those questioned indicated that they were spiritually unfulfilled and fundamentally unhappy with their church situation before finding something new in the Charismatic Movement.

Spiritual Satisfaction Before "Spirit Baptism"

Not at all	15.9%
A little	25.0%
Quite a bit	34.1%
Extremely so	22.7%
No reply	2.3%

Source: Russell P. Spittle. Ed., Perspectives on the New Pentecostalism (Grand Rapids: Baker, 1976), 143.

7. Fascinating reading: Thomas C. Reeves, The Empty Church: The Suicide of Liberal Christianity (New York: The Free Press, 1996).

8. In the era of the "megachurch," this probably remains the world's "gigachurch."

9. Paul Yonggi Cho, The Fourth Dimension (Plainfield, NJ: Logos International, 1979). By the way, on June 28, 1997 Schuller was sued for $5 million by a flight attendant. Schuller disrupted a United Airlines flight from Los Angeles to New York, violently shaking the flight attendant, after experiencing dissatisfaction with the in-flight service. "I'm a 'hands-on' person," Schuller later joked, after apologizing and paying an $1100 fine. Source: Christianity Today (October 6, 1997), 85. Crystal Cathedral Ministries filed for bankruptcy in October 2010 and in February 2012 sold the building and its adjacent campus to the Roman Catholic Diocese of Orange for use as the diocese's new cathedral.

10. Mel Tari, A Mighty Wind (Carol Stream, Illinois: Creation House, 1972), 61.

11. If the counter argument is made that charismatics are not actually advocating idolatry, Galatians 1:6–9 and 2 Corinthians 11:3–4 will prove helpful.

12. Although I try to keep an open mind, far too much of what happens in supposedly spiritual circles is hard to take seriously. For example, consider the following report:

> Oak Ridge, Tennessee—Sam Brobst took a "Learning Your Spiritual Gift" course at Full Life Center, a charismatic church, and felt the Lord leading him to prophesy during meetings. But when Brobst opened his mouth the first time, he and others were surprised by what came out: pirate speak.
>
> "We were in the middle of worship, when this voice rings out, 'Yar! Hear the word of the Lord—the Lord of the mighty seas!'" says one witness. "It was straight out of a Disneyland ride." Christianity Today 38, January 2008, by way of LarkNews.com

11. Hot Line to God?
Divine, Psychological or Diabolical?

When I was a teenager, my parents gave me my own telephone line—with a red phone. On this line I conversed with school friends, ordered pizzas, made prank calls, talked with girls and even played chess. My own private line! I must confess, I felt mighty presidential with that red telephone. (Plus, we lived in a white house!) It was my "hot line"!

We all have a need to feel important. But at times people compensate for loneliness, low self-esteem or perhaps guilt, by living in a fantasy world. They imagine they have their own "hot line" to God, meaning a link so sure and direct that they do not need to test what they hear with Scripture or with the counsel of others. The appeal of this hot line is extremely strong in Neopentecostal circles.

Raising the Dead?

My fellow minister Douglas Arthur came across a woman at Boston University who claimed she had a hot line to God. She was so spiritual, she said, that she could do miracles. Douglas asked her if she had ever raised a dead person.

"As a matter of fact, I have," she replied. "I arrived on the scene of a car crash, and there was this man lying dead on the pavement. I laid my hands on him, said a prayer and raised him from the dead."

Douglas was stunned and asked, "Are you certain that he wasn't still alive? People involved in car crashes are knocked unconscious all the time."

"Well, he was definitely dead," she retorted.

"Okay. I'm just asking how you could be sure he was dead." "Oh, I could just sense it," she replied.

"You don't say!" Douglas said. "Do you think you could ever do it again?"

"Sure, if that was God's will."

"I suppose the Spirit would tell you if that's what he wanted to be done."

"That's right—the Spirit would tell me."

"The Spirit would tell me"? This is the hot line to God. Of course, it is not possible to reason with everybody who claims to be this plugged in to the Deity!

As we saw in Chapter 5, the search for shortcuts to spirituality is one of the ways modern culture has infiltrated would-be followers of Jesus Christ. Everybody wants to cut corners. As one example, for decades now, America has had "drive-in churches." There is one church in Florida where you drive in and deposit a coin in the machine and out comes a bread wafer and a small quantity of grape juice. After hearing the "thought for the day," you drive off. Imagine that! Church in less than ten minutes. How convenient! Faith on the run; painless Christianity—no sacrifice—which is the exact problem.

In this chapter we will take a look at ten areas of confusion about knowing God's will. And we will see that no one today has "a hot line to God"!

The Gift of Prophecy

Many modern-day groups boast "prophets and prophetesses." It is certainly a nice thought that God would single you out as a channel for communicating his word. Whether such people are connected to God or not is another matter.

Ephesians 2:20 teaches that the Christian prophets, along with the apostles, formed the foundation of the church. In Ephesians 2:20, 3:5 and 4:11, it is the New Testament prophets that are in view, not Old Testament ones. The miraculous "prophetic" office was probably exercised in the evangelists' writing of the four Gospels. It also seems to have been at work in the prophesying of Agabus, as well as with Philip's daughters (Acts 11:28, 21:9-10). However, this is no longer present today. Once the foundation was laid, the structure was built upon it. Therefore, there is no need to lay the foundation again; there is no need for the first-century prophetic office again. If prophets were here today, then there would be no reason why apostles would not also be with us, as they go together in Ephesians 2:20, 3:5 and 4:11. There are, however, no apostles. To be an apostle one had to be an eyewitness of the resurrected Christ (1 Corinthians 9:1, Acts 1: 22), as well as work miracles, signs and wonders (2 Corinthians 12:12). Apostles were also miraculously equipped by the Spirit to remember the words Jesus had spoken to them, among other things (John 14:26, 16:13). (The Mormon church's claim conflicts with Scripture.)

Once again, since there are no apostles anymore, and since apostles and prophets are coupled in the New Testament, it follows that there are no prophets with "foretelling" abilities today. (We still, of course, need plenty of preacher/ prophets who are "forth tellers," and who call us powerfully back to God and his word.)

Discerning the 'Spirits'

1 Corinthians 12:10 speaks of discerning the spirits, while 1 John 4:1 instructs us to test the spirits. Neopentecostals will say they can "just tell" whether someone has a good spirit or whether God wants them to do this or that. I think this has nothing to do with the biblical texts. Those who claim to have

this spiritual gift are not, in this case, particularly "discerning"!

A "spirit" actually stands for a prophetic message. Strange as that may sound, in 2 Thessalonians 2:2 the Greek word "spirit" is usually rendered "prophecy" or "prophetic message." When we read the word "spirit," we think immediately of an incorporeal being. Yet this is not always correct. The spirit can be the message itself. 1 Thessalonians 5:19–22 and 1 Corinthians 14:29 deal with the same subject: what to make of prophecies.

The conclusion: "Discerning the spirits" meant nothing more than weighing the prophetic messages delivered to the first-century churches through those with the miraculous gifts of prophecy.

'Fleecing'

In Judges 6:36–40, the wavering Gideon puts out a fleece to know the certainty of God's will—not that God hadn't already spoken! "Fleecing" is, in effect, putting a kind of ultimatum to God: "God, if this is what you want me to do, give me the sign I'm asking you for; if it doesn't happen, I'll assume this isn't your will."

When I was part of the Charismatic Movement, my usual "fleece" for decision making was a simple traffic light. "Lord, if it's green, I'll do it; if it's red I won't; and if it's yellow, I'll hold off for now and try later." The sign-seeking mind-set looks for indications of God's will. Putting out a fleece is a common and accepted practice. But is it really a spiritual practice? Some considerations:

1. Gideon had a weak faith, despite the revealed word of God for his life.

2. He is nowhere commended for his "fleecing." In fact, it is clear from Isaiah 7:11–12 that asking for a sign is "putting the Lord to the test."

3. Jesus refused to put God to the test in Matthew 4:7. (It must be conceded that in Deuteronomy 6:16, which Jesus quotes, the "testing" was being done from selfish and rebellious motives, which was different from Gideon's situation.)

4. A major problem with the fleecing approach is that one never knows whether God has agreed to play along with the game or not, since the outcome does not provide a definite indication of the will of God. (Even if the light were green, there would always be room to doubt whether God was really answering my prayer or that he considered it a worthy test of his will.)

5. God is in no way obligated to play our games. He is in heaven, and he does whatever he wills (Psalm 115:3). We are not the ones to dictate the bases upon which we will obey his word.

6. Fleecing must not be confused with asking for an open door (1 Corinthians

16:9, 2 Corinthians 2:12, Colossians 4:3, Revelation 3:8). With the fleece, you are free to "go" regardless of the result of the fleece test. But with a door, you can "go" only if God opens it. (Unless you want to break your nose!)

The 'Peace of Christ'

Many teach that you can know God's will through this simple process:

1. Pray about the matter.
2. See whether your heart is at peace with a certain decision or course of action or not.
3. If not, keep submitting your request to God until you are at peace about it.
4. Once your heart is at peace, you know you have found the will of God.

This interesting view is based on Colossians 3:15, where the peace of Christ is to rule our hearts. But look at the context of the passage; it has nothing at all to do with discerning God's will but rather is discussing our one-another relationships! Another common support for the view is found in 2 Corinthians 2:12–13, where Paul says he had felt uneasy about ministering in a certain city because he felt the need to work with his fellow evangelist Titus, who was in another location. The "peace of Christ" notion is stretching things a bit, don't you think?

Answered Prayers

If you can be one hundred percent certain that God has heard you, that your prayers are answered, then, it is surmised, you have a direct line to God. You are probably saved, in God's good books. Ah—but the first notion must be challenged. While we may be reasonably sure God has answered certain of our prayers, giving us what we asked for, in other cases this is far from certain. Besides, God is not the only power with the ability to arrange events.

I am not saying, by the way, that God has never answered my prayers in a fairly clear manner. It is also clear that he has provided on many occasions when I did not even ask him to. Prayer is powerful, and no disciple can fail to experience its value and the sense of majesty it allows us to feel as we enter the presence of God. Yet prayer concerns faith. There is always *some* room for doubt—if only a one-percent margin. Is total certainty required for faith? No, for then it would not be faith! (2 Corinthians 5:7).[1] In short, answered prayers are (1) difficult to assess, (2) not open to scientific verification and, moreover, (3) within reach even for an unbeliever.

Hearing Voices

When people say they hear God's voice in their head, is it psychological or satanic? Such people do have problems, and I have attempted to study the Bible with several persons convinced that God or some other power is speaking to them. I knew one woman who had received many "prophecies" from God. She was so eager for God to speak to her that one day she "heard" the word "Ishmael," the Hebrew for "God is listening," which is precisely what she was straining to do! (Curious reversal.)

While we can never (biblically) rule out God's speaking to us in an audible voice, the claim seems improbable to the highest degree. The jury will probably be out a long time on whether the source is demonic or psychotic.

What is the theological justification for hearing voices? Some consider Isaiah 30:21 to support the notion of the "inner voice." Yet in context, the voice is that of spiritual teachers or true prophets, not the mystical whisperings of the Holy Spirit. (For more on this passage, see the entry in Chapter 27.) In biblical history God did, on rare occasion, speak to an individual human being. Abraham and Solomon, for example, each heard God's voice two or three times. We have three occasions when Jesus himself heard the voice of God. The Spirit does speak once each to Peter, Philip and Ananias in Acts. With such occurrences so rare in Scripture, is it not odd that some today would report so many visitations?

In summary, voices, because they are experienced in the brain, cannot be refuted. But since voices are heard by all kinds of people with all kinds of agendas and problems, we can draw no conclusions about spirituality from them.

Dreams

We all have dreams. As a teenager, I used to have recurring dreams about tornadoes. The dark funnel cloud was on the horizon, and I was trying to warn everyone else, who often did not take me seriously. I have dreamed about vampires and other creatures of the darkness. Many times I have been on the run from Hitler's Nazis, and several times from Mafiosi. (Too many movies!) Before the Soviet coup in July 1991, I dreamed I was walking on water in the USSR! Another time I dreamed I was being held and drugged by the KGB, though I managed to escape. Did I dream this because I had been to Russia and was connecting loose thoughts? Or was it a premonition to warn me to be careful on future visits? Or was it to prepare me for a lunch my wife and I actually had with a KGB agent? Or did I have these dreams simply because I am interested in Russia? Who knows?

We all tend to dream about the things most important to us, and dream theory has discovered a more or less standard array of symbols.[2] Dreams in biblical times were an occasional means of divine communication. However, there is no evidence that God continues to speak to mankind in this way. (If you are interested, Chapter 27, question 14 addresses the question at length.)

Do not be overly impressed or alarmed by someone's dream, even if it includes Jesus, the devil and you! While we cannot rule out the possibility that God is getting our attention, we can never know for sure (Job 4:12–17 and 33:14–18).

No-Cost Exegesis

The common Neopentecostal approach to the interpretation of Scripture is that, as you read the Bible, the Spirit reveals the meaning of the passage to you. If your attitude is right, or you "have the peace of God in your heart," then whatever you sense in your spirit will be trustworthy. This position hinges on a rather dubious interpretation of 1 Corinthians 2:14, as well as on John 16:13 and 14:26, which, though addressed specifically to the apostles, are wrested from their context and turned into a promise for all believers.

The fruit of this subjective approach is that scriptures are taken out of context. The pastor of a London congregation had a dream about the "end times"— complete with rapture, tribulation, the conversion of all Israel, the beast from the sea, Armageddon, the Antichrist, political intrigue in the Politburo, etc. How did she know this vision was from God? "Because the book of Revelation verifies it." And how did she know that this is what Revelation is talking about? "Because God showed it to me in my dream." This amounts to circular exegesis.

I remember one fellow who was beginning to attend church and study the Bible. Like all of us, this young man had a lifestyle adjustment he needed to make. (The Bible calls it repentance!) When we pointed out that homosexuality is a sin, he squirmed. Even when he finally agreed that the Bible says it is wrong, he still claimed, "But the Spirit is telling me it's okay. I'm an exception." What? The Holy Spirit is at odds with the Bible, the Spirit in tension with the Word? If so, the Spirit is at cross purposes with the "sword of the Spirit" (Ephesians 6:17). Does this make sense to you? It didn't to us, either. Needless to say, that man did not repent and make Jesus his Lord.

Few believers go so far as to consciously demean the authority of the Bible, though in an unwary moment some will inadvertently tip their hand. "You have to realize that it [prophecy] isn't exactly God doing it. It is men doing it by the inspiration of the Spirit of God. Anything that man has to do with is not perfect...."[3] So they pick and choose what they want to accept? Like the previous errors, this one founders because of its utter subjectivity.

Casting Lots

Will the Spirit show us his will today through the casting of lots? We read in Proverbs 16:33, "The lot is cast into the lap, but its every decision is from the Lord," and further in Proverbs 18:18, "Casting the lot settles disputes and keeps strong opponents apart." Ancient peoples often cast lots[4] to know the will of heaven. For example, the ancient Persians threw the pur, as we read about in the book of Esther. Unlike the other peoples, the Hebrews were assured by God that when they sought his will he would give accurate answers.

Also, under Levitical law, the priest wore a special vestment called an ephod, to which were attached Urim and Thummim[5]—a priestly method for knowing God's will. (One stood for Yes, the other for No.) Drawing straws isn't a bad idea for settling disputes—even today in certain circumstances!—but can we be certain the outcome truly reflects the will of God?

The confusion arises because we do not discern the two covenants. Under the old covenant, the final time lots were cast to make decisions, as far as we can see, was when the apostolic group needed a replacement for Judas. The lots were cast and the Lord's choice was clear (Acts 1:21–26). (We have no reference to this very Jewish custom ever being used by those under the new covenant.)

There is no warrant today for casting lots to discern God's will. We have all the principles, precepts, commands and guidelines we need—in the Bible!

'From the Lord'?

What does this curious phrase mean? "A beautiful girl walked into my life, and even though she's not a Christian I feel I should go out with her. The Lord sent her to me. This was definitely from the Lord."[6] The problem is that "from the Lord" can mean that something is (a) good or (b) bad—in the sense of painful or unfortunate. Either one! The term "from the Lord" means that God has allowed or caused something to happen—that it fits within his plans and his providence.

In 1 Samuel 26 Saul's bodyguard let him down. David and Abishai could easily have killed Saul, but instead they only took his spear and water jug. Abishai's interpretation of the situation: "Today God has delivered your enemy into your hands" (26:8). Abishai was arguing, in effect, "Look, it's from the Lord; this turn of events reveals God's will for you, David." The man of God, however, knew that a higher principle was at stake. A similar situation occurs in 1 Samuel 24:6, where Saul, having entered a cave to relieve himself, was completely off guard, and yet David refused to lay a hand on the Lord's anointed (as in 26:11.)

It is clear from 1 Kings 12:15 that "from the Lord," here used of the unwise rejection of advice by Rehoboam, does not mean the individuals involved are following a spiritual course of action. Rehoboam's folly led to the total rift between Israel and Judah, and yet it is described as "from the Lord." A similar instance is found in Judges 14:4, where Samson enters an unspiritual marriage.

No, events are not a trustworthy indicator of God's will. Yes, whatever happens God has allowed to happen and thus is part of his sovereign will, but God tests our motives and actions through events.

My favorite passage demonstrating this important truth is Numbers 20:2-12. Here Moses disobeys the Lord; in anger he strikes the rock instead of speaking to it. As a result water does not come out—or does it? (Look for yourself!)

You see, the ends do not justify the means; the outcome does not justify the path taken to it. Many assume that they have done what is right in God's eyes because their course of action seems to have been "blessed" by God; there was a happy ending. Praise the Lord that he works through all of our mistakes! But that in no way puts his seal of approval on our moments of rebellion.

Helping the Confused

In order to help those whose religion has been conditioned by any of the ten misconceptions treated above, "great patience and careful instruction" will be required. We will need to:

- Listen carefully to what they are saying.

- Teach people to be logical. Correct them when they reason illogically, being sure to walk them through the steps in our line of reasoning.

- Point out to them when they are following their emotions.

- Keep reminding them that God speaks to us in the Scriptures, not through subjective experience.

- Be patient.

- Be logical ourselves!

- Use the Scriptures as we teach.[7]

Confusing the Helpful

When religious persons with delusions of divine grandeur imagine they have their personal hot line to God, what should be helpful (the Scriptures) becomes totally confused. Everything gets twisted around! Their need for the Bible is nullified by their "direct access" to God. As Peter comments, speaking of the letters of Paul,

He writes the same way in all his letters, speaking in them of these matters. His letters contain some things that are hard to understand, which ignorant and unstable people distort, as they do the other Scriptures, to their own destruction. Therefore, dear friends, since you already know this, be on your guard so that you may not be carried away by the error of lawless men and fall from your secure position (2 Peter 3:16–17).

The Scriptures get twisted. They are read only to justify the preconceived positions of persons who take the law (God's law) into their own hands. Some "ignorant and unstable people" are gravely confused.

Soon after I became an evangelist, a visitor came to the door of the London church office. I saw an imposing figure with angry, dark eyes, dressed in sandals, turban and flowing robe, holding a staff in his hands. I asked him who he was.

He replied, "Do you not know?" Realizing at once that this poor fellow had some problems, I decided to play his game.

"Please tell me," I said.

"I am the Alpha and the Omega." He had chosen a title of God from the books of Isaiah (41:4, 44:6) and Revelation! (Revelation 1:8, 21:6, 22:13). "Mr. Alpha," I replied, "why don't we sit down over there?" He followed me, and we looked one another in the eyes. "What languages do you speak?

Do you speak French?" (I guessed that this man was from North Africa.) "The Alpha and the Omega speaketh every tongue."

"Well then," I said, "*Verba mei potes comprehendere? Loquirisne Latinum?*" I spoke to him in Latin, though he only stared back at me, dumbfounded. "*Hellenidzeis?*" I added, this time speaking in Classical Greek. Still, no recognition.

"I am afraid I don't know what you mean," Mr. Alpha finally responded.

"Surely the Alpha and the Omega understands the Latin and Greek languages! Since you do not, I can only conclude that you are not who you say you are." The man still had that wild look on his face, and I began to feel a bit nervous about what he might do, especially with his heavy staff. "It is time to go," I concluded. "Let me walk you to the door. Good day." And that was the last I saw of him.

Agreeing with Ourselves?

Obviously not everyone is as self-deceived as "Mr. Alpha." And yet churches are full of men and women who believe they have an inside track on the mind of God, without thoroughly studying his word. They affirm they believe in the Bible; yet when shown scriptures that challenge them to change, they say, "I don't think that verse is inspired," or "That part no longer applies," or "That's just your 'interpretation.'" In fact, they believe only in themselves, and the Bible happens to back them up here and there. When there is any conflict, what is the authority? Not the Word!

When these people say they believe in the Bible, what they should really say is, "I believe in me, and quite often God has the good sense to see things my way. When he doesn't, that's too bad. I know I am right." This is a deep deception and not at all the spirit in which God wants us to receive his word (1 Thessalonians 2:13, 1:5).

The fundamental question is, How do we know the truth? Watch out! Many people have managed to circumvent the Bible by coming up with their private hot line to God. Many claim to follow only the Bible, but their unwillingness to be consistent when confronted with the truth penetrates the thin veneer of religion.

Psychological, Diabolical or Divine?

When you next meet someone with a hot line to God, you can be sure that a game is being played. What is taking place is, in my opinion, only psychological. (Certainly not divine!) It may not be inspired by a demon, and yet the confusion and distraction it breeds serves the purposes of the devil quite well. To that extent it is diabolical.

Those vehement about their direct connection with God may be zealous, but their zeal is not based on knowledge (Proverbs 19:2, Romans 10:2). Once again, no one today has a hot line to God! Those who say they do bring the gospel into derision and contempt and distract others from the Spirit's real work of changing lives and advancing the kingdom. Let's put an end to playing games.

QUESTIONS FOR THOUGHT

- *Do I know anybody who is deeply confused about God and his Spirit, somebody who would be helped by this information?*

- *Do I tend instinctively to trust my first interpretation of a passage of Scripture, or am I willing to work at it until I understand the text?*

- *Is it possible that I have retained some of my old superstitious nature from pre-Christian days?*

_____ NOTES _____

1. See the excellent discussions of prayer in the works of C. S. Lewis, for example, *Miracles* (New York: Macmillan, 1978). More on this in Chapter 17.

2. One need not become a total Freudian to acknowledge that dreams do tell us something about our subconscious.

3. Kenneth Hagin, *You Can be Led by the Spirit of God* (Tulsa, Oklahoma: Faith Library Publications, 1981), 109.

4. See Leviticus 16:8–10; Numbers 26:55-56, 33:54, 34:13, 36:2; Joshua 14:2, 18:6, 8, 10–11, 19:1, 10, 17, 24, 32, 40, 51, 21:4, 10; Judges 20:9; 1 Samuel 14:41–42; 1 Chronicles 6:54, 24:5, 7, 31, 25:8–9, 26:13–16; Nehemiah 10:34, 11:1; Esther 3:7, 9:24; Psalm 22:18; Proverbs 16:33, 18:18; Ezekiel 21:21–22, 24:6; Joel 3:3; Obadiah 1:11; Jonah 1:7; Micah 2:5; Nahum 3:10; Matthew 27:35; Mark 15:24; Luke 1:9, 23:34; John 19:24; Acts 1:26.

5. See Exodus 28:30; Leviticus 8:8; Numbers 27:21; Deuteronomy 33:8; 1 Samuel 28:6; Ezra 2:63; Nehemiah 7:65.

6. In Genesis 24:12–50 we see the legitimate sense of something being "from the Lord," but this is often abused.

7. A suggested Bible study you can share with your friends is "Feelings":

- Proverbs 3:5, 14:12, 16:2, 28:26, Jeremiah 17:9—Feelings are unreliable as a spiritual guidance system.
- 1 Samuel 13:12, 1 Kings 13:lff, 2 Kings 5:10–15—We can land in serious trouble when we follow our emotions!
- Galatians 1:6–9, 2 Corinthians 11:3–4—No one has the right to modify the gospel! Watch out for variations on the message which condone a lower standard of commitment than that which Jesus preached.
- Jeremiah 23:16ff—Ten points emerge from this study: 1. The false prophets claim to speak from God (v. 16). 2. Their messages are of purely psychological origin, not from God (v. 16). 3. They water down the word of God (v. 22). 4. Their dreams (cp Numbers 12:6) are delusions, merely psychological (vv. 25-26), and lessen the commitment of the people by imparting false hope (v. 27). 5. Although they fancy God to be speaking his word through them, he is not; their messages have nothing to do with the word of God (vv. 28-29). 6. They borrow "messages" from one another; they exchange "oracles" (v. 30). 7. They do not benefit the people (vv. 31–32). 8. They do sincerely expect the Lord to speak to them (v. 35). 9. They suffer terrible theological confusion as God's word and their words are completely confused (v. 36). 10. The end result: They distort God's word (v. 36).
- Jude 19—Unspiritual persons divide the body of Christ.
- Luke 9:23—Discipleship becomes a matter of denying your feelings, not following them. Christ taught the opposite! Deny feelings; follow Christ. Follow feelings; deny Christ.

• Matthew 7:21-23—Surprised, and quite possibly sincere, miracle workers were not saved because they did not obey the word of God. (See also 1 Corinthians 8:3 for an explanation of Matthew 7:23.)

Upside Down

In the third section we witnessed a good deal of zeal that is not grounded in spiritual reality. Ultimately, such religion is powerless to change us at the deepest level.

The true Spirit of God changes us from the inside out—the first transformation. Then and only then can the second transformation occur: the salvation of the world. Comfort-loving men and women, however, are hardly the types who will "turn the world upside down" (Acts 17:6 RSV).

The fourth section calls all of us to clear thinking about the issues and to total commitment to Jesus Christ. When you are following Jesus, the sacrifice of comfort is a foregone conclusion. May the Spirit of God shake us from our complacency!

12. A Zeal That's Real
The 'Holy' Spirit

God's Spirit isn't called the Holy Spirit without reason. To most people "holy" means serious, mystical, otherworldly, maybe even eerie. But disciples know holiness has to do with devotion, dedication, sanctity.

We're talking about commitment to God, about setting our life aside for him. We're talking about doing great things for God and for this world. We're talking about thinking, believing, dreaming, living and dying heroically. As Horace Mann remarked, "Be ashamed to die until you have won some victory for mankind."[1] And as Paul remarked, "Grace to all who love our Lord Jesus Christ with an undying love" (Ephesians 6:24). True zeal is more than skin deep. It is not some ephemeral, Sunday costume one dons weekly. For God's claim on our life is total, not partial.

Slain by a Fierce, Wild Beast!

Ever since I was a little boy I knew (from Sunday school) that we were supposed to live for God. I heard about people who sold everything and lived in poverty—and something in my soul responded, "I should live that way, too." There was a certain attractiveness to the grand old hymns, waxen candles, walks through cemeteries, thinking about God. Even confirmation classes intrigued me! And I still remember the words of a song I heard when I was six or seven years old:

> I sing a song of the saints of God,
>> patient and brave and true:
> They toiled and they fought and they lived and they died
>> for their own good Lord they knew.
>
> And one was a doctor and one was a priest
>> and one was slain by a fierce, wild beast;
> And there's no, not a reason, no not the least
>> Why I shouldn't be one too!

My conscience was mildly haunted by the words of that song for another twelve years—especially by the thought of being slain by a beast! Could there be something so worth living for that it was also worth dying for? The words remained in my heart, until I began to consider the Bible more seriously. Looking back now, I believe I was just waiting for a chance to become committed. (Maybe you were, too!) When I met men and women who lived as committed a life as the one they taught (and sang) about, the old chords were set vibrating, and I knew my quest, in one sense, was at an end.

The world is looking for a cause, something to live for. Usually people rally behind one cause or another, but seldom the right one. It is up to us to show them that Jesus Christ is worth living for. And dying, if that is what we are called to do.

Holiness an Option?

Is holiness only an option? In these days of "church of your choice" and "nonjudgmentalism," is holiness just another dispensable variation on a jaded theme that we could just as well do without? Or is this not the narrow path that Jesus walked and which he bade us come and walk as well? The Hebrew writer stated it lucidly:

> Make every effort to live in peace with all men and to be holy; without holiness no one will see the Lord (Hebrews 12:14).

The Scriptures are clear: Holiness is no option. Let the world mock, and let the religious world defend its shallow religiosity with theology even Felix would have applauded (Acts 24:25). Lukewarmness is not an option, because God, the holy God, is not an "option." God commands us to be holy because he is holy (1 Peter 1:15–16, Leviticus 11:44–45, 19:2, 20:7).

Holiness Comes from the Spirit

It should be no surprise that the Holy Spirit makes us holy. It flows through our veins, a transfusion of life and determination coursing through every artery and capillary. The person who claims to have the Spirit must live a holy life, or the game is up! By their fruits you will know them (Matthew 7:20). Without holiness no one will see the Lord.

Although in time the emphasis on holiness declined, especially after the legalization of Christianity in the 300s, God never lowered his standard or the requirements for discipleship.[2] That's why we read in Romans 12:11, "Never be lacking in zeal, but keep your spiritual fervor,[3] serving the Lord." This fervor, energy or heat, is the difference between pulseless, morbid religion and vibrant, vital faith. No amount of explanation about why a corpse is really "alive" is going to convince anyone with eyes in his head. Living faith has a pulse because it is energized by the very Spirit of God (James 2:26).

'When You're Hot, You're Hot'

"When you're hot, you're hot. And when you're not, you're not," the saying goes. God's word demands that we be hot, not cold or lukewarm:

> "To the angel of the church in Laodicea write: These are the words of the Amen, the faithful and true witness, the ruler of God's creation. I know your deeds, that you are neither cold nor hot. I wish you were either one or the other! So, because you are lukewarm—neither hot nor cold—I am about to spit you out of my mouth" (Revelation 3:14–16).

These words are addressed to a church that used to be hot, but had slipped into the self-satisfaction of lukewarmness. Sadly, only a few decades later this church seems not to have repented. Other churches who received letters in Revelation 2–3 were still in existence (like those in Ephesus and Philadelphia, for example), but to the church of Laodicea the second-century writers have nothing to say. It seems this first-century church dwindled in faith and in numbers and ultimately vanished off the screen.

Jesus Christ looks not just at heart, faith and intent, but also at deeds. "Holy" and "hot" are nearly synonyms when it comes to commitment. Furthermore, the Scriptures affirm that cold is actually better than lukewarm (Malachi 1:10, Revelation 3:15). Religious experiences are no substitute. Truly spiritual people don't just gather "miracle" stories and seek after some spiritual buzz; they do the work of God (Matthew 7:21–23).

Can you honestly say that you are "hot" for God, his word, his will, his people, his plans?

'Inwardly Boiling'

Hundreds of millions claim to be Christians, despite the fact that their "pulse" is next to impossible to locate. Dead faith creating dead weight in dead churches proclaiming a cause long dead.

Imagine your friend asking you to check a pot of water on the stove. "It should be boiling by now," he says.

You check it, swiftly dipping in your finger (just to be safe), only to feel tepid water. "Still cold!" you reply.

"No, it should be boiling by now," he returns, "please go back and check again."

You check once more, and feel only lukewarm water.

What would you think if he said, "I know it's hot; it must be boiling. Yes, it must be 'inwardly boiling'"?

What if he persisted in spouting off slogans like "What counts is heart, not heat," and "Lukewarm water needs time to 'mature'"; wouldn't you eventually come to question his sincerity, or his understanding of words such as "hot," "cold" and "boiling"? He then further defends his doctrine: "No water is perfect"; "All water has the right to seek its own temperature"; "Being nice is what counts, not being hot"; or perhaps "The warming up is more important than the heat." The theology of lukewarmness continues to blossom: "We truly believe in inner boiling," and "Judge not water's heat," and finally, "'Hot-water-only-groups' are too exclusive!" Would you not be right to question his logic?

So it is with holiness. The commitment of discipleship is nonnegotiable. The fervor of spiritual zeal is defined by God, not by man. No one has the right to dilute holiness then say, "It's good enough."

Fake Versus Real Zeal

Do you have a zeal that's real, or are you the hype type? What does God think about faking dedication, feigning devotion, falsifying discipleship, fudging holiness? The tale of Ananias and Sapphira (Acts 5:1-11) reveals the heart of God on this matter. When this couple faked commitment instead of being honest about where they were, we read that they were lying to the Holy Spirit (v. 3) and testing the Spirit of the Lord (v. 9). God the Spirit is offended when, instead of allowing him to make us holy, we make a farce of faith.

No more showy, shallow, sham religion! Let's all strive for a zeal that's real.

White-Hot Commitment

How can we claim to be God's people when we are lacking in zeal? Many people lack the truth and sometimes are just as zealous in their religion as Christians are (Romans 10:1-2). Zeal does not mean loud "Amens" and boisterous behavior, but being filled with the Spirit of God and modeling the walk we talk about. After all, as Mark Twain said, "Few things are harder to put up with than a good example." When people see that kind of zeal, they will know it's real.

Never, ever forget who you are and whose you are. We are holy people on a holy mission in a holy church serving a holy God. The zeal has got to be real! Then and only then will we turn the world upside down.

QUESTIONS FOR THOUGHT

* Am I a zealous Christian? Am I lukewarm or hot? Is anything holding me back?

* Do I realize holiness has nothing to do with feelings and everything to do with being on fire for God?

* Am I the "hype type"? Are my roots deep or shallow?

* Am I done with lukewarm religion that exalts "spiritual buzz" over knowing Christ?

_____ NOTES _____

1. Or, in the words of Theodore Roosevelt, "Far better it is to dare mighty things, to win glorious triumphs even though checkered by failures, than to rank with those poor spirits who neither enjoy nor suffer much because they live in the gray twilight that knows neither victory nor defeat."

2. The concern for holiness continued unabated for nearly three centuries before the early church cooled off. Take the second-century sermon called 2 Clement, for example. Clearly, at this time, there was still a concern for holiness. "What assurance do we have of entering the kingdom of God if we fail to keep our baptism pure and undefiled? Or who will be our advocate, if we are not found to have holy and righteous works?" (2 Clement 6: 9b) Reading the "Church Fathers," or Patristic writers can be enormously beneficial, affording clearer insight into how the original church evolved into the confused state of modern Christendom and bringing us closer to the radical spirit of our earliest brothers and sisters in the faith.

3. "Fervor" is the Latin word for "seething, heat; ardor, passion." The verb *fervere* means "to boil."

13. 'The Spirit Insists!'
World Evangelism

Mission and purpose are two different things, as we have discussed earlier (Chapter 4). Our purpose: to enjoy our relationship with God and make it to heaven; our mission: to change the world. (When the two become confused, spiritual burnout is not far away.)

The mission is twofold. We are called to preach the Word and to help the poor. Although ultimately one's spiritual condition, not one's medical or economic situation, is what counts, still we are called as the people of God to both facets of the mission. True Christians love the poor. True Christians love the lost and share what they have found with them. It is fundamentally unrighteous to neglect one or the other.

In this chapter we zero in on our evangelistic responsibility; in the next on our obligation to the needy. Just as Jesus sent his disciples out to preach the Word and to minister to the needy, so the Spirit sends us today on the same twin mission (Mark 3:14).

The Lifeblood of the Church

World evangelism is our absolute passion as disciples. It was the will of God in the first century, the mountaintop mandate of the Lord Jesus and the lifeblood of the New Testament church. The situation is no different today! While we humbly realize it is possible, our generation may well not be the last in human history (1 Thessalonians 5:1). Surely our common goal must be to bring Christ to every nation—to saturate the earth with the gospel in our generation, by all means possible.

Our first-century brothers and sisters, moved by the Holy Spirit, caused quite a stir when they preached the radical message of the gospel. The inspiring theme song of the musical Upside Down, which brings the book of Acts to life, calls us to the same quest which fired the hearts of disciples of old:

Upside down, the world needs shakin',
    rattle the cages, the chains that need a-breakin'!
Two thousand years and here we are, just a world of waste and screams,
But just a ragged band of men can reawaken all those dreams.

There's a way to take this planet and turn everything around—
    Or, a better way to say it:
Let's turn the whole thing upside down![1]

The Spirit insists that we work together to turn the world upside down.[2] How do we know that? Because the Spirit inspired the entire Bible, and the Bible is loud and clear on this one. Europe, Asia, Africa, Australia, the Americas—the entire world!—can be and must be evangelized if we, as God's children, are to be faithful to our Father's wishes. On this there can be no compromise. So let us never leave our "great work" in order to negotiate with the critics (Nehemiah 6:1-14).

Good News Preaches Itself

When you have good news, when you are really excited about bringing someone in on the best thing ever, it isn't hard to share it! The day I wrote this chapter we celebrated my son James' ninth birthday. My wife Vicki and I had talked about getting a dog on and off through the years, but had decided to forgo expanding the household in this way, in part because the kids were quite young. I knew in my heart that once we visited the kennel and actually looked the little critters in the whites of their eyes, the chances that we would capitulate were very high! In the end, we chose a beautiful cocker spaniel pup and brought him home, secreting him in the basement until all the kids were home from school. Vicki and I sat the kids down in the kitchen, blindfolds on. At this point, our hearts were racing; we were so excited! Vicki held the camera in place to catch my son's expression when he first saw his birthday present—the one with the waggling tail. I trotted down to the basement and carried up the pup. Placing it in my son's lap, I removed his blindfold and—*voilà!* The rest is history. My nine-year-old dubbed him "Columbus."

Our good news felt so "good" that it was explosive (Jeremiah 20:9). If we didn't share it soon, it would have leapt out (literally). News like that preaches itself. Similarly, as someone has said, "The Spirit of Christ always insists on making Christ known" (see John 15:26).

We're Outta Here!

How determined are we to follow the Spirit and to refuse to tolerate un-spirituality? Years ago, my brother and I were driving down the East Coast, attending various Christian conferences. The first message at one conference we had registered for was on the topic of evangelism. The speaker began by describing evangelism as a "talent" or "gift." The experts, according to this man, had calculated that only ten percent of Christians can be expected to evangelize, since for ninety percent of us, it is not our gift.

But there is a difference between gifts and commands. For example, we are all commanded to encourage others (Hebrews 3:13), yet some have the gift of encouragement (Romans 12:8) and will find that what may be hard for others is relatively easy for them. While it is true that some of us find some of the commands easier to obey than others, we must never minimize a command into an option under the claim that "It's not my gift"! Evangelism is not an option.[3]

As the conference speaker was going on, I thought of the ten lepers (in Luke 17) and how only one out of ten had the gratitude to return to thank Jesus for his healing. (Yes, only "ten percent" had the decency to show their appreciation for what God had done in their lives. The "ten-percent rule" applied here, though not as meant by the speaker!) After the talk, I turned to my brother Steve and said, "I'm outta here!" We walked out, because we were not interested in explaining away the Great Commission or consoling ourselves on our lack of commitment.

How about you? Are you hanging out only with those who have low expectations for world impact? Are you attracted to a church or religion that says "I'm okay; you're okay," "Judge not," and "Lukewarm is acceptable"? Putting it another way, do you count the hours that go by between times of sharing your faith, or the days? How often do you bring friends to church? Remember, the Holy Spirit is not a spirit of timidity, but one of power, love and self-discipline. The next time a thought of compromise starts to "lecture" you on why you do not have to obey the Great Commission, say "I'm outta here."

The Acts of the Spirit

After Pentecost, first-century Christians were not interested in concealing the gospel—only in revealing it. When the church was scattered in the Great Persecution after the martyrdom of Stephen, everyone shared their faith, not just the top leaders! (Acts 8:1, 4). Acts (often called the Acts of the Apostles) records the birth and growth of the church during its first three decades. Several aspects of the explosive expansion of the church are noteworthy:

- The bold proclamation of the message by all the disciples
- The universal opposition met with by the church
- The rapid growth of the movement

Since the same Spirit empowers us today, is there really any reason not to expect the same working of the Spirit in our own lives? Why not study Acts with an eye on the spirit of the Christians as the Spirit impelled them to take the Word to a lost world?

The title "The Acts of the Apostles" is really a misnomer, since only Peter and Paul receive significant coverage in this book. Many scholars contend that Luke's second volume should really be called "The Acts of the Spirit," since it is the Holy Spirit who essentially serves as "Director of Evangelism" and "Chief Empowerer of the Christian Movement."[4] This is key in understanding the plan of Acts. In our lives we have no more powerful advocate in evangelism than the Holy Spirit himself. Let's examine a few of the ways the Spirit assists us.

Boldness Booster

Timidity has never been the way of the Spirit![5] The Spirit will help us to change in any area of our life necessary in order for us to become effective evangelistically. Have circumstances gotten you down? Are you not as bold lately as you have been in the past? If so, claim the power of the Spirit as the early Christians did when under great pressure: "Now, Lord, consider their threats and enable your servants to speak your word with great boldness" (Acts 4:29). Was that prayer ever answered! (Would God let any prayer like that go unanswered?)

> After they prayed, the place where they were meeting was shaken. And they were all filled with the Holy Spirit and spoke the word of God boldly (Acts 4:31).

A miracle? Perhaps. (The shaking is immaterial.) They sincerely desired boldness, prayed a prayer for boldness and emerged from that prayer meeting bolder than ever! Coincidence? Hardly! God is waiting and willing to fill with his Spirit any of us who need to grow in the area of boldness.

Spirit-Directed Outreach

The book of Acts shows just how involved the Holy Spirit is in the enterprise of evangelism.[6] Let's take a quick tour through Acts and notice how often the Spirit is mentioned in connection with outreach:

- Through the Spirit Jesus briefed his apostles, explaining the kingdom of God and preparing them for the mission soon to commence (Acts 1:2).

- The Spirit would empower the Christians to systematically evangelize the world: first, the city; then, the outlying towns and villages; finally, faraway lands (Acts 1:8).

- The Spirit brought the international crowd together to hear the good news of Jesus Christ (Acts 2:5).
- The Spirit filled the disciples with evangelistic boldness (Acts 4:31).
- The Spirit equips obedient disciples to speak even in the face of opposition (Acts 5:27–32).
- The Spirit made it clear that racial divides are no obstacle to the kingdom of God (Acts 8:14–17).
- The Spirit advised the early missionaries where to preach and when to move on (Acts 8:29, 39).
- The Spirit encouraged the church, leading to numerical growth and spiritual sobriety (Acts 9:31).
- The Spirit made it dramatically clear that we are to focus on the central elements of the gospel, not the peripheral ones, when the Gentiles were ushered into the kingdom (Acts 10:44–48, 11:12–18).
- When the Spirit and faith fill a person, many people are brought to the Lord (Acts 11:24).
- The Spirit conceives missions plans (Acts 13:2) and sees them through (Acts 13:4).
- The Spirit sometimes blocks missionary plans (Acts 16:6–7).
- The Spirit places leadership, particularly eldership, over those who have been led to Christ (Acts 20:28).

Surely we can be confident that the same Spirit has been working in our generation to raise up leaders and bring down walls of Communism and apartheid, thus opening the door to the evangelization of our world. Jesus concluded the Great Commission by saying, "I am with you always, to the very end of the age." Is it not through the continuing work of the Spirit that his promise is being fulfilled?

The Spirit Changes Hearts

The Spirit works with us in our evangelism. We do not need to rely on our own wisdom, but on the power of the Spirit (1 Corinthians 2:1–5). According to John 16:8, the Spirit convicts the hearts of non-Christians.[7] Here is the world evangelism plan in a nutshell:

- The Spirit changes the hearts of disciples of Christ.
- Disciples of Christ preach the Word wherever they go.
- The Spirit works through the Word to change the hearts of nonbelievers.

Conclusion

The early church took the Great Commission (Matthew 28:18–20) to heart and made a concerted effort to implement Jesus' clear command to preach the gospel. Most of the territory around the Mediterranean was evangelized within the lifetime of the apostles, and many inroads were made deep into Africa, Asia and Europe. In the following centuries, before the legalization of Christianity in 313 AD, the fledgling faith continued to expand, the message being carried nearly worldwide—in some form at least—by the time of the Protestant Reformation.

Although the original nuclear church exploded into action, it later slackened. Yet today again the Spirit of God is moving in the world so that the torch is being rekindled. Patristics[8] researcher David Berçot has written this:

> Christianity was originally a revolution that challenged the attitudes, lifestyle, and values of the ancient world. It was more than a mere set of doctrines—it was an entire way of life. And all the military, economic, and social forces of the Roman world couldn't stop it. But after 300 years, the revolution partially faltered.
>
> It ran aground because most professing Christians lost their obedient trust in God. They imagined they could improve Christianity through human means, by adopting the methods of the world. But they didn't improve Christianity; they gutted it.... There was nothing wrong with early Christianity. It didn't need "fixing." But the fourth-century Christians became convinced they could improve Christianity. "If Christianity meant material blessings and prosperity instead of suffering and deprivation, we could convert the whole world," they reasoned. But in the end, the church didn't really convert the world. The world converted much of the church....
>
> The church is still married to the world, and Christians still think they can improve Christianity through human means. But Christianity will not improve until the church returns to the simple holiness, genuine love, and cross-bearing of the early Christians. Our divorce from the world is long overdue, and this is one divorce that would have God's unequivocal blessings.
>
> The cross and revolutionary banner of early Christianity are still lying where the martyrs left them. It's not too late for the church to return and carry them again.[9]

Yes, we are called by God to turn the world upside down. Let's preach the Word and pray for God to (1) saturate the earth with the message, (2) saturate it in our lifetime and (3) help us to be the very best ambassadors we can be. The Spirit insists!

QUESTIONS FOR THOUGHT

- Do I have a true passion to see the world evangelized in my lifetime?

- How often am I aware of a spiritual impulse to share Christ with others?

- Am I excusing myself from evangelism, claiming evangelism is a "gift" instead of a command?

- Do I resist the Holy Spirit by not speaking out and sharing the truth with others?

- Would I be willing to join a mission team, preaching the Word where Christ is not known (Romans 15:20)?

_____ NOTES _____

1. *Upside Down.* Lyrics: Steve Johnson. (New York: NYC Church of Christ, Inc., 1994.)

2. The phrase "turned the world upside down" comes specifically from Acts 17:6 (RSV). Technically, the verb means "to upset" ("disturb," as in the sense of "disturbing the peace") more than to "up-end." When the Latin Vulgate translation was produced, Jerome chose the word *concitant,* which means simply "rouse, stir up."

3. As previously noted in Ephesians 4:11, the gift is not evangelism, but evangelists—a leadership position.

4. In Acts alone, the Spirit is mentioned more than sixty times! For comparison, the four Gospels together mention the Holy Spirit some eighty times.

5. In fact, verses 2 Timothy 1:8, 12, 16 and 2:15 all speak of not being ashamed. This is integral to being a disciple and to making it to heaven! (See Mark 8:38, Luke 9:26, Romans 1:16, Philippians 1:20, 1 Peter 4:16.)

6. Much has been made of Acts 17:26-27, "From one man he made every nation of men, that they should inhabit the whole earth; and he determined the times set for them and the exact places where they should live. God did this so that men would seek him and perhaps reach out for him and find him." Is it true that God *directly* determines where people live—125 Main Street (as opposed to 127 Main Street)—in order to place them in proximity to disciples? God's providence is awesome and evident everywhere. But when Acts 17:26–27 is preached this way we are not talking about providence, but a subtle form of predestination.

The theological problem is that if God has determined where those who will be saved live, and when they will be there, then he has *de facto* consigned others to situations in which they will not have an opportunity to respond to the gospel. Then there is the textual problem. The RSV, among many good translations, renders Acts 17:26 more accurately in this instance than does the NIV. We read, "And he made from one every nation of men to live on all the face of the earth, having determined allotted periods and the boundaries of their habitation" (RSV). There is an allusion here to Deuteronomy 32:8. Paul is not talking about local geographical predestination, but rather God's providence.

7. The Word is the sword of the Spirit (Ephesians 6:17).

8. "Patristics" is the study of the writings of the "church fathers," such as Clement, Ignatius, Tertullian, and Origen—men who wrote in the earliest centuries of Christianity.

9. David W. Berçot, *Will the Real Heretics Please Stand Up* (Tyler, Texas: Scroll, 1989), 158. Berçot is a Patristic scholar and friend of the author.

14. The Spirit of the West
The Curse of Consumerism

In case you were wondering, the spirit of the West—the wild, wild West—has nothing to do with cowboys, sagebrush, tumbleweed and rodeos. We're using the word in its sociopolitical sense to refer to affluent Northern and Western Europe and North America.[1] The spirit of the West is the spirit of materialism and of the society that lives to consume, and consumes to live: a vicious cycle of emptiness (1 Peter 1:18) that leaves us with a deep sense of meaninglessness (as in Ecclesiastes). Every nation of the world breathes this spirit, whether its citizens fall into the category of "haves" or "have-nots."

None for Me, Thanks

The other day I heard the most unusual news in a long time. A 72-year-old woman had won the New Jersey State Lottery, taking a purse of $11.2 million. How did she spend her newly gained fortune? Contrary to expectation, she did not keep a single penny for herself. Ever since she started playing the lottery, she had said, "If I ever win the lottery, I'm giving it all away." And so she did: to her church, as well as to not a few jubilant nonprofit organizations!

How can you help but admire someone willing to give it all away? Whether or not it was the wisdom of years that had taught her the true value of money, her selfless decision is honorable. Surely there is a lesson in there for us all.

Neither Poverty nor Riches

The challenge of the Spirit is not to win the lottery and give it all away. It is to love those less fortunate than us, to live more simply and to keep ourselves from being "polluted by the world," as James put it.[2] The spirit of materialism (a.k.a. Mammon) is everywhere, and it can be difficult even for disciples of Jesus Christ to navigate between the treacherous rocks of indulgence and indigence.

The Scriptures urge modesty in our use and possession of material goods:

> [7]Two things I ask of you, O LORD;
>   do not refuse me before I die:
> [8]Keep falsehood and lies far from me;
>   give me neither poverty nor riches,
>   but give me only my daily bread.

⁹Otherwise, I may have too much
    and disown you and say, 'Who is the LORD?'
Or I may become poor and steal,
    and so dishonor the name of my God (Proverbs 30:7–9).

I suspect that far more of us pray, "O Lord, don't let me become poor" than "O Lord, don't let me become rich." Yet the Scriptures teach that there are dangers in both extremes.

The World Is Too Much with Us

If we aspire to riches, truly "the world is too much with us." As Wordsworth aptly described the curse of consumerism some two hundred years ago,

> The world is too much with us; late and soon,
> Getting and spending, we lay waste our powers:
> Little we see in Nature that is ours.[3]

All this getting and spending, spending and getting, is the nub of consumerism. And consumerism is the bane of our culture.

Materialistic Christians?

We as Christians claim to value the spiritual over the material, but do our lifestyles back up our claim? If we do not have a passion to help the poor (Galatians 2:10), it is unlikely we have escaped the virus of materialism unscathed. The Bible is full of warnings against materialism (1 John 2:15–17, Revelation 3:14–20, Ecclesiastes 4:4). Sometimes it takes a visit to the Third World[4] to appreciate the plight of the poor.[5]

Don't just assume that, because you have repented, been baptized and attend church you are free of materialism. The spending habits of many Christians vary little from those of their unbelieving friends. When I read Richard Horsley's The Liberation of Christmas, I was astounded by its opening exposé of the rampant materialism of our country, where twenty-eight percent of the world's resources are consumed in the month between Thanksgiving and Christmas![6] Isn't there inequality here—some gross distortion?

The Incubator

The virus of materialism is inculcated through parental upbringing and our educational institutions. The lack of spirituality in modern culture has seriously weakened our immune system: We succumb easily to the spirit of materialism.

If the virus enters through the values we have inherited, surely it is fed through the message we read, hear and see enfleshed in those around us every day. The message: Money is the bottom line. Your "net worth" is defined solely as your monetary worth. If you are not affluent, you are worth little. If you are rich, you are valuable. If you are living in poverty, you do not exist. This is clearly at odds with everything God tells us in his word. Instead of loving people and using things, we have been discipled to love things and use people.

How does this pernicious virus incubate in our hearts? Television is the incubator, and it breeds materialism quite effectively, and in particular consumerism—where we buy far more than we truly need, and find value in material things rather than in the things of the Spirit.

Television and the entertainment industry has also effectively inoculated us against caring for the poor. A few shots of poverty now and again keep its grinding reality mentally at bay. Images of the needy and of war numb our consciences. But how does Jesus Christ feel about it?

Television and Consumerism

Yes, TV is the primary medium through which consumerism, violence, immorality and secularization are brought into our lives. Nearly every American household owns at least one television set. (When I was little, our home had one black and white model; by the time I left for college, the number had swelled to five.) What are the results of our TV-driven consumerism?[7] Consider the social erosion facilitated by the greed of big business and its slick advertisers:

- *Financial shipwreck.* Impulse spending, unprincipled and unbudgeted personal finances, credit card "slavery" and staggering personal (and national) debt plague most of us. Such recklessness is powerfully promoted by the corporations and their cronies. Money is one of the most common subjects of marital disputes. To make things worse, we deprive our children of the opportunity to learn from our mistakes by keeping the subject of money "hushed."[8]

- *Disintegration of relationships.* The basic social unit is being reduced to the individual alone, as we are tempted to sit at home in front of the TV set. Alienation results when social erosion affects the familial level.

- *Disintegration of health.* Television has wrought great harm in its contribution toward nicotine addiction, alcoholism, etc. Laziness is condoned in principle as the lives of the "rich and shameless" are paraded on screen. We as a nation are grossly out of shape.

- *Ruin of family values.* TV eats up precious family time. A 1996 *USA Today* poll found the average male watches twenty-eight hours of TV a week; some children, to their detriment, watch even more.[9] In TV-land marital infidelity is depicted as "natural," family dysfunction as normal. "Family," thanks to some of the media, is gaining negative overtones.

- *Pathetic role models.* When convicted felons are kids' role models, we are in trouble!

- *Erosion of morality.* Violence, promiscuity and materialism are glorified in the media and are prime agents in our moral decline. This clearly translates into injustice, crime and hedonism.

- *Secularization.* These days, money is the bottom line. When worth is defined as financial worth, humanity is emptied of that which is truly valuable. Jesus noted that the Pharisees loved money, yet he assures us that what is highly valued by men is detestable in the sight of God (Luke 16:15).[10]

Yes, TV is, for better or worse, the most influential "educational institution" of the world today. How much are you watching? Perhaps more important, how much do you allow your children to view "the tube"? Stating there is a direct connection between television viewing and materialism is like saying there is a correlation between warfare and bloodshed. As the younger generation is fond of saying, "Duh"!

Consumerism is a form of slavery at best and the suicide of the family at worst. Truly it is the curse of Western culture.

The following excursus is written as a challenge to full-time ministers of the gospel. (If you are not in that category, you can still take a peek!)

Excursus: Suggestions for Preachers

Here are ten suggestions that can be easily modeled and preached at the congregational level:

1. *Explain why Big Business wants us to watch their programs and commercials.* This may seem self-evident, but it is amazing how far an occasional reminder will go.
2. *Emphasize how much extra time, energy and money will be available when TV viewing is reduced.* Advertising increases our consumption. TV

ties up valuable time—not just for industrious activity, but also for relationships, especially marriage and parenting relationships. Those who watch much TV are often sluggish and "dumpy" in appearance. Suggest alternative recreational activities, like taking up a new sport or reading.

3. *Explain how corporations target kids in their advertising.* It has been my experience that the less kids watch TV, the less they say "gimme," especially at such times as birthdays and Christmas.

4. *Admonish parents to limit their children's viewing hours.* For younger children especially, it is easy to simply tell them, "No, not now."[11]

5. *Preach against TV addiction and expect the church to change.* It is my conviction that churches generally do what preachers expect them to do. If we expect them to change and are (patiently) willing to follow through, change comes! Pathetic is the preacher who blames the flock before blaming self.

6. *Model it!* Restrict our own viewing of TV, focusing mainly on news, some sports and educational programs. Really, the minister who is about the Master's business will have little time for the "tube."

7. *Limit the number of televisions in a household.*[12] This wise decision will go far in promoting family life. Sell or give away extra sets.

8. *Make specific suggestions about what to watch and not to watch.* Know the stations in your area and what programming they broadcast. The more specific you can be, the better.

9. *Encourage the people to come to their own personal and specific convictions about this issue.* Avoid legalism. Preach from such passages as Ephesians 5:3-10 and Philippians 4:8-9.

10. *Follow up instruction with practical financial advice.* Many of our people are "out of control" in personal finances. Help them to see connections between worldly values and their own indebtedness, unhappiness and manipulation. Stress that we all have choices.

'The Spirit Says'

If we claim to be led by the Spirit, surely we cannot afford to ignore the words of the Spirit, which delight in helping the needy and in living simply. Let me suggest here that you take your Bible and read carefully Isaiah 58:1-10, and meditate on the kind of religion God accepts.

The Spirit says here (and throughout the inspired word of God) that our inwardly directed spirituality as the people of God (fellowship, worship, meditation) must be balanced by an outward focus (letting our light shine, evangelism, care for the needy). But should we be surprised? Consider Jesus: "Though he was rich, yet for your sakes he became poor, so that you through his poverty might become rich" (2 Corinthians 8: 9). Since Christ identifies with the poor, and not just with the rich, does he not expect us to follow in his footsteps? Let's now take a panoramic look at biblical teaching on the poor. Should this be in a book on the Holy Spirit? Absolutely! But it frightens me that some readers may be tempted to skip this part and move on to something more "exciting" or controversial. I hope you will not be one of those.

Biblical Teaching on the Poor

The plight of the poor and needy is a frightening one, and often followers of Jesus Christ do not know how to react.[13] For the first ten years of my Christian life, my attitude was "spiritual needs are more important than physical needs." Although in one sense this is true, it also played into my own convenience. I can remember arguing in seminary with a man who reminded me that the Bible commands us to fight for the rights of the poor. *"That's Old Testament,"* I adamantly proclaimed. "Under the New Testament we have *permission* to help the poor, but no *commission*." Needless to say, that man was not greatly impressed with my spirituality!

Before I had studied what the Scriptures teach about poverty and the proper response, I blocked the horrors of the needy out of my mind, focused on the "spiritual," refused to give to beggars and hermetically sealed my heart off from the reality of a world in need.

Everything changed for me in Calcutta, India. In a city of twelve million, built to accommodate merely one million, the excess population literally overflows into the streets, home to numberless men, women and children. I spent that first night awake, sitting on the floor, stunned. The shock of my first real exposure to staggering poverty jolted loose the barricade I had put in front of my heart. At last I was free to read the Bible without the presupposition that my church had the correct interpretation of the Christian response to poverty. I want to share with you what I learned.

Gospel Truth

I discovered that everywhere—in both the Old Testament and New Testament—we are encouraged time and time again to remember the needy. Of the scores of passages dealing with the subject, I was deeply convicted by such verses as Deuteronomy 15:4–5, 11; Job 31:16–23; Isaiah 58:6–10; Amos 6:1a, 4–7; and the piercing Ezekiel 16:

> "Now this was the sin of your sister Sodom: She and her daughters were arrogant, overfed and unconcerned; they did not help the poor and needy. They were haughty and did detestable things before me. Therefore I did away with them as you have seen" (Ezekiel 16:49–50).

The deepest sins of Sodom were not things like sodomy, which are merely symptoms of a self-seeking and depraved heart. The real sin is specified clearly: They were smug and aloof from the poor.

My heart was bombarded over and over by the teaching of Proverbs 3:27–28, 14:31, 19:17, 21:13, 28:27, 30:7–9, 31:8–9. But this wasn't only an Old Testament teaching. In the New Testament, Luke, with his emphasis on poverty and wealth, shouted loudest (Luke 3:10–11, 6:20b, 6:24-25a, 6:30–31, 35, 10:25-37, 12:33–34, 16:19–24). Acts, also written by Luke, followed suit (2:44–45, 4:32-35, 6:1-7, 11:27–30, 9:36, 10:1-2, 4b...), and then there were all those passages in the letters, like James 2:14–26 and Galatians 2:10. One passage that speaks with perfect clarity is Luke 10: 25–37, otherwise known as the Parable of the Good Samaritan.

The 'Good' Samaritan

Jesus never actually calls this man "good." That's our adjective. Is it because by contrast we are not so good that we elect to call the hero of the story "good"? Let the simplicity and the truth of its words penetrate your heart:

> On one occasion an expert in the law stood up to test Jesus. "Teacher," he asked, "what must I do to inherit eternal life?"
>
> "What is written in the Law?" he replied. "How do you read it?"
>
> He answered: "'Love the Lord your God with all your heart and with all your soul and with all your strength and with all your mind'; and, 'Love your neighbor as yourself.'"
>
> "You have answered correctly," Jesus replied. "Do this and you will live."
>
> But he wanted to justify himself, so he asked Jesus, "And who is my neighbor?"
>
> In reply Jesus said: "A man was going down from Jerusalem to Jericho, when he fell into the hands of robbers. They stripped him of

his clothes, beat him and went away, leaving him half dead. A priest happened to be going down the same road, and when he saw the man, he passed by on the other side. So too, a Levite, when he came to the place and saw him, passed by on the other side. But a Samaritan, as he traveled, came where the man was; and when he saw him, he took pity on him. He went to him and bandaged his wounds, pouring on oil and wine. Then he put the man on his own donkey, took him to an inn and took care of him. The next day he took out two silver coins and gave them to the innkeeper. 'Look after him,' he said, 'and when I return, I will reimburse you for any extra expense you may have.'

"Which of these three do you think was a neighbor to the man who fell into the hands of robbers?"

The expert in the law replied, "The one who had mercy on him." Jesus told him, "Go and do likewise."

What do you notice about this parable? Often it is used to exhort us to evangelize, and rightly so, since meeting the needs of strangers is Jesus' whole point in the parable. But taken at face value, this contains a plethora of principles on meeting the needs of the poor. What was the situation?

The Samaritan was aware of a need. The unfortunate victim had a raw deal. So do those in the world today born into inequality, limited opportunity, poverty, moral decay. Through the mass media, most of us too are aware of their needs; we cannot plead ignorance. Neither could the priest and the Levite.

The race of the victim was irrelevant to the Samaritan. Even though the victim was a Jew, the Samaritan hero did not let that prejudice his love for his neighbor. How many of us would react differently if the disadvantaged of the world belonged to our own comfortable social and racial set? Do we allow differences of skin color and other outward features to distance us from the world of human suffering?

Others were not meeting his needs. The ones who had the least excuse (here representing respectable religion) actively went out of their way to avoid the conscience pangs that might have prodded them to show mercy, like the God they claimed to know would have done.

The victim could not help himself. He was in no position to help himself. There is a world out there of countless millions—hundreds of millions!—who are in legitimate need. Unless we help them, it is unlikely anyone will. The various relief organizations barely begin to meet their needs. No, we cannot excuse our inactivity with the rationalization that others are getting the job done.

This, then, is the situation. What does the Samaritan do?

• He sees the need.

- He takes pity on his neighbor. Let us not argue about who our "neighbor" is; our fellow human being is our neighbor!
- He provides medical care and meets physical needs.
- He gives money to a responsible agency (the innkeeper).
- He does not limit his liability, but is willing to "go the extra mile."

When it comes to meeting the needs of the world's poor, Jesus bids us "Go and do likewise."

'Status Quo' Christians?

The world needs turning upside down, in more ways than one! Woe to us if we merely support the establishment![13] The way of Jesus Christ stands in judgment on all materialism, consumerism and apathy.

Our mission: to bring good news into the lives of every person on the planet. We need to share the gospel and our lives as well. We are called to give spiritual blessings, and material blessings, too. Beware the preaching that divorces the two. Feeling challenged? The Spirit of God would have it no other way!

> The Spirit of the Sovereign LORD is on me,
> because the LORD has anointed me
> to preach good news to the poor.
>
> He has sent me to bind up the brokenhearted,
> to proclaim freedom for the captives
> and release from darkness for the prisoners,
> to proclaim the year of the LORD's favor
> and the day of vengeance of our God,
> to comfort all who mourn (Isaiah 61:1–2).

Where Do I Start?

1. Study out the topic. Weigh all the verses you can find on money and wealth. Nothing is so motivating as being personally convicted from the Scriptures. For an excellent follow-up meditation, see Isaiah 5:8–25.
2. Sell some of your possessions, as Jesus taught in Luke 12:33.
3. Scrutinize your expenses and lifestyle. When tempted to make a purchase, ask yourself these four questions:[14]
   - Do I really need it?
   - Would I buy it one month from now?
   - Can I buy it somewhere else for less?
   - Does it appeal to my status-seeking ego?

4. Make a budget, and stick to it! Decide how much you need to live on, balance your checkbook, and determine to become a disciplined person with your personal finances.[15]

5. Fast regularly. This will help you maintain awareness of the dire straits in which the poor find themselves as you develop solidarity with them. It will add concentration and pungency to your prayers. And it will leave you with more money to give to those who truly need it.

6. Make a concrete plan to sacrifice to help the poor. For example, consider adopting a child.[16]

7. Pray: Right now! Tell God how you feel about these things and what you plan to do about it. Keep your resolve fresh. Ask God to make it clear if he wants you to dedicate your life to a career of helping the poor and needy.[17]

QUESTIONS FOR THOUGHT

- *Am I in bondage to consumerism? Am I ready to alter my lifestyle?*

- *Do I have a biblical care for the poor and the needy?*

- *Do I sacrifice financially each year for the cause of the down- trodden?*

NOTES

1. Certainly, Western culture is prevalent also in Australia and in several other geopolitical regions. The term is intended more for clarity than exactitude.

2. "Religion that God our Father accepts as pure and faultless is this: to look after orphans and widows in their distress and to keep oneself from being polluted by the world" (James 1:27).

3. William Wordsworth (1770-1850), *"The World Is Too Much with Us"* (1807).

4. The "Third World" is the developing world, most of which lies in the more southerly land masses of the planet. The "First World" is the developed, highly technological world. "The Second World"—although the term is rarely used—is the former Communist Bloc, which in economic terms, lies somewhere between the other two "worlds."

5. After my first few visits to the Third World, I was haunted by the sense that not only I, but my entire Christian culture, had been ignoring the clear teachings of the Bible vis-à-vis the poor. One invaluable resource was Ronald J. Sider's *Rich Christians Living in an Age of Hunger* (London: Hodder and Stoughton, 1977). I would also highly recommend Steve Kinnard's *Jesus and the Poor* (Spring, Texas: Illumination Publishers, 2017).

6. "In the United States, which consumes 70 percent of the world's resources, 40 percent of all goods retailed annually are sold during the four weeks between Thanksgiving

Day and December 25," in *The Liberation of Christmas* (New York: Continuum, 1993), ix.

7. This consumerism, by the way, finds nearly universal denominational support.

8. As sociologist Robert Wuthnow has demonstrated. See *Poor Richard's Principle: Recovering the American Dream Through the Moral Dimension of Work, Business, & Money* (Princeton: Princeton University Press, 1996), 138, 147, 166. Why not bring our kids in on our financial thinking as we go? Isn't this the best training they could receive?

9. The average preteen spends several hours a day watching the "tube." I believe the ones who need the challenge are not so much the youngsters as their parents, who must take their God-given responsibility to nurture their children during the formative years.

10. Sociologists recognize that secularization takes place through three avenues: (1) the media, (2) the technological explosion, and (3) the university. Might we not add a fourth: the traditional church? Truly the church has lost its moorings, and is now ethically adrift on the sea of relativity! The problem: It is "politically incorrect" to speak clearly and authoritatively, to give the direction people so desperately need. But speak we must.

11. We allow our children (all of whom live at home) to watch only a few selected channels. As ministers, we are clearly going to need to confront lazy parenting which claims to prefer not to "dictate" morality. It has been my experience that the more involved parents are, the more moral guidance they give *and the more they unhypocritically model morality in their own lives,* the more happy and thankful their children are.

12. We have one TV in our house. We simply don't want it to interfere with family life.

13. Adapted from Douglas Arthur and Douglas Jacoby, *I Was Hungry! The Christian Response to Poverty* (London: CLCC, 1987).

14. Created by Karen Louis of Singapore.

15. Furthermore, reduce your use of fuel, electricity and so forth. Set the thermostat lower in winter and higher in summer. Use public transport. Owning a smaller car will cut insurance costs and consume less fuel.

16. My wife, Vicki, and I took that step and adopted a girl from Shanghai, China.

17. *I Was Hungry*, an English poem, has been adapted for a primarily American readership. Source unknown.

I Was Hungry

You fed my food to your pigs
You blamed it on the markets, you blamed it on the Marxists
You told me the poor were blessed
You really did mean to write to your congressman
You used me as a dumping ground for your food mountain
You promised to pray for me
You were sure I could manage on welfare
You switched the channel to avoid the sight of me
You paid a pittance for my harvest
You sold my government arms to keep me quiet
You used my land to grow flowers for your table
You told me to get lost

15. Free in the Spirit
Freedom False and True

From one perspective, this has been a book about how the Holy Spirit does and does not work in our lives. Conflicting notions of obedience and freedom lie at the core of the discussion. Paul certainly teaches that the Spirit brings freedom:

> Now the Lord is the Spirit, and where the Spirit of the Lord is, there is freedom. And we, who with unveiled faces all reflect the Lord's glory, are being transformed into his likeness with ever-increasing glory, which comes from the Lord, who is the Spirit (2 Corinthians 3:17–18).

But what is the nature of the freedom the Spirit brings into our lives? In many ways, this question strikes at the heart of spirituality; it separates true religion from pseudoreligion.

Feeling or Following?

Liberation is a powerful motif, whether spiritual, political, economic or otherwise. Yet there is a tremendous difference between the false freedom promised by self-seeking varieties of religion and the true freedom God promises us in the Scriptures. Wherever the Spirit is, there is freedom. Not irresponsibility, not euphoric obliviousness to the biblical call to holy living, and definitely not exemption from obedience. For the sons and daughters of God, our sense of freedom does not diminish as the Spirit's transformation continues—it only deepens year after year, as we hold on to the truth.

Freedom, which is attained only at a great price, is not cheap. Though often counterfeited, genuine Christian freedom (Galatians 5:1) is found only in Christ. Consider the false freedom promised not only by the world, but even in the name of Christ. The appeal to an easier way has always lain at the heart of false teaching. Hence the modern day call to "free the spirit," "go with the flow" and "trust your heart."

Feeling or following: That is the question. When we become fixated on *feeling* God, we are headed the wrong way; when we resolutely decide on *following* God, we are headed the right way. (And the great feelings will come in time.)

Jumping the Tracks

"Come follow me, and I will set you free—free from duty, free to interpret the rules as you like, free to determine what you think is right." This is the promise of Satan, if only we will forsake Christ and return to the world. As tempting as flypaper to a housefly, as the worm to the fish, as peanut butter to the mouse, as the Edenic hanging fruit to the first couple, so is the appeal of returning to the world.

Peter describes the false teachers: "They promise...freedom, while they themselves are slaves" (2 Peter 2:19).[1] But how can a slave offer freedom? Can a poor man pay the ransom of a rich man? He cannot, plain and simple.[2] So what sort of freedom is it they are promising? I believe it is a destructive flight from reason and responsibility.

Imagine you are a train. You have been taught that you can go wherever you like, as long as you stay on the tracks. You have heard, however, of self-made, "independent" locomotives who have jumped the tracks in the headlong pursuit of "freedom." These trains refused to accept "the system," with its strictly gauged tracks, tunnels, crossings and signals. They had the guts to buck the system and, they boast, it is worth it. "Why," you wonder wistfully, "couldn't I, too, experience the freedom of going wherever I want to go—instead of only along these narrow, confining tracks?"

We are all like that train and have all been tempted to look longingly at the world and the empty freedom it promises. And we also know, every one of us, that no one who "jumps the tracks" is "free" for long. Sooner or later—and usually sooner!—we meet with harm and pain, twin rewards for our audacity.

True spiritual freedom apart from the precepts of the Scriptures and obedience to the commandments is an illusion. It just does not exist. New Age religion, Neopentecostalism, Zen Buddhism—no alternative can possibly improve on the truth God has revealed to us, because no alternative can change us from what we are ("trains") to what we are not (flying mystics with spiritual jet packs). We were created and designed to stay "on track," and as long as we do so, life, despite those "light and momentary troubles," will remain relatively smooth. But once we leave the "confines" (and protection) of God's paths, turbulence and tragedy are weak words to describe what comes next.

Yet where the Spirit of the Lord is—yes!—that's where real freedom is found.[3]

God's Spirit, Not Yours

"I did it my way," says a popular song of the past. Sad but true, as a picture of a world gone astray. We have all tried to do it our way, to follow our own spirit. How much better to sing, "I did it God's way"! (See Matthew 7:21-27.)

God's Spirit will fill us and change us, from the inside out, to be powerful, loving and disciplined. This is the triple winning combination if you want to enjoy your relationship with God, as well as win friends and influence people—for Christ. But character change takes time. Don't think for a minute that you can "test Christianity out" for a few years, then get your money back if you are not satisfied with the results. Becoming Christlike in our character is a lifelong endeavor. Be encouraged by your progress (Philippians 1:25).

His Spirit gives us gifts, grace and guidance. Those gifts are meant to be used for the good of others. That grace covers all sins, past and future, and provides confidence as we enjoy our freedom as God's children. The guidance is from the Scriptures, which are inspired by the Holy Spirit, as well as from persons in whom the wisdom of the Scriptures is living and active.

His Spirit, because it is *holy,* will make us holy as well. The Spirit insists that we carry out our divine commission, with its two aspects: world evangelism and generosity toward the needy as we live modest lives. When this is our lifestyle, we are truly free in the Spirit!

Inside Out and Upside Down!

Hopefully, your understanding has deepened as you have read this book. If so, what are you planning to do about it? What will change? Winston Churchill once said, "Men stumble over the truth from time to time, but most pick themselves up and hurry off as if nothing happened." The human capacity for complacency and inertia in the face of truth is truly amazing (James 1:24, Ezekiel 33:30-32). Let this not be true of us, for we have an inner power that strengthens and drives us to live heroically, daringly and spiritually. That unseen but highly visible power is the Holy Spirit! The Spirit of God, who dwells in our hearts and will direct our lives if only we'll not resist, is urging us to follow Scripture and seek the will of God with all our hearts. If we are willing to do so, we will be transformed—from the inside out—and, in the process, turn the world upside down!

QUESTIONS FOR THOUGHT

* *Am I enjoying my salvation? Do I feel a sense of freedom?*
* *What has the Holy Spirit attempted to show me this week? How might*

my life be lighter and freer if I followed the Spirit's cues?

• *Do I want to go deeper? The second half of the book is waiting!*

_____ NOTES _____

1. For false freedom as exposed in the Old Testament, see Jeremiah 2: 21–32.

2. "No man is free who cannot control himself" (Pythagoras).

3. Recommended: Steve Brown, *A Scandalous Freedom: The Radical Nature of the Gospel* (West Monroe, LA: Howard Publishing, 2004).

PART TWO

Sense & Nonsense

The second half of this book consists of material that was originally conceived as a series of appendixes. These chapters are of a somewhat more technical nature and address a wide variety of issues, especially those arising in connection with Neopentecostalism.

- From Chapter 16 to Chapter 25, questions about miracles are treated. Chapters 26 to 29 are more general, covering an assortment of problems and questions. The appendix is a Spiritual Gifts Worksheet, supplementing Chapter 7, on the gifts of the Spirit.

- A selected bibliography has been provided for those who wish to go further. Approximately fifty sources are referenced.

- Finally, you will find a glossary of terms. Approximately forty are explained. It is hoped that this will serve as a helpful companion as you read through Part Two.

16. Miracles Today?
Pull the Other Leg!

The saying "You're pulling my leg" applied literally in my case. As a high school junior, I had taken up an invitation to attend a charismatic prayer meeting.[1] After the meeting, four of the members of the group took me into a back room, sat me down in a chair and asked if I would like to be healed.

"Healed of what?" I asked, rather perplexed.

"You know, one of your legs is longer than the other. Did you ever realize that?"

"Well, I suppose that's true," I responded, thinking that it's really unlikely both legs are exactly the same length. The same would probably be true of our arms, toes, ears...(the only disappointing thing about the bilateral symmetry God gave us).

"We would like to pray for you. Would you like us to pray about your legs?" I didn't want to embarrass them, so I agreed to their suggestion. They had me hold my legs outstretched, and sure enough, one seemed shorter than the other (by a fraction of a centimeter at the most). I could see this was not going to be the most sensational healing ever performed.

The four men prayed for my leg. Laying hands on me, they called on the healing power of Jesus. "There—everything's okay. You're healed," they said. There followed a few quiet "Hallelujah's" and "Amen's."

Although I was most unimpressed with the "miracle" itself, I was intrigued by the strange faith of these people who believed that with just a little faith, people in prayer can move God to do something he might not otherwise do. I came back for the next meeting. "Is there a God powerful enough to heal?" I wondered. "Could I have a genuine relationship with God?"

Slain in the Spirit?

On another occasion, at a Full Gospel Businessmen's Fellowship International (a.k.a. FGBMFI) meeting, the guest speaker was "slaying" people "in the Spirit." In a heated and frenzied atmosphere of expectation, he would give a firm push to the man or woman whose turn it was to be "slain," sometimes after they had made a special request for prayer or "healing." They would fall backward, to be caught by two ushers standing either side of them. The "rush" this sort of activity gives people ought not to be underestimated. From the Neopentecostals' perspective, the people were being "slain in the Spirit." From mine, they were being pushed over by a man who was capitalizing on the gullibility of a superstitious crowd.

When my turn came—it took me nearly an hour to work up my nerve—I was going to ask him to heal me of my nearsightedness. I was to be the very next "slayee" when the program stopped. Oh well!

'Miracles' Every Day?

I have three problems with the signs and wonders of Neopentecostalism. First, I cannot accept them as bona fide miracles at all. The unimpressive and laughable aspects of the rigmarole, the irritating plea for money and the remarkable similarity to signs and wonders in other world religions, or even tricks at magic shows, is embarrassing and disturbing.[2] The events recounted above are all too typical of this superstitious form of religion.

Second, biblical miracles were performed for clear theological purposes. People were *really* helped—medically, for example, or to better understand the nature of God. Biblical miracles were neither for show nor to encourage viewers to make a "donation." Why should we be parted with our hard-earned money to line the pockets or tickle the egos of grown persons who should be ashamed of themselves?

My third objection is that the Charismatic Movement would have us believe that miracles are daily occurrences in the Bible. The shallow argument based on Hebrews 13:8 ("Jesus Christ is the same yesterday and today and forever") is appealed to as proof that New Testament miracles were meant to take place in every generation of Christians.

No, Miracles Are Rare!

C. S. Lewis, in his classic book *Miracles*, pointed out that if miracles happened every day, we would soon cease to appreciate them as miracles at all.[3] By definition, a miracle is a rare occurrence, something out of the ordinary, a bypassing of the laws of nature by God. The fact is that miracles were not normal occurrences in Bible times. If you were the average man or woman living in Bible times, you could easily live your entire life without ever seeing a miracle. Yet Neopentecostals speak of biblical times as though miracles were happening every day.

As scholars have noted, there is a marked decrease in frequency of miracles from the gospels to Acts and an even greater decrease from Acts to the letters.[4] In the New Testament miracles are relatively infrequent. The New Testament itself can reinforce the impression that miracles were everyday occurrences, especially the gospels and Acts, which record only the "highlights," compressing into a few scrolls what transpired over a period of many years. Are things any different in the Old Testament?

Although there is the occasional miracle in the Old Testament, most miracles are clustered around two events: the Exodus and the rise of the prophetic movement (starting with Elijah and Elisha).

Accounting for 'Miracles'

The difference between biblical miracles and the "miracles" of today is clear. But how do we account for the more dramatic claims made today? Let us confine our discussion to "faith healing."

- Healings could be psychosomatic. Never underestimate the connection between mind and body. About thirty percent of all medical "cures" are psychosomatic.
- It could be a case of fraud (2 Corinthians 11:13–15), especially where money is involved (2 Corinthians 2:17).
- It could be a paranormal occurrence[5] which, in time, will be capable of explanation.
- Exaggeration of claims must always be taken into account. It is good to ask, "Did you see this yourself, or did someone pass the story on to you?" Claims are not always exaggerated, but this is a common and very human tendency.
- Satan has the ability to counterfeit miracles (Revelation 13:13, 2 Thessalonians 2:9). God alone does true miracles (Psalm 72:18, 136:4). Pharaoh's magicians approximated what God did through Moses (Exodus 7:12, 22), but there were limits to what they could do (Exodus 8:19). Still, I hesitate to ascribe alleged "miracles" to the devil.
- The miracle may simply be the answer to the prayer of a sincere seeker after God. God does hear the prayers of the unsaved (Acts 10:4, 1 Kings 8:43). The prayers he will not listen to (answer) are those where deliberate sin is involved (Psalm 66:18, John 9:31).

Some Claims Legitimate?

Let us elaborate on that last possibility, the sincere seeker's answered prayer, for a moment. There is nothing in the Bible to say that God cannot or will not answer the prayer of a non-Christian. How can God not answer the prayer of the sincere person who prays that he can find God? And why wouldn't God occasionally answer a prayer—perhaps a prayer for healing—in order to assist someone in seeking him, or, in the event that the miracle had no effect, to leave him (and any witnesses as well) without excuse on the last day. It is a starchy mentality that will not allow God to answer prayers of his lost children.

If you are having a hard time with this, consider an analogy: In a household there is a domestic servant, and there is a son. The servant does not belong to the family and cannot legitimately call the master "Father." But he may approach the master with various requests. The father would gladly allow his son to borrow his car, but the servant does not have that privilege. The servant may, however, ask the master for the time of day, or for a cup of water. The master would give these to his son as well.

The analogy does not support the idea that non-Christians have a personal, saved relationship with God; but there is some sort of relationship, and who is to say that it is not personal? Of course, if God responded to Solomon's petition that he answer the prayers of noncovenant people so that they could come to know him, that would be nothing new (1 Kings 8). God's love for individual men and women has never changed.

We will needlessly offend sincere people and shut the doors of the kingdom of heaven in their faces if we insist that all of their spiritual experiences are from the devil. Let us learn some wisdom in this area. Too much of Christian apologetics is a matter of trying to explain away the experiences of others.

Observations About Healings

- Few have actually witnessed healings. Most reports come from second-hand information.
- Most "healings" are frivolous (colds, undiagnosed "cancers," etc.).
- Many healings are psychosomatic. Positive attitudes effect or speed up the healing process. Many illnesses are psychosomatic.
- God may still answer our prayers for healing, even though the gift of healing has passed away.
- God's usual way of working in this world is through natural processes. When your body heals itself, God should receive the thanks. He may also work through doctors.

Are Miracles Necessary Today?

Miracles are certainly not essential, if Luke 16:19–31 and John 20:30–31 are to be believed. The recorded miracles in Scripture are sufficient; no more are needed. But are we really missing them? Do we really need miracles to get the Word out in our generation? There are so many advantages we have over our first-century brothers: fast travel nearly anywhere on the planet, the printing press, telephones, fax machines, email and a relatively efficient postal service, radio and television, the completed New Testament, two millennia of history and mistakes to learn from, not to mention religious freedom in many countries.

Besides the occasional miracle, what did they have that we do not? Slow travel (usually on foot), a dismal legacy of national spiritual failure under the old covenant, no printing press (manuscripts that had to be painstakingly copied), widespread illiteracy, no telephone (although private letters could reach any part of the Roman Empire in a matter of days), no electricity, radio or television technology, only the completed Old Testament (which few were privileged to possess), open and virulent persecution. When you think about it, it is obvious that God has blessed us with many advantages our first-century brothers and sisters did not enjoy. Take your choice. As for me and my house, we will take modern times any day!

Night and Day Contrast

So what is the difference between false, modern-day miracles and biblical miracles? Or is there any difference? Is one counterfeit and the other genuine? Might not the same arguments explaining away pseudomiracles be used to explain away miracles in the Bible? Let's look at the differences, for they are major. In fact, the contrast is night and day!

1. Biblical miracles were clear-cut and well documented.

Most "miracle stories" are not. It is one thing to repeat a story of a healing that someone else told you, but quite another to be healed or to perform the healing yourself. It is one thing to babble with syllables that defy analysis, perhaps with the occasional foreign phrase mingled in; it is quite another to speak fluently in a language you have never studied. It is one thing to deliver a vague prophecy that has the applicability of a horoscope, quite another to provide accurate and detailed information that is of value to others. I once studied with a man who was convinced he had AIDS, although this had not been verified by any doctor. One day he "felt" God had come into his life—as well as a surge of energy and complete "healing" from AIDS. Hallelujah?[6]

2. In the Bible people were healed indiscriminately.

Personal faith was not always essential for the healing to take place. Mark

6:5 shows that a faithless religious climate could hinder even Jesus, but we still see many healed in the Bible who do not have personal faith (Luke 13:13, Matthew 8:13). Modern faith healers frequently attribute failure to heal to lack of faith on the part of the one in need of healing. In the Bible, people were not first "screened" in order to assess their suitability as candidates. In modern charismatic healing services, ushers "screen out" the "hopeless" cases: amputees, the deformed, etc. Some faith healers go even further in efforts to put on a good show. A well-known TV evangelist and faith healer, Peter Popoff, was "debugged" on national television when it was revealed that his wife was sending him messages from the audience about people's illnesses via FM transmitter. He in turn was "miraculously" diagnosing them on the platform! I am also reminded of a scandal that surfaced when a reporter unknowingly entered the dressing room while the "wheel chair crew" (who were to receive healing later that evening) were all being coached on how to behave.[7]

3. Biblical miracles were carried out in any type of environment.

An ecstatic, artificially contrived atmosphere was unnecessary. No prelude or patter was needed, and often miracles were performed despite a hostile audience. Today's charismatic revival meetings occur, for the most part, in synthetic, controlled environments.

4. In the Bible, any miracle could and did occur.

Men walked on water (Matthew 14:25, 29). Men disappeared and reappeared (Luke 24:31, Acts 8:39-40). Large bodies of water were rearranged (Exodus 14:21) and storms were rebuked into calmness (Mark 4:39). Very large meals were catered (John 6:1–13). Heavenly limousines were dispatched (2 Kings 2:11). Ears were replaced (Luke 22:51). There were miracles of radical fishing (Luke 5:4–6), radical body-building (Judges 16:30), radical gardening (Mark 11:21) and radical physics (2 Kings 6:6). Miracles of instantaneous transportation occurred (John 6: 21, 1 Kings 18:12). Armies were blinded (2 Kings 6:18), shackles fell from the wrists of the saints, and iron gates opened of their own volition (Acts 12:6–10). Legions of demons took up new residences (Mark 5:1–13). Any condition was curable, from blindness to leprosy to death itself. Although not all diseases were healed, no job was too difficult, providing there was a reason in God's economy for the miracle to take place. Modern claims pale into insignificance by contrast. They are limited almost exclusively to trivial or unverifiable events: "cured" colds and backaches, visions, tongues, and so on.

5. Healings in the Bible were almost without exception instantaneous.

If the miraculous gift of healing is still here today, let one who possesses it drop in on a hospital ward and free up some beds, or visit a cemetery and make the gardener work overtime. It is asked why Jesus said, "Lazarus, come out!" in John 11:43. If Jesus had not said, "Lazarus, come out!" everyone in the graveyard would have come out! Not so with today's faith healers, who cannot replicate New Testament raising from the dead, as practiced by Jesus and the apostles (Matthew 10:8, Acts 9:40).[8]

One recent story was tragicomic:

> "FATAL DIAGNOSIS: Two witchdoctors in Zimbabwe who claimed they could cure AIDS have died from the disease after having sex with patients they believed they had healed.—AFP"

6. Biblical healings were complete.

There were no partial cures, slight improvements or relapses. Modern "healings" are usually one of the above. Truly, God's word shows up modern "wonders" for what they are (Isaiah 44:25).

7. Biblical healings were effected by persons of known integrity.

They did not try to milk money from those they helped, nor did they dazzle for their own ego (Acts 8:10-11). Sadly, the same cannot be said of "wonder-workers" today.[9]

8. The purpose behind biblical miracles was to bring to mankind the word of God.

For the most part, biblical miracles produced faith in the word of the speaker. They were to confirm the divine authority of those who spoke it and to certify their message (Exodus 4:1–9, 1 Kings 17:24, Mark 2:10, Mark 16:20, John 20:30–31, Acts 14:3, Hebrews 2:4).

Conclusion

What a contrast to modern day "signs and wonders"! Only God can work miracles; all others are counterfeit. In my view, the pseudomiracles far, far outnumber the genuine ones. If those who follow after would-be faith healers would study their Bibles more carefully, they would not be so quickly impressed. Go on, pull the other leg!

NOTES

1. On an autobiographical note, I am rather indebted to the Charismatic Movement as a whole, in which I was involved for two years in the 1970s. Though I cannot endorse their theology of discipleship or conversion, and no longer agree with their interpretation of the work of the Spirit, these men and women were the first people I had ever met who took their faith seriously. It was through my involvement with them that I came to accept the basics: the power of God, the Bible as God's word, the certainty of heaven or hell, the necessity of rebirth—along with the bankruptcy of traditional Christendom. Much of the material I present in this book is a direct result of the process of finding answers to the many questions I had as a result of my involvement.

2. Recommended: The movie *Leap of Faith,* starring Steve Martin. Although there is a serious point to the film, the exposé of so-called faith healers' tactics is illuminating indeed.

3. As John Donne said, "There is nothing that God hath established in a constant course of nature, and which therefore is done every day, but would seem a miracle, and exercise our admiration, if it were done but once" (*LXXX Sermons* [1640], xxii, Easter Day, 25 March 1627).

4. For example, Jimmy Jividen, *Miracles: From God or Man?* (Abilene, Texas: ACU Press, 1987).

5. An event lying outside of the range of current normal scientific investigation.

6. Some people believe in "healing" inanimate objects, for example, "The pastor laid hands on my car and healed it." (The spirit of 2 Kings 2:21?)

7. See James Randi, *The Faith Healers* (Buffalo, New York: Prometheus Books, 1987). James Randi is a magician who has undertaken a thorough investigation of the best-known faith healers such as Oral Roberts, Pat Robertson, Peter Popoff, W. V. Grant, A. A. Allen, Leroy Jenkins, Earnest Angley and even Catholic healers and shrines. He has attended many healing services, conducted extensive interviews, used video and audio tapes, checked available records, written letters, even examined trash left from healing services. His book is a thorough and complete indictment of all faith healers.

Randi says he has not found a single case of a genuine miracle, defined as a case with an independent medical investigation both before and after the healing, no medical treatment that might have affected the ailment, and a type of condition not subject to psychological impact or spontaneous reversal. He finds no case by any healer that meets such qualifications. His best-known exposé is the one telecast on the Johnny Carson Show. He presented a videotape of a Peter Popoff healing session in San Francisco. Randi had spotted a hearing device in Popoff's ear and suspected that it was a radio receiver through which he received information from someone off stage. Randi's associate used a scanner to find the frequency on which the information was being broadcast and then re-corded the secret messages. On the Carson telecast, Randi first showed Popoff approach someone and reveal information about them that he had apparently learned by divine revelation. Then Randi showed the tape again, superimposing the recorded messages to reveal that someone offstage, who apparently had engaged the person in conversation previous to the session, was feeding Popoff all the information for his supposed divine revelation.

Randi's book is filled with descriptions of other deceptive techniques, such as supplying wheel chairs to those not actually needing them so that they can appear suddenly to be able to walk, even though they had not come to the service in a wheelchair; using staff members as shills who pretended to be healed; rejecting from the healing line those with observable conditions such as a missing hand or withered arm, while accepting those with nonobservable ailments; and the old trick of making a "shortened leg" appear to lengthen by manipulating the shoe on one foot.

Acknowledgment: R. Stafford North's review of Randi's book in *The Christian Chronicle*, Vol. 45, No. 5 (Oklahoma City, May 1988), 23.

As for "leg-lengthening," the first time I visited a charismatic group, the leaders invited me into the back room, where they seated me with my legs extended. The manipulation was just that—manipulation. I was too embarrassed to tell anyone about it!

See also https://grahamghana.wordpress.com/2011/02/10/pastor-you're-pulling -my-leg/.

8. Mark 8:22ff and Numbers 12:10ff are certainly not the model for progressive healings taking days or even months to happen!

9. One of the most stunning and shameless appeals for money was made by Oral Roberts in the early 1980s. He claimed he had seen a vision of Jesus, who was 900 feet tall and instructed him to ask for increased contributions for the completion of one of Roberts' projects.

17. Nothing New Under the Sun
Miracles Outside Christianity

If Solomon's astute observation (Ecclesiastes 1:9) applied in his day, how much more does it apply now. In one sense claims of miracles are nothing new under the sun, as we shall soon see. There have always been "miracles": in the religions of the world through all generations, in the first-century Mediterranean world and in Christendom at large. In this chapter we make a lightning survey of miracles the world over, suggesting some explanations for these phenomena.

Miracles in World Religions

As long as there has been religion, men have sought the miraculous. There are "charismatics" in every significant religion of the world. From Hinduism to Shinto, from the religions of the South Sea Islands to the semi-Christian cults, the miraculous—especially healing, prophecy and tongue-speaking—has captured the hearts of men and women from time immemorial. Consider a few examples from Indian, Asian and Middle Eastern religions.

Hinduism[1] is the oldest continuously existing religion on the face of the earth, if we allow that Judaism, based on the Old Testament Law, begins at least a millennium later. Miracles have always interested the inhabitants of the subcontinent of India, and stories of the miraculous abound. Modern times prove no exception. Many gurus and spiritual masters hail from India, as those of us living in the West know. One Indian charismatic sect, which follows Sai Baba, claims over fifty million adherents, and incredible miracles, particularly healings, are reported to come as a result of the power emanating from that man.[2]

In the early period of Chinese religion, we find descriptions of shamans with remarkable powers. Like those who performed the native American rain dances, shamans were responsible for making rain. In addition they healed disease and communicated with the gods and with the departed spirits of ancestors. (To this day, ancestor worship is part and parcel of traditional Chinese religion.) Most interesting for our survey, they are known to have worked themselves into frenzied states of ecstasy, opening themselves up to the influence of spirits and departed ancestors, who appeared to speak through them (prophecy). They even exorcised demoniacs, who jerked violently and spoke in tongues. And all of this was taking place while the Israelites were still slaves in Egypt (Shang Dynasty China, 1766-1122 BC).

There were also shamans in Shinto (the religion of Japan), who communicated with the *kami*, "superior ones" or divinities. Remember the World War II kamikaze pilots? (*Kamikaze* means "divine wind.") Both male and female shamans danced themselves into a frenzy and became mouthpieces for the gods.

Meanwhile in India, after Israel and Judah returned from Babylonian and Persian captivity, the Buddha (563-483 BC) died, and soon thousands of miracles were attributed to him. If they were genuine, he would have been one of the most charismatic men ever to have walked the face of the earth.

Of all the brands of Buddhism[3] I have studied, the most fascinating is Tibetan Buddhism. Holy men using white magic (which is for good purposes, unlike black magic) launched hailstorms from their fingertips, flattening the crops of their enemies. They lived in mountain caves with virtually no clothing or food, keeping themselves warm by sheer willpower. They also had the ability to fly through the air—to transport themselves here and there by mere thought. (Carlos Castañeda, watch out!) One fellow I knew at Harvard, a Tibetan monk, was supposed to be the reincarnation of one of the lamas. (A lama is a holy priest; the Dalai Lama is the supreme spiritual leader of Tibet.) One day in class I asked him whether he really believed he was that reincarnation; he humbly admitted that he had his doubts!

Islam[4] (founded in the seventh century) gave birth to the Sufi order. Sufism was originally a reaction against the materialism and theological contortions of mainline Islam, and the Sufis are the mystics of their religion. Union with Allah became the supreme goal, and some Sufis took this so far as to virtually usurp divinity. One Sufi exclaimed, "Glory be to me!" Another less fortunate fellow was crucified in 922 AD after claiming "I am the truth." Sufis are not only the mystics of Islam; they are the charismatics of Islam as well. Supernatural abilities are attributed to the dervishes, religious men vowed to poverty whose physical powers, enhanced through their states of ecstasy, are considerable. Dervishes are known to speak in tongues. The wildest of the lot were the Rifaiya, or "howling dervishes."[5] Working themselves into a frenzy by chanting in a circle and violently jerking their bodies, they demonstrated their faith by eating glass, falling on sharp knives, walking on fire, swallowing red-hot coals and even handling vipers. (Appalachian rattlesnake handlers, move over!) A contemporary order of "whirling dervishes" is famous for the swirling dances by which they bring themselves into a state of ecstasy. Space prohibits describing the strong charismatic element in African and Caribbean religion (for example, the Santeria religion).

All the major religions of the world claim miraculous happenings—and so do the minor ones! From the tropics of Africa and Melanesia to the frigid climes of the Himalayan hermits and the Hudson Bay Eskimos, men and women prophesy, speak in tongues and claim the miraculous.

How much of it is genuine? That is a question we will attempt to answer shortly, but first a visit to the Mediterranean world of the first century AD.

First-Century Mediterranean Area

When Paul says to the Corinthians, "You know that when you were pagans, somehow or other you were influenced and led astray to mute idols" (1 Corinthians 12:2), he is alluding to the pagan religious background of the Corinthians. In Corinth, as in all the cities of the Roman world, there were many charismatic cults, and these cults stressed several things seemingly within the repertoire of the Corinthian church. The Christians were influenced and led astray because they had absorbed the popular religious mentality of the day, surrendering their will to an experience.

Let us start with the cult of the god Asklepios, the god of healing. Significant shrines of Asklepios remain at both Cos and Epidaurus (in Greece), and from them we learn much about the approach to healing among the ancient Greek people. People would visit the deity's temple, make an offering and undergo ritual bathing in a sacred stream. Spending the night in the shrine precinct, they would pray for a visitation from the god in a dream (during which the deity advised them of the correct form of treatment). Treatment included religious rituals, magic formulae, physical and drug therapy, and even sacred drama and music. After devotees had been healed they would give an offering of thanks to the god, usually in the form of a plaster replica of the member of the body that had been healed. The cast would then be attached to the temple wall. (Not unlike some church buildings today, where one finds crutches, wheelchairs, and so forth attached to the wall of the building!)

In light of this, one can see that experiences of healing are nothing new in the religious history of mankind. We could discuss the charismatic cults of Aphrodite, Attis (or Hermes), both long established in Corinth by the time of 1 Corinthians (55-57 AD). Literature on Dionysus (the god of wine) is always interesting. How do you suppose one went about pleasing the god of wine? Adherents of his cult paid their respects by drinking (and eating) as much as possible, sometimes in wild orgies. States of ecstasy were thus induced. But perhaps the cult of Isis and Sarapis is most interesting for the present study, as this religious group practiced tongue-speaking, as well as prophesying and healing, and there were five temples in Corinth alone. Isis is an Egyptian goddess, whose worship can be traced back to the fourth millennium BC (over a thousand years before the time of Abraham), while Sarapis is a Canaanite deity. As in the case of many Greek religions, the worshiper would fall under the influence of the deity and begin to speak frenziedly in an unknown tongue (known only to the god), but which could be interpreted by a miraculously endowed prophet. As for the healing abilities of Isis, there is the statement of Diodorus Siculus, who reports the nocturnal visits of Isis to those in need of healing:[6]

> Standing above the sick in their sleep she gives aid for their diseases and works remarkable cures upon such as submit themselves to her; and many who have been despaired of by their physicians because of the difficult nature of their malady are restored to health by her (*L.C.L.* I.25.5).

Does this sound familiar? Such claims of healing, as this chapter contends, are as old as the sun. The modern Neopentecostal movement is but an expression of the age-old religious impulse of mankind.

In some generations more than others, zeal for the miraculous is exceptionally strong. It is in such a climate that Jesus lived and in such an environment that the missionary church of the first century was planted. If anyone doubts this, let him take a look at the pagan milieu of the book of Acts (see Acts 8:9–11, 13:8–10, 16:16–18, 19:13–16).

Miracles in Christendom at Large

After the apostles died, the supernatural gifts of the Holy Spirit passed away as well. That of course does not mean that God never heals in response to prayer; he is sovereign and does whatever he pleases. Early church history indicates that the miraculous gifts of the Spirit were not present after the latter part of the first century. Even as early as the second century, the charismatic Montanist movement was denounced, not only for being heretical, but also because its so-called miracles were *unbiblical,* not at all corresponding to the sound doctrine of apostolic times.

By the third century, however, as the message of the gospel became more and more diluted, increasing numbers of people were claiming miraculous experience. Experiences focused especially on the departed saints, who in time became regarded as suitable intercessors for saints on earth. Eventually an entire pantheon of "saints" was created! With the rise of the cult of relics[7] and the revival of pagan superstition, often under a Christian guise, a rational, commonsense religion gave way to an irrational, whimsical and emotional spirituality.

Although there have been cycles of charismatic revival and decline, no generation of Christendom has been without its enthusiasm for the miraculous manifestations of the Holy Spirit. Instances of prophecy, tongue-speaking and interpretation are too numerous to even attempt to recount. Stories of healings are as commonplace in popular Christianity as they are in the other religions of the world. That miracles are claimed in so many different Christian denominations is no insignificant fact; surely God cannot be placing his stamp of approval on every conflicting doctrine and practice! Some groups deny the divinity of Christ. Others water down discipleship to little more than pew-warming. Still others disagree on basic moral issues on which the Bible is crystal clear.

It should not be surprising to us to find that the miracle-seeking movement has infiltrated nearly every major denomination. A writer speaking of how Roman Catholics came to speak in tongues stated that with some people "the beginning comes quietly, gently and effortlessly; with Tom N., it was as he was finishing his rosary; with Rita M., it was while she was singing a hymn at Mass; with Sister M., it came as she knelt in silent prayer to the Blessed Virgin."[8]

And what about the cults? Many groups outside the orbit of traditional Christendom claim the miraculous. For example, the Mormons speak in tongues, as their scriptures dictate (Alma 9:21, 2 Nephi 32:2[9]).

Knock Three Times

There are more charismatic sects than most of us have ever dreamed of. Once I was sharing my faith in the streets near our home in London when I met a chap who said he was a member of "The Brotherhood of the Cross and Star." I had stopped him on the sidewalk to invite him to our church's invitation worship service, when he said that he had just left a service in progress, and then invited me to come along. I consented, realizing I might well have an opportunity to invite the whole group.

After entering a dilapidated church building, I was led down the stairs into their basement meeting room and asked to remove my shoes, which I did. I instantly became aware of two significant differences between me and my hosts: They were, without exception, African or West Indian, while I am white; they all wore shining white robes—I wore a conservative, dark English suit. I took a seat, and the group were probably more surprised to see me than I was to see them.

I kept hearing references to a certain "Olumba Olumba Obu," but did not know what they meant. Then the leader of the service shouted, "All give praise!" I was instructed to bow to the ground and knock my forehead three times on the hard floor, which I did (all things to all men!). I turned and asked the woman seated next to me if the group spoke in tongues and prophesied and received an affirmative answer. After another round of "All give praise" and a few more knocks of my head on the floor (this time I was told to remove my glasses), I heard the reader mention "Father Olumba, the Alpha and the Omega, the supreme head of the universe. All give praise!" (Needless to say, this time I did not go down.) Suddenly the woman on my right sprung to her feet and "screamed in the Spirit," twisting her body violently, her white robe nearly knocking me out of my seat. I asked the man in front of me where "Olumba Olumba Obu" lived. His reply: "Father Olumba lives in our hearts. He also has his headquarters in Nigeria." I was smack in the middle of a cult!

Enduring another twenty minutes of tongue-speaking, dancing and an appeal for money (of course), I was asked whether I had any words for the group. Indeed I did! I challenged them to study the Bible consistently, to deal with their lukewarmness and to live as disciples. Then I invited everyone to our invitation service.

As we can see, Neopentecostalism has spread into every nook and cranny of Christendom. From Catholicism to Orthodoxy to Protestantism to the cults, the Charismatic Movement is here to stay!

The $64,000 Question

Are we to discount miracles in the various world religions just because they do not acknowledge Christ? And if so, are we to reject the charismatic experiences of Mormons and the Olumba Olumba Obu sect, who do (technically) acknowledge Christ, just because they are heretical in their doctrine? And if we are willing to dismiss the experiences of these groups because they teach a corrupted gospel, do we have any more reason to defend the "miracles" in more mainstream Christian groups?

The $64,000 answer: No, we do not. Charismatic claims are no more a priori legitimate than the claims of the Hindus or the Mormons. The Charismatic experience is essentially the same the world over, regardless of the beliefs of those who seek it.

It is quite possible to have miraculous experience without even believing in Christ, and so charismatic experience in itself establishes nothing. There is, as Solomon wisely observed, "nothing new under the sun." Do not be too quickly impressed by rumors of the miraculous.

_____ **NOTES** _____

1. Hinduism is the principal religion of India and was institutionalized c. 1500 BC.

Popular Hinduism boasts tens of thousands of miracle stories, as well as countless charismatic sects.

2. Sai Baba's following, strongest in South India, are in my opinion the unfortunate victims of fraud.

3. Buddhism originally denied personal individual existence. Popular Buddhism propagated countless miracle stories, both of the life of the Buddha as well as of the Buddhist "saints."

4. Islam is the youngest of the major religions of the world, and was founded by Mohammed (570–632 AD) in Arabia. Islam is based on Judaism and Christianity and was historically a reaction against the corruption of Arabian polytheism and decadent Judaism and Christianity.

5. "Dervishes" are Muslim holy men vowed to a life of poverty. Many dervishes practice ecstatic dancing and speaking in tongues.

6. See also Apuleius, *Metamorphoses II.*

7. Relics were sacred objects, articles or scraps of clothing supposedly connected with Jesus, members of his family or other saintly men and women and out of which magical powers and blessings were said to flow.

8. Edward O'Connor, *The Pentecostal Movement in the Catholic Church* (Ave Maria Press, 1971), 128.

9. "Do ye not remember that I said unto you that after ye had received the Holy Ghost ye could speak with the tongue of angels? And now, how could ye speak with the tongue of angels save it were by the Holy Ghost?"

18. Miracles in Acts
History, Rhyme and Reason

This chapter approaches the Spirit in the book of Acts from the perspective of God's historical purposes:

- The first section, "History," differentiates between the two covenants and brings the discussion into the light of prophecy and fulfillment.
- Questions about the miraculous gifts and outpourings—whether they are intended to describe spiritual experience for the first, apostolic generation, or for believers of all generations—are covered in the second section, "Rhyme."
- Finally, "Reason," the third section, illuminates the game plan of Acts and places the first two sections in perspective.

History: The Spirit Had Not Been Given

The dramatic difference between the old covenant (the age of Law) and the new (the age of the Spirit) cannot be overstated. Before Jesus was glorified, the Holy Spirit was for only a select few.[1] Let me suggest a helpful way to distinguish between the presence of the Spirit in the two testaments. Broadly speaking, under the Old Testament, God's Spirit was among his people; under the New Testament, the Spirit lives within his people. In fulfillment of many prophecies, the new covenant was to be a time when all disciples—not just a few of God's special leaders—would have the Spirit living in their hearts.[2] The imminence of this change is referred to in John 7:39, a crucial verse to keep in mind as we consider texts on the Spirit in both testaments:

> By this he meant the Spirit, whom those who believed in him were later to receive. Up to that time the Spirit had not been given, since Jesus had not yet been glorified.

Until the day of Pentecost, 30 AD, men and women of faith did not generally possess the Spirit. Yet, as Jesus said, "he who is least in the kingdom" (Matthew 11:11) has the very special privilege indeed of the indwelling of the Spirit!

The giving of the Spirit bisects human history. Any understanding of the Holy Spirit that minimizes the radical change after Pentecost is thus deficient. For before the church, "the Spirit had not been given" (John 7:39).

The Outpouring of the Last Days

The Scriptures promised that the Spirit would be poured out, bringing blessing and a new beginning. These prophecies were fully fulfilled only in the Pentecostal outpouring of the Holy Spirit.

[1]"But now listen, O Jacob, my servant,
    Israel, whom I have chosen.
[2]This is what the LORD says—
    he who made you, who formed you in the womb,
    and who will help you:
Do not be afraid, O Jacob, my servant,
    Jeshurun, whom I have chosen.
[3]For I will pour water on the thirsty land,
    and streams on the dry ground;
I will pour out my Spirit on your offspring,
    and my blessing on your descendants" (Isaiah 44:1–3).[3]

"I will no longer hide my face from them, for I will pour out my Spirit on the house of Israel, declares the Sovereign LORD" (Ezekiel 39:29).

"And I will pour out on the house of David and the inhabitants of Jerusalem a spirit of grace and supplication. They will look on me, the one they have pierced, and they will mourn for him as one mourns for an only child, and grieve bitterly for him as one grieves for a firstborn son" (Zechariah 12:10).

[28]"And afterward,
    I will pour out my Spirit on all people.
Your sons and daughters will prophesy,
    your old men will dream dreams,
    your young men will see visions.
[29]Even on my servants, both men and women,
    I will pour out my Spirit in those days…
[32]And everyone who calls
    on the name of the LORD will be saved;
for on Mount Zion and in Jerusalem
    there will be deliverance,
as the LORD has said,
    among the survivors
whom the LORD calls" (Joel 2:28–29, 32).

Pentecost is the point in history at which the Spirit was made available to all. The last text above is the exact passage Peter quotes in his sermon at Pentecost. In other words, all the prophecies about the Spirit converge on one Spring day in Israel in 30 AD:

> [16]"This is what was spoken by the prophet Joel:
>
> [17]'In the last days, God says,
>   I will pour out my Spirit on all people.
> Your sons and daughters will prophesy;
>   your young men will see visions;
>   your old men will dream dreams.
> [18]Even on my servants, both men and women,
>   I will pour out my Spirit in those days,
>   and they will prophesy'" (Acts 2:16–18).

Many assume that religious revivals, with the spiritual manifestations, must indicate the end of the world is near. But is there another way to look at this?

Excursus: The Last Days?

This is an area of tremendous confusion for most charismatics, most of whom are premillennial in theology.[4] They usually claim that the last days started somewhere in the twentieth century, although pinning people down to exact dates is a tricky business.

What exactly are "the last days"? The Neopentecostal interpretation is that we are living in the last days, which began, at most, a century ago and will culminate in the Second Coming. Many of us have been taught that the last days reach from the year Jesus poured out his Spirit on the church at Pentecost all the way, once again, to the Second Coming. I would like to offer a third interpretation.

Acts 2:16-17 shows us that outpouring of the Spirit on the day of Pentecost occurred in the last days. When Peter explains the phenomenon of Acts 2:4ff, he refers to Joel 2:28–32 (Acts 2:16–21). It is clear Peter considers the event predicted by Joel, about 800 years beforehand, to be fulfilled in the Pentecostal outpouring (Acts 2:16, 17, 33). Joel was not the only prophet to predict an outpouring of the Spirit in the last days. He is joined by Isaiah (32:15, 44:3), Ezekiel (39:29) and Zechariah (12:10), to name a few. As a result of this event at Pentecost, we live in the age of the Spirit. God did a wonderful thing in 30 AD starting in Jerusalem: He poured out the Holy Spirit, who continues to guide and bless his people.

However, this passage does not logically prove whether the outpouring commenced, concluded or was merely contained in the time frame of the last days. James 5:3, 2 Peter 3:3, and 2 Timothy 3:1 indicate that the first-century church was living during the last days. So what happened? Was Jesus delayed (à la Daniel 10:13)? Are the Jehovah's Witnesses right? Were Jesus' attempts to set up an earthly kingdom thwarted?

One verse that brings into question the two most common views is Hebrews 1:2, where we read that Jesus Christ spoke to us "in these last days." The problem with the last days starting at Pentecost is that Jesus, by that time, had not "spoken" at all for ten days. Why not ask the obvious question: "Last days *of what?*"

Unless we subscribe to the premillennial view, if these are the last days of the world (Pentecost to Parousia, the Second Coming), are we not just stating the obvious? We are saying, in effect, "The period of time from two thousand years ago to the end of the world is the final period of human history." But what if the last days are *the last days of Judaism?*[5]

The prophets had predicted the supersession of the old covenant by the new (Jeremiah 31:31–34, e.g.), and Jesus himself had said that the kingdom would be removed from the Jewish people and given to others (Matthew 21:43). Between Pentecost and the Destruction of Jerusalem in 70 AD was a forty-year period. In my view, the last days are this "grace period," one final (and full) generation between the spiritual end of the old covenant and the physical, formal end of the entire Old Testament system (Hebrews 8:7–13).

The last days of biblical Judaism ended in the first century. So are we living in "end times" or not? Is this the final generation of humanity? God only knows! (1 Thessalonians 5:1–3).

At Pentecost the Spirit was poured out and made available to all—high and low, master and servant, prophet and common man. This awesome promise is available in baptism (Acts 2:38) and for all generations (Acts 2:39):

> [38]Peter replied, "Repent and be baptized, every one of you, in the name of Jesus Christ for the forgiveness of your sins. And you will receive the gift of the Holy Spirit. [39]The promise is for you and your children and for all who are far off—for all whom the Lord our God will call."

Outpouring Versus Indwelling

One way to visualize the difference between the Spirit under the old covenant and under the new is to picture a glass of water. It's nice to cool down (if it is summer, pour some on yourself!), but even more refreshing to drink some. In the same way, the indwelling of the Spirit changes us from the inside out; this must not be confused with the various external receptions or outpourings of the Spirit which we find throughout the Old and New Testaments. Although at first this distinction may be confusing, it is essential to keep it in mind.

> External reception: The Spirit on a person
> Internal reception (or indwelling): The Spirit in a person.

Rhyme: It Sounds the Same, But Isn't

One problem facing the reader of Acts is discerning what is exceptional and what is normative. In other words, which of the miracles and the various outpourings of the Spirit are intended by Luke to portray daily life (as in the church capsule, 2:42–47) and which are included for historical purposes? I believe a careful examination will show that a good portion of the events recorded in Acts are meant to be understood as unique.

Rhymes are similar, but not necessarily the same. The words "road" and "toad" sound alike, but there is no inherent connection between the two—unless the unfortunate amphibian gets run over! "Rice" and "mice" rhyme too, but here again, the imagination is required to find any connection. They rhyme but are completely different words.

Studying the topic of the Holy Spirit in the Bible brings up many similar passages; they "rhyme" but are not easily extrapolated to today. The Bible reader naturally studies the passages on the Spirit together (as one would find them compiled in a concordance), and it seems reasonable enough to expect the Spirit to "behave" the same in each passage read. Constructing a picture of the "normal" or "biblical" action of the Spirit in our lives today is easier said than done. We should be as careful about positing connections between the Spirit passages as we are about connecting mice with rice or fox with socks!

Before and After?

Some people say that nowadays it is possible to receive the Spirit after salvation, as in the case of the Samaritans (Acts 8) or even *before* salvation, as in the case of the Caesareans (Acts 10). This assumes that the Samaritans did not receive the indwelling until the apostles arrived; and conversely, that the Caesareans did receive the indwelling before they were baptized into Christ. While this seems plausible, logically it will not do. After all, what makes a right relationship with God? (1) Forgiveness of sins is necessary, since sin is what places man in spiritual darkness (Colossians 1:13–14). (2) The Holy Spirit, which makes us children of God, guarantees our final redemption, makes us Christians and so forth (Romans 8:9). These two spiritual blessings ought to be received simultaneously.[6] In Acts 8 and 10 the *outward* outpouring of the Spirit (8:18, 10:44) should not be confused with indwelling (2:38–39).

Location	Historical purpose	Normative?	How forgiven	Comments
Acts 2	Outpouring of the Spirit; launching the new covenant.	2:4 - no 2:28-41-yes.	Repentance and baptism (2:38)	The foundation of the church is being laid.
Acts 8	Samaritans' inclusion in the gospel. gospel. Severe prejudice.	No.	Faith and baptism (8:12)	Meets the requirements of Mark 16:16.
Acts 10	Gentiles included in the new covenant. Severe prejudice.	No.	Faith (10:43) and baptism (10:47-48)	More "conversion" of Peter than Cornelius!

These special receptions of the Spirit occur for specific historical purposes, which are taken up in the following section. They punctuate biblical history at the three points specified in Acts 1:8. There is absolutely no reason any of them should have to be repeated in our day.

Reason: The Game Plan of Acts

The book of Acts has a definite outline, and the expanding concentric circles of evangelism follow the instruction of Jesus before his ascension. The three-part structure corresponds to Luke's portrayal of the scope of the evangelistic mission:

> "But you will receive power when the Holy Spirit comes on you; and you will be my witnesses in Jerusalem, and in all Judea and Samaria, and to the ends of the earth." (Acts 1:8).

The gospel was first to be preached in the Holy City, then in the geographical territory of Israel and finally to the Gentiles. This tripartite plan is realized in, respectively, Acts chapters 1–7, 8–12 and 13–28.

Acts 2: Launching the Church

In Acts 2 the outpoured Spirit heralds the new covenant and inaugurates the coming of the kingdom of God in the church. For this reason, highly visible, spectacular spiritual manifestations occurred. Pentecost, the Feast of the

Ingathering, has been called "Babel in Reverse." The nations are being summoned back to God; the curse of tongues (Genesis 11) is being undone.

Two historical observations should be made. (1) The tongues of fire and miraculous languages did not occur in the audience, which probably numbered in the tens of thousands.[7] (2) The miracles in the early Christian community were done by the apostles (Acts 2:43). The Pentecostal outpouring was to grab the attention of the remnant people of God—those Jews who would accept Jesus as the Messiah and, in fulfillment of the prophecies, be gathered as his flock under one Shepherd.

Acts 8: An Historical Exception

The significance of the Samaritans being evangelized should not be underestimated. When the gospel of Christ reached Samaria (c. 39 AD) through the preaching of Philip the Evangelist, a number of Samaritans were immersed into Christ (Acts 8:12). Even Simon the sorcerer became a Christian (v. 13). The stir this caused back in Jerusalem among the Jewish Christians was sensational. The deep-seated prejudice against the Samaritans dated back to the Assyrian captivity (722 BC onward), when many Israelites intermarried with Assyrians and produced a race of half-breeds, the Samaritans. It was one thing for a Jew to become a Christian, quite another for a Gentile to become a Christian (after circumcision, on which many early Christians insisted), but another thing altogether for a Samaritan to become a Christian. These betrayers of the nation, these low-down, good-for-nothing vermin deserved no place in the kingdom of God, in the mind of temple-going Jews! Yet the disciples were commanded to make disciples of all nations.[8] Jesus had reached out to the Samaritans, had made them the heroes in a parable.

You would think that people transformed by the Spirit of Christ would have overcome their prejudice, but that was not the case. In fact, the number one "issue" in the first-century church was the "Jew-Gentile controversy," over the terms on which non-Jews were to be accepted into the church. Must they follow the law of Moses or not? Must they be circumcised or not? It was a serious issue, threatening to divide the church, which explains Paul's alarm as he writes letters to churches involved in the controversy, such as those in Galatia.

The First Denomination?

In Acts 8 we are standing at an historic juncture. Were it not for the intervention of the apostles, it is quite possible that a separate Samaritan brotherhood would have arisen. What a tragedy that would have been! Denominationalism is antithetical to the will and prayer of Jesus Christ (John 17:22–23). We all have our differences, yet we are one body. May disciples of Jesus Christ never divide; may the seamless garment of Jesus never be rent asunder!

When word returned to the leaders in the "mother church," two of the three main apostles were dispatched to the scene.

> When the apostles in Jerusalem heard that Samaria had accepted the word of God, they sent Peter and John to them. When they arrived, they prayed for them that they might receive the Holy Spirit (Acts 8:14–15).

Most people read this far and jump to the conclusion that they were already Christians but that God delayed their reception of the Spirit for a special purpose, or that they had received the Spirit and the apostles were preparing them for "Holy Spirit baptism."

> ...because the Holy Spirit had not yet come upon any of them; they had simply been baptized into the name of the Lord Jesus. Then Peter and John placed their hands on them, and they received the Holy Spirit (Acts 8:16–17).

But the text says the Spirit had not yet "come upon" the Samaritans. That short phrase shows the sort of reception of the Spirit that occurred in Samaria: an *external* reception. In other words, this was not the indwelling of the Spirit that was being conferred. Acts 2:38–39 does not seem to allow for such exceptions.

Pentecostals and Catholics alike appeal to Acts 8 to support their doctrine that the Spirit is received in a special manner *after* conversion: the former through the laying on of hands to confer "Holy Spirit baptism," the latter through the laying on of a bishop's hands in "confirmation." Both groups fail to understand that we receive every spiritual blessing once we are "in Christ" (Ephesians 1:3, Romans 6:3).

The Samaritans were baptized "into the name of the Lord Jesus." Which baptism is this? Baptism *in Jesus' name* (Acts 2:38) is normal Christian baptism, bringing forgiveness and the Spirit. They were already saved. The outward reception of the Spirit (visible to Simon [v. 18], who "saw" something that amazed him) was given by God through the apostles as a sign to the brothers that God had accepted the Samaritans; there was to be no further requirement for salvation. So we see that Acts 8 is no exception to the rule (Acts 2:38).

Acts 10: An Historical Exception

In this passage, yet again, we see that the Spirit's outpouring is not an experience to be sought. Rather, it is a miracle of God for an historical purpose. Here we have Samaria in reverse, for the audience received the Spirit externally *before* they were saved.

Peter had preached up to verse 43 of Acts 10 (emphasis added): "All the prophets testify about him that everyone who believes in him receives forgiveness of sins *through his name*." Forgiveness is available only when one obeys Acts 2:38. "Through his name": baptism in Jesus' name brings forgiveness of sins.

At this time a stunning thing happens: God pours out the Spirit on the Caesareans—the first Gentiles to respond to the gospel (with the partial exception of Acts 11:20, a Gentile mission that did not involve the leaders of the Jerusalem church).

> While Peter was still speaking these words, the Holy Spirit came on all who heard the message. The circumcised believers who had come with Peter were astonished that the gift of the Holy Spirit had been poured out even on the Gentiles. For they heard them speaking in tongues and praising God (Acts 10:44–46).

Was this the *indwelling* of the Spirit that was being given? No, for they had not yet been baptized. This was an external reception.

Why did it happen this way? A cursory reading of the following verses, and especially Acts 11:1–18, makes it clear that God was making a point. Peter had begun to grasp it (10:35), after three visions from God and a command to preach to the Gentiles, but the others in his company needed some reassurance. After all, allowing Gentiles into the church was a big step. It was one thing to let them attend, submit to circumcision and Sabbath law, and then be immersed, but quite another to bring them into the fold without some indoctrination in Judaism.

God pours out the Spirit not for the benefit of the Caesareans, but for the benefit of the Christians. And even after that miracle, there were many offended brothers, much debate, and eventually a whole council to further discuss the issue (Acts 15).

> Then Peter said, "Can anyone keep these people from being baptized with water? They have received the Holy Spirit just as we have." So he commanded them to [or ordered that they] be baptized in the name of Jesus… (Acts 10:46b–48a).

Peter wraps up his sermon, which he had only just begun to deliver (Acts 11:15), and gives the "invitation"—in this instance an apostolic mandate! They are then immersed in Jesus' name (clearly the "baptism in Jesus' name" of Acts 2:38) and are saved.

Acts 10–11 has rightly been called "the conversion of Peter" more than the conversion of Cornelius! Peter's prejudicial thinking—as well as that of the early church—needed "converting."

Conclusion

Sensitivity to God's historical purposes and to the distinction between the indwelling and the outpouring of the Spirit are key to making sense of the exceptional in Acts 2, 8 and 10. God's purposes were accomplished through the first-century miracles in the apostolic generation. These purposes revolved around breaking the gospel out of its chrysalis of Judaism, for the metamorphosis of the world.

If we are willing to study the scriptural texts in context—in other words, to work hard—passages will be clarified, and the rewards of Bible study will accrue quickly. For God is the Author, Creator, Sculptor, Poet par excellence. Even when it does not meet the eye, be assured, rhyme and reason are there!

_____ NOTES _____

1. Before the New Testament indwelling of the Holy Spirit, from Pentecost onward, some of biblical history's more important men and women had the Holy Spirit in some outward sense. Here is a condensed list of texts describing persons living under the Old Covenant whom the Spirit filled or on whom it fell: Numbers 11:25 (the 70 elders), Numbers 24:2 (Balaam), Judges 3:10 (Othniel), Judges 6:34 (Gideon), Judges 14:6, 19, 15:14 (Samson), 1 Samuel 10:10, 16:23, 19: 23 (Saul), 1 Samuel 16:13 (David), 1 Chronicles 12:18 (Amasai), 2 Chronicles 15: 1 (Azariah), 2 Chronicles 20:14 (Jahaziel), Ezekiel 11:5 (Ezekiel), Luke 1:15 (John the Baptist), Luke 1:41 (Elizabeth), Luke 1:67 (Zechariah).

All of these men and women, living before the new covenant, possessed the Holy Spirit in some way, but only as a foretaste of the indwelling Spirit promised to New Testament believers (Acts 2:38–39, 5:32, Romans 8:9, Galatians 3:26–27, 4:6).

2. For example, Isaiah reads, "'The Redeemer will come to Zion, to those in Jacob who repent of their sins,' declares the Lord. 'As for me, this is my covenant with them,' says the Lord. 'My Spirit, who is on you, and my words that I have put in your mouth will not depart from your mouth, or from the mouths of your children, or from the mouths of their descendants from this time on and forever,' says the Lord" (Isaiah 59:20–21).

3. See also Isaiah 32:15.

4. Premillennialism is the system of doctrines asserting that Christ's second coming will precede his literal thousand-year reign on the earth. Premillennialists try to find support for their views by taking literally many passages that are metaphorical in nature, mainly from the Old Testament prophets, Jesus' prophecy of the destruction of Jerusalem in Matthew 24/Mark 13/Luke 21 and (especially) from Revelation. In this view, the church is not equated with the kingdom of God, which is yet to come. Most charismatics are premillennialists.

5. For an interesting, if overstated, analysis of this view and associated implications, see Max R. King, *The Cross and the Parousia of Christ: The Two Dimensions of One Age-Changing Eschaton* (Warren, Ohio: Warren Printing Inc.: 1987) and *The Spirit of Prophecy* (Warren, Ohio: Warren Printing Inc.: 1971).

6. For example, let's say that someone has been forgiven, but he does not yet have the Spirit. That would mean he is saved, but he is still not a Christian. Or let's say that someone has the Spirit, but he has not yet been forgiven. That would mean he is a Christian, but he is still lost: Both situations are impossible! Again, forgiveness of sins and the Spirit are received simultaneously. According to Acts 2:38, when someone is baptized, he is forgiven and receives the Spirit—*simultaneously.*

7. As three thousand were baptized, and Luke is using the Jewish method of counting males only (see 4:4), the actual number of persons who were added to the church was probably much larger. Biblical headcounts are normally of adult males only. (What would happen if modern churches adopted this practice?)

8. "But was Samaria even a nation?" some wondered. As the apocryphal book of Ecclesiasticus (c. 180 BC) said, "There are two nations that my soul detests, the third is not a nation at all: the inhabitants of Mount Seir, the [Edomites], and the Philistines, and the stupid people living at Shechem [the Samaritans]" (50:25–26). The prejudice and antipathy of Jews against Samaritans this reveals should not be underestimated.

19. Confirmation of the Word
The Biblical Purpose of Miracles

Before we consider the attitude of Jesus toward miracles and the sign-seeking mentality, afterwards moving on to consider the phenomenon of modern tongue-speaking, Spirit baptism, the occult, and much more, let us train our attention on something often missed in the study of the supernatural side of God's working in history. The function of miracles in the plan of God (this chapter) and their relation to the apostles (Chapter 20) are the subject of our present study.

The Bible Itself

One of the greatest miracles of all time was God's giving us the Bible itself! It is our guide for life, and usually without it we cannot survive (Matthew 4:4). The complete Bible has been with us for over nineteen hundred years, though not in collected form, but how easy it is to forget that during a period almost as long, from Moses (c. 1500 BC) to the latter part of the first century AD, the Bible was still in the process of formation.

Most scholars believe that the Old Testament scriptures were not completely collected or "canonized" until the first century AD, while the New Testament was probably not completely assembled until some time in the second century AD, at the earliest.[1]

Imagine being a member of a congregation that possessed the gospel of Mark, one letter of Paul and perhaps a copy of 1 Peter—and nothing else from the "New Testament," which would not be completed for another ten or fifteen years! For many of our first-century brothers and sisters, the Old Testament was the only scripture they ever knew (2 Timothy 3:15).

Because God chose to work through human beings and through history to bring his word to us, the entire process of inspiration, writing and canonization took centuries. Like many of the finer things in life, the Bible could not be rushed. Solomon's temple took seven years to build, Herod's temple forty-six, and Noah's ark a hundred. Ask Noah if it was worth all of the time he put into building it! (He had only one chance to get it right.)

Throughout most of the period of recorded biblical history, the word of God was in the process of becoming. Now it just is. But before it became what it is—written, complete, available—it was in need of confirmation.

Confirmation for the Spoken Word

The thesis of this chapter is that the purpose of biblical miracles was to bring us the word of God. Yes, of course, they were for confirming the Word, and I understand that to be the primary function of miracles, but it took many miracles just to produce the Scriptures: miracles of inspiration, for example. God's Spirit worked in the Old Testament writers. 2 Peter 1:19–21 discusses the inspiration of the Old Testament prophets. Ephesians 3:5 talks about the inspiration of the New Testament apostles and prophets (Ephesians 2:20, 4:11). If we understand the thesis, we will have a totally changed perspective on miracles.

If there were miracles of *inspiration*, there were also miracles of *certification*. Not just anyone could proclaim the word of the Lord—although many tried, as we read in Jeremiah 23. True prophets and apostles required credentials to establish their authority to speak for God—or, to put it another way, to confirm their word.

Confirming the Law and the Prophets

In the Old Testament, both the Law and the Prophets received certification. When Moses was a bit nervous about becoming God's spokesman, God showed him a clever trick with his staff. Moses didn't quite understand what God was up to, so God told him:

> "This," said the LORD, "is so that they may believe that the LORD, the God of their fathers—the God of Abraham, the God of Isaac and the God of Jacob—has appeared to you" (Exodus 4:5).

The miracles Moses performed—and there were *many* during the forty years he led Israel—were to establish his authority. During these years, the Bible was just beginning to be written. It had been a long time since God had last spoken, maybe centuries, and it is easy to see the vital role the miracles would play in convincing the people that the words Moses spoke had the full authority of the Lord God behind them. And if anyone dared challenge that word—watch out! (Numbers 16:28–35). Often the miracles associated with Moses were done by God himself (Exodus 20:18–19). Miracles also served to convince outsiders (those of them who were open to believing) that the God of Israel was the true God and his servants should be heeded (Exodus 7–14).

As for the prophets, miracles are associated with the rise of the prophetic movement more than with the later stages. Elijah was a man with a lot of spark. Who could forget the way he outran the wicked Ahab's chariot for thirty miles

(1 Kings 18:46), or the way he used miracles to call Israel back to God? (1 Kings 18:21-39). Perhaps the widow of Zaraphath put it best:

> Then the woman said to Elijah, "Now I know that you are a man of God and that the word of the LORD from your mouth is the truth" (1 Kings 17:24).

When the Law and the Prophets were committed to writing, there was no need for further substantiation.

Do you remember the rich man's plea to Abraham to send Lazarus back to his brothers? They would repent, so he reasoned, if only they could see a miracle. Yet they already had the Scriptures (Moses and the Prophets), which should have been enough. The rich man failed to appreciate this—like many today—and actually had a disagreement with Abraham:

> Abraham replied, "They have Moses and the Prophets; let them listen to them."
>
> "No, father Abraham," he said, "but if someone from the dead goes to them, they will repent."
>
> He said to them, "If they do not listen to Moses and the Prophets, they will not be convinced even if someone rises from the dead" (Luke 16:29–31).

Confirming the Gospel

Jesus' miracles were what convinced Nicodemus that he was a teacher sent from God (John 3:2). When John the Baptist was having problems with his faith, what did Jesus encourage him to consider? His miracles (Matthew 11:4-5). Jesus' challenge to all of us comes ringing through his words to Philip:

> "Believe me when I say that I am in the Father and the Father is in me; or at least believe on the evidence of the miracles themselves" (John 14:11).

The miracles of Jesus were not primarily to meet people's physical needs—for if that were the case, all Jesus needed to do was snap his fingers and every lame person in Palestine would have been healed. They were not even primarily a demonstration of his love, which was shown in his service (John 13:1) and pre-eminently in his crucifixion (Romans 5:8). No, the signs Jesus did were to leave no doubt as to his authority (Acts 2:22)—and no excuses, either! The conclusion of the gospel of John presents a profound and most important truth:

> Jesus did many other miraculous signs in the presence of his disciples, which are not recorded in this book. But these are written so that you may believe that Jesus is the Christ, the Son of God, and that by believing you may have life in his name (John 20:30–31).

The miraculous signs of Jesus point to his authority and to his Lordship, and they back up the message of the man whose life already perfectly embodied that message.

The apostles were *all* accredited by miracles, which is one reason Paul lays emphasis on his own miracles as a witness to his apostolic authority, since he was not one of the original number (Romans 15:19, 2 Corinthians 12:12).

Look through the book of Acts, and realize that most of the wonders there were effected through the apostles or those on whom the apostles had laid their hands. Miracles performed by the apostles themselves are found in Acts 2:43, 3:7, 5:12, 5:15,16, 9:34, 9:40, 13:11, 14:3, 14:10, 15:12, 16:18, 19:6, 19:11–12, 20:10, 28:8, 9.

Why was this so important? The early church devoted itself to the apostles' teaching. Imagine what would have happened if just anybody had been accepted and followed, an uninspired man in an age when God's inspired word was still not complete (1 Corinthians 13:10). In fact, this happened in some congregations (2 Corinthians 11:3–6, 12:11–12). In these passages Paul affirms his apostolic authority, particularly on the basis of his ability to work miracles. Pay special attention to Acts 14:3:

> So Paul and Barnabas spent considerable time [at Iconium], speaking boldly for the Lord, who confirmed the message of his grace by enabling them to do miraculous signs and wonders.

What was the reason God enabled them to perform miracles? To encourage Paul and Barnabas? To impress people? Was it not so that the message they preached would be accepted as the word of God? And what were they preaching? Can you imagine Paul saying, "Turn with me to Luke chapter 9, verse 23, and we will begin our lesson today"? They were not preaching out of an NIV Bible! Today we are blessed by God to have his completed and complete Word for teaching the lost and each other; we have need of nothing beyond this (2 Timothy 3:16–17), including miraculous confirmation.

Also helpful for our study are Mark 16:19–20 and Hebrews 2:2–4, which speak of the miraculous confirmation of the word of God:

> After the Lord Jesus had spoken to them, he was taken up into heaven and he sat at the right hand of God. Then the disciples went out and preached everywhere, and the Lord worked with them and confirmed his word by the signs that accompanied it (Mark 16:19–20).

> For if the message spoken by angels [the Old Testament] was binding, and every violation and disobedience received its just punishment, how shall we escape if we ignore such a great salvation? This salvation, which was first announced by the Lord, was confirmed to us by those who heard him. God also testified to it by signs, wonders and various miracles, and gifts of the Holy Spirit distributed according to his will (Hebrews 2:2–4).

There is no excuse for ignoring the word of God. As the Hebrew writer argues, the message of salvation was announced by Jesus, then confirmed by the apostles. The confirmation has *already* taken place. And although the past tense is not conclusive, the implication is that the age of miracles is past.

Confirming Revelation

Although there is the occasional miracle throughout the Old Testament, most miracles are clustered around two events: the Exodus and the rise of the prophetic movement (starting with Elijah and Elisha). One will realize that at these two times God was giving his people revelation: the Law and the Prophets. That is why another burst of miracles was only to be expected in New Testament times with the revelation of the gospel.

Many Old Testament passages confirm this view. The withdrawal of God's prophetic Spirit was seen as a sign of judgment (Isaiah 29:10, Lamentations 2:9, Micah 3:6.) As we saw in the previous chapter, Psalm 74:9, written during the exilic period, could apply to many periods of Old Testament history other than the exile:

> We are given no miraculous signs;
>> no prophets are left,
>> and none of us knows how long this will be.

Notice that prophets (with their revelation from God) and miraculous signs (confirming that revelation) are mentioned together.

Finally, during the "Intertestamental" period (c. 435 BC–30 AD), the voice of prophecy was stilled. From the last books written during the Persian period (Esther, Ezra-Nehemiah, Malachi, 1–2 Chronicles) to the next and final "Old Testament" prophet, John the Baptist, there is an astounding gap of nearly five centuries! This period of prophetic silence is acknowledged in the Rabbinical writings[2] as well as in the apocryphal books.[3] Consider 1 Maccabees 9:27, written in the period of Maccabean persecution (second century BC):

> A terrible oppression began in Israel, there has been nothing like it since the disappearance of prophecy among them (Jerusalem Bible).

Few are aware of the stilling of the voice of prophecy. The cessation of prophecy, tongue-speaking and miraculous healing in Neopentecostal circles is unthinkable! But God stopped the prophetic stream on more than one occasion, and there is reason to believe he would do it again (1 Corinthians 13:8). To sum up, biblical miracles were:

(a) rare occurrences
(b) clustered around revelational events
(c) for the primary purpose of confirming the spoken word of God

Conclusion

We have seen the central role of miracles in confirming the word of God, and that it was always the spoken word of God that received confirmation, not the *written* word (Scripture). John 20:30–31 shows that once the miracles were written down, just reading of them should be sufficient to bring us to faith in Christ. For the most part, we must adopt the attitude expressed in Psalm 77:11:

> "I will remember the deeds of the Lord;
> yes, I will remember your miracles of long ago."

But many do not understand this. They reason that there have to be miracles today for people to turn to God. The strange thing is that, like the rich man (Luke 16), this is how many unbelievers also reason. People are always saying things to me like, "If there really is a God, then let him make a special appearance to me. I'm an open-minded person." According to John 20, however, even if Jesus came back to visit a devout atheist and performed before his very eyes every miracle he had ever performed during his life on earth, that would make no difference!

Make no mistake about it: Many people today have really missed the boat when it comes to understanding the purpose of miracles. Paul Cho of Seoul, one of the foremost charismatic leaders and opinion-makers in the world, says, "Without seeing miracles people cannot be satisfied that God is powerful."[4] How different are Abraham's words, which have a common sense and wisdom lacking in most "charismatic" pulpits:

> "If they do not listen to Moses and the Prophets, they will not be convinced even if someone rises from the dead!" (Luke 16:31).

The purpose of biblical miracles was to bring the word of God to man. Now there is a "back cover" to the Bible, and so miracles have served their purpose: We have the complete Bible. As we have stated before, this does not mean that God's hands are tied, or that he does not answer prayers for help or healing, only that there is no need for miracles today in the way that there was in the first century.

The miracles served a great purpose, in confirming the message of the preacher beyond a shadow of a doubt. And once the word of God had been confirmed, there was no need of further confirmation.[5]

NOTES

1. The Muratorian Canon, providing roughly the same list of New Testament books as we have today, dates from c. 180 AD and is the earliest surviving New Testament canon.

Suggested reading touching on the canonization issue: Philip Wesley Comfort, Ed., *The Origin of the Bible* (Wheaton, Illinois: Tyndale House Publishers, 1992); Neil R. Lightfoot, *How We Got the Bible* (Grand Rapids: Baker, 1988).

2. E.g. T. Sota 13:2.

3. The word *Apocrypha* comes from the Greek for "hidden things," and are Jewish religious writings dating from around 200 BC to 100 AD. They were never universally received as scripture by the consensus of the church. The Apocrypha contain many historical contradictions and unscriptural teachings. They were only officially accepted as scripture in the Catholic Counter-Reformation at the Council of Trent (1546).

4. Paul Yonggi Cho, *The Fourth Dimension* (Plainfield, NJ: Logos International, 1979), 64.

5. To call up our fourth-century brother John Chrysostom from the dead: "[1 Corinthians 12–14, which discusses the miraculous gifts of tongues and prophecy] is very obscure, but the obscurity is produced by our ignorance of the facts referred to and by their cessation, since they used to take place then but now no longer occur." 1 Corinthians 13:8-10 states that the miraculous gifts were to cease some day. They ceased, and history recorded their cessation.

Once again, this is not to say God never performs miracles today in answer to prayers of faith. Nor is it to deny that the Charismatic Movement has undergone revivals among the various sects and world religions from time to time. But the authentic gifts, history shows, are no longer among us.

20. The Hands of an Apostle
How Miraculous Gifts Were Transmitted

We saw in the last chapter the role miracles played in confirming the spoken word of God. Now let us shift from the confirmatory nature of the miracles to how New Testament miraculous gifts were received or transmitted. The thesis of this chapter is simple: The supernatural gifts of the Spirit were normally transmitted through the laying on of the hands of an apostle. If this is correct, the implications for Neopentecostalism are significant.

Apostolic Miracles

Throughout the New Testament one gets the impression that whenever a miracle happens, the apostles are usually close by; in fact, the chances are very high it is an apostle who is doing the miracle. As we have observed before, most of the miracles in Acts have to do with the apostles. Luke certainly leaves us with the impression that it was God's will that the apostles perform miracles. Consider these passages:

He appointed twelve—designating them apostles—that they might be with him and that he might send them out to preach and to have authority to drive out demons (Mark 3:14–15).

When Jesus had called the Twelve together, he gave them power and authority to drive out all demons and to cure diseases, and he sent them out to preach the kingdom of God and to heal the sick (Luke 9:1–2).

Everyone was filled with awe, and many wonders and miraculous signs were done by the apostles (Acts 2:43).

"Now, Lord…stretch out your hand to heal and perform miraculous signs and wonders through the name of your holy servant Jesus."… With great power the apostles continued to testify to the resurrection of the Lord Jesus, and much grace was upon them all (Acts 4:29–30, 33).

The apostles performed many miraculous signs and wonders among the people (Acts 5:12a).

When Simon saw that the Spirit was given at the laying on of the apostles' hands, he offered them money (Acts 8:18).

Then there is the helpful 2 Corinthians 12:12:

The things that mark an apostle—signs, wonders and miracles—were done among you with great perseverance.

If miracles were commonly performed by all Christians, why does Luke emphasize the apostles' miracles and play down everyone else's? If the average Christian of the first century had the power to perform miracles, why are miracles an apostolic prerogative? Remember, extremely few qualified as apostles:

- An apostle was a witness of Jesus' resurrection (Acts 1:21–22, 1 Corinthians 9:1).
- The Christians devoted themselves to the apostles' teaching (Acts 2:42, Ephesians 2:20), as Jesus promised that the Spirit would equip the apostles to recall Jesus' teaching and lead them into all truth (John 14:26, 16:13).
- The apostles confirmed the gospel through signs (Acts 14:3, Hebrews 2:3). The implication is that most first-century Christians did not perform miracles.

Usual Transmission of Gifts

In those few cases where nonapostle Christians had miraculous powers, how were these received? It is certainly possible that the Pentecostal outpouring enabled young men and women, among others, to speak prophetically (Acts 2:17–18). For example, is it not likely that Philip and his daughters, even Agabus, were in Jerusalem at Pentecost, as all faithful Jews would journey up to the city to observe the feast? (Acts 21:9, 11:28). Yet in the vast majority of cases where the supernatural charismata were exercised, they were transmitted through the direct agency of the apostles.

Hands-On Leadership

The New Testament says that however the *charismata* were meted out, it happened in accordance with God's will. The Hebrew writer makes a helpful comment (parallel to the closing words of Mark's gospel):

This salvation, which was first announced by the Lord, was confirmed

to us by those who heard him. God also testified to it by signs, wonders
and various miracles, and gifts of the Holy Spirit distributed according to
his will (Hebrews 2:3b–4).

The gifts were distributed according to God's will (1 Corinthians 12:11),
but notice what is said first: The word was confirmed by "those who heard [Je-
sus]"—a reference to the apostles (Galatians 1:11–12). How else was it confirmed?
Through the recipients of the miraculous gifts. Allow me the liberty to rewrite
the passage, in the light of 2 Corinthians 12:12: "This salvation...was confirmed
to us by the apostles. God also testified to it by the marks of the apostles and gifts
of the Holy Spirit distributed according to his will."

It would be no surprise if there were also some apostolic factor associated
with the distribution of the gifts. But is there any evidence that this was how the
gifts were transmitted? Indeed there is!

For this reason I remind you to fan into flame the gift of God, which is
in you through the laying on of my hands (2 Timothy 1:6).

Timothy had received a miraculous gift through the laying on of the hands
of an apostle: Paul. The gift was not something Timothy could ever have attained
on his own, even though he was personally acquainted with Paul (Acts 16:1).
God gave him his gift through the laying on of the hands of an apostle. A similar
situation is found in Acts 19:6:

When Paul placed his hands on them, the Holy Spirit came on them,
and they spoke in tongues and prophesied.

Tongues and prophecy were supernatural gifts of the Spirit (1 Corinthians
12:10). They were usually received only at the laying on of the hands of an apostle. The clearest illustration of the doctrine is found in Acts 6 and 8. Consider the
following series of texts from Acts of the Apostles:

This proposal pleased the whole group. They chose Stephen, a man
full of faith and of the Holy Spirit—also Philip, Procorus, Nicanor,
Timon, Parmenas, and Nicolas from Antioch, a convert to Judaism.
They presented these men to the apostles, who prayed and laid their
hands on them (Acts 6:5–6).

Notice two of those on whom the apostles lay their hands: Stephen and Philip.[1]

> Now Stephen, a man full of God's grace and power, did great wonders and miraculous signs among the people (Acts 6:8).

Stephen was filled with the Spirit (Acts 6:3, 5) even before the apostles laid their hands on him, so that does not account for his miraculous ability. It seems that his miraculous power resulted from the apostles' laying their hands on him. But the evidence mounts even higher:

> When the crowds heard Philip and saw the miraculous signs he did, they all paid close attention to what he said. With shrieks, unclean spirits came out of many, and many paralytics and cripples were healed (Acts 8:6–7).

Here Philip, another of the men on whom the apostles laid their hands, demonstrates his miraculous ability. Is it mere coincidence that these two men, Stephen and Philip, are recorded as doing miracles after the apostles laid their hands on them, but not before? Is it not possible that, like Timothy and the Ephesian disciples, they received the miraculous manifestations of the Spirit when the apostles laid their hands on them?

The most conclusive evidence is found in the events surrounding the conversion of the Samaritans. You will recall that the Samaritans had been baptized in Jesus' name, receiving (according to Acts 2:38–39) the forgiveness of sins and the indwelling of the Holy Spirit. They had not, however, received the Spirit in any external, visible way. Confirmation (see Chapter 19) was given because a new frontier was being crossed, and God wanted there to be no doubt that their past national unfaithfulness was not to hinder their full acceptance as believers in Christ.

Was Philip able to transmit the miraculous gifts of the Spirit to the Samaritans, thus proving their acceptance by God, and so driving the nails into the coffin of the anti-Samaritan prejudice? And if he was, why did he delay? It would appear that he had no authority to transmit the gifts. Let's pick up the narrative in Acts 8:14:

> [14]When the apostles in Jerusalem heard that Samaria had accepted the word of God, they sent Peter and John to them. [15]When they arrived,

they prayed for them that they might receive the Holy Spirit, [16]because the Holy Spirit had not yet come upon any of them; they had simply been baptized into the name of the Lord Jesus. [17]Then Peter and John placed their hands on them, and they received the Holy Spirit. [18]When Simon saw that the Spirit was given at the laying on of the apostles' hands, he offered them money and said, [19]"Give me also this ability so that everyone on whom I lay my hands may receive the Holy Spirit" (Acts 8:14-19).

We suspect Philip was not able to transmit the gifts for the following reasons:

- He made no effort to transmit the gifts to the Samaritans, even though that was precisely what was needed to settle the imminent controversy.
- The Samaritans received the Spirit (outwardly) only when the apostles Peter and John placed their hands on them.
- Simon, who saw a chance for financial gain in this ability to transmit the Spirit, offered money to the apostles.

Acts 8:18 is the most succinct statement in the New Testament of the position presented in this chapter: "The Spirit was given at the laying on of the apostles' hands." The miraculous gifts were passed on at the imposition of the hands of an apostle. If this statement is indeed correct, it would explain why Corinth, where Paul had spent quite some time, lacked no spiritual gift (1 Corinthians 1:7), whereas Rome, which he had not visited, possessed only the nonmiraculous spiritual gifts: "I long to see you so that I may impart to you some spiritual gift to make you strong" (Romans 1:11).[2] His presence was required if they were to receive some spiritual gift(s).

Is this line of reasoning airtight? No, it is not. Is the argument sound? Yes, it is. Apart from the historical exceptions of Acts 2 and 10, for example, there is no conclusive evidence against the argument.[3] In the light of the evidence, it can be said that this theory is the best explanation we have of how the gifts were passed on.

Implications

The implications of this doctrine are easy to follow: After the death of the last apostle, the supernatural gifts were no longer transmitted. And after the death of the last person still to possess a miraculous gift—if not before—the gifts died out altogether. If this is true, then charismatic claims to possess various miraculous gifts of the Spirit are either fraudulent or wishful thinking.

NOTES

1. We hear nothing else of the others from here on, unless the Nicolaitans of Revelation 2:6, 15 are followers of an apostate Nicolas.

2. Even if "prophesying" in Romans 12:6 is miraculous, there is no reason to think Rome must have been completely cut off from any apostle, or that there was no one on whom an apostle had laid hands who later moved to Rome.

3. Is Ananias (Acts 9:17-18) an exception? We will never know, since little is known of his association with apostles—although it would be strange if the Syrian disciples had no contact with the leaders of the church in Jerusalem. The miracle of Acts 9:18 and 22:13 has nothing to say for or against the doctrine that the miraculous gifts were transmitted by apostolic hands.

Is 1 Timothy 4:14 proof that nonapostles could relay the gifts? Not at all. (1) The reference is almost certainly to the same gift mentioned in 2 Timothy 1:6, as Timothy has to be reminded again in Paul's second letter not to neglect it; and if Timothy had more than one gift, it would not be obvious which gift 2 Timothy 1:6 referred to. (2) It is unlikely that Paul, Timothy's mentor and immediate superior, would not have been present at his ordination, or whatever event was attended by the body of elders. Nor does 1 Timothy 5:22 present any problem for our view, since Paul does not specify what the purpose of this laying on of hands was. (It would seem, in the light of 1 Timothy 3:6, that Paul is talking about appointing people as evangelists or sending them out into the ministry before they are ready.)

21. No Sign Will Be Given!
Jesus: Playing Down the Miraculous

At this point in the book, you may be thinking, "Why did Jesus do so many miracles anyway, if they weren't really necessary?" Now, we never said they weren't necessary! For one, the word of God had to be brought to men, and we see the valuable role miracles played, both in inspiring and in confirming the Word. Also, the miracles were a demonstration of God's character and will. Furthermore, they had to be performed to fulfill what the Scriptures had predicted about Christ, so that we would have a solid basis for our faith. Do remember, however, that once the miracles were recorded, there was no need for an encore (Luke 16:31).

Some are discouraged with this conclusion. "Wouldn't it be more exciting if we had miracles? Wouldn't we be able to get more visitors to church? Wouldn't it advance the kingdom more in the long run if we had the supernatural gifts?"

There is no denying that things would be more sensational if we could perform miracles, especially considering present trends in church growth. And it would be foolish to deny that attendance numbers might increase. But is that what it's all about? Normal Christianity is quite exciting in itself, and attendance numbers are not the only indicator of how a congregation is doing, important as they are. Conversions, long-range retention, spiritual maturity and the multiplication of leaders are surely more important considerations.

Think about it: How many loyal followers did Jesus have at the end of his own ministry? One hundred and twenty in the area of Jerusalem and five hundred in Galilee. How many had seen his miracles? Many of the crowds that assembled to hear his teaching numbered in the thousands (Luke 12:1). How many people did Jesus preach to in his lifetime? A few hundred thousand? Or several million? Let's be realistic! The deciding factor in the effectiveness of a ministry could never be miracles; it is the hearts of the lost and the zeal of the laborers.

We mustn't look for shortcuts to numerical growth. What happened in the fourth century when the Roman Empire decided Christianity was to be the official religion (381 AD)? The pagans streamed into the church! "Attendances" were at an all-time high, as the heathen temples emptied in favor of the Christian churches. But there was a heavy price to pay: All the worldliness of the pagans was imported wholesale into the church; the whole situation became very political. The church never recovered from the blow.

No, there are no shortcuts. The only way to build a dynamic and expanding ministry is hard work! Yet how easy it is to be unrealistic about the whole thing, to think that miracles would really advance our evangelistic thrust! We can end up reasoning as Jesus' brothers did:

> Jesus' brothers said to him, "You ought to leave here and go to Judea, so that your disciples may see the miracles you do. No one who wants to become a public figure acts in secret. Since you are doing these things, show yourself to the world." For even his own brothers did not believe in him (John 7:3–5).

If Jesus really knew what he was doing, so they reasoned, he would use the miracles to build up his image, to gain notoriety for his work. But the point of the ministry is not publicity; it is to save souls. His brothers' philosophy was worldly, unrealistic and selfish. Jesus would have nothing to do with it! But Jesus knew exactly what he was doing. Often we read of his refusal to grant a sign, for he knew the hearts of men. It is abundantly clear that Jesus discouraged the sign-seeking mentality. Let's look at seven reasons why he was so reluctant to play to the crowds:

1. People would follow him from wrong motives.

Jesus knew that it is much easier to get caught up in the excitement of miracles than in the business of repentance. When the crowds followed him in John 6, Jesus challenged their motives:

> Jesus answered, "I tell you the truth, you are looking for me, not because you saw miraculous signs but because you ate the loaves and had your fill. Do not work for food that spoils, but for food that endures to eternal life" (John 6:26–27a).

Whereas the miracles should have convicted them of their need to become committed disciples, instead self-interest was why they were following Jesus. Even after this stiff challenge they remained unrepentant:

> So they asked him, "What miraculous sign then will you give that we may see it and believe you? What will you do?" (John 6:30).

And this was after he had miraculously fed many of them! (John 6:1–15). Things come to a head later in the chapter, after they realize what sort of commitment Jesus is expecting. Their response?

> On hearing it, many of his disciples said, "This is a hard teaching. Who can accept it?" Aware that his disciples were grumbling about this, Jesus said to them, "Does this offend you?" …From this time many of his disciples turned back and no longer followed him (John 6:60–61, 66).

Their motivation was sinful from the beginning. Such people can be persuaded to associate themselves with Jesus as long as there is something they think they can get out of it, but as the saying goes, "When the going gets tough, the tough get going."

2. Miracles don't guarantee faithfulness.

Experiencing great miracles is no guarantee of long-term fidelity. It's like a close brush with death—how many people are significantly changed by it? When I was younger I had two "close calls": Once I nearly drowned in the ocean, and the other time my bicycle was snapped in two when a car struck me. When things like this happen, it is easy to become "religious" for a time, but how quickly the effect wears off! Jesus knew there is no comparison between a momentary conviction based on circumstances or feelings and the lasting commitment of a solid decision. Jesus saw this in his ministry over and over again.

Sadly, even the people of God are not innocent of such selfish forgetfulness of what the Lord has done (2 Peter 1:9). Is this not a lesson taught us time and time again throughout the wilderness period of Israel?

> [11]They forgot what he had done,
>> the wonders he had shown them.
> [12]He did miracles in the sight of their fathers
>> in the land of Egypt, in the region of Zoan.
> [13]He divided the sea and led them through;
>> he made the water stand firm like a wall.
> [14]He guided them with the cloud by day
>> and with light from the fire all night.
> [15]He split the rocks in the desert
>> and gave them water as abundant as the seas;
> [16]he brought streams out of a rocky crag
>> and made water flow down like rivers.
>
> [17]But they continued to sin against him,

rebelling in the desert against the Most High.
¹⁸They willfully put God to the test
    by demanding the food they craved (Psalm 78:11–18).

Jesus knew that the hearts of men and women needed to be won to him not on the basis of unusual events they had witnessed, but on the basis of an appreciation of God's love for them in sending himself to die for their sins (John 12:32).

3. The Scriptures are sufficient.

As we have repeatedly discussed already, the Scriptures are all we need to have a solid faith in God. Abraham tried to enlighten the rich man on this point, who had a difficult time grasping how a stunning miracle would not create moral change in the hearts of his family members. How much more does this apply when the Scriptures record miracles! If we want to be impressed, all we have to do is read the Bible. If that does not impress us, it is not too likely witnessing a bona fide miracle will bring about a profound change in our heart and conduct.

4. Not even "doubters" need signs.

Some try to use Gideon or Thomas as justification for their own weak faith and commitment. The astute reader will notice that Gideon was not commended for his procrastination, nor was Thomas commended for his skeptical attitude concerning Christ. He had no excuse for his doubts, for he had seen countless miracles at the hands of Jesus, and Thomas was present on several occasions when Jesus prophesied his resurrection. How did Jesus deal with "doubting Thomas"?

Then he said to Thomas, "Put your finger here; see my hands. Reach out your hand and put it into my side. Stop doubting and believe" (John 20:27).

No, Thomas is not commended for his "scientific" attitude; he is rebuked! Nor is it suggested that he work through his doubts; he is commanded to stop doubting. Now are we becoming irrational? No, because for Thomas this did not even come close to a "leap in the dark." He had seen plenty of evidence!

A friend of mine was studying the Bible with a non-Christian. Things seemed to be going well, until what appeared to be a total impasse. Despite all the evidence Joyce had shown her in the Scriptures, she said she wasn't sure she could accept the whole Bible after all, since she had never really believed in the devil and wasn't sure sin was "sin." Joyce's response? She challenged her to be reasonable—to stop doubting and believe. "How superficial of her," I thought at the time; "Joyce should have given her a book on evidences and suggested a few useful passages to read." (God has shown me many things about the ministry since then!) The woman became a Christian just days later!

Most of the would-be Thomases of today have no need of miracles. What they need is a good challenge to repent! However, when someone's faith is weak, undeveloped and legitimately needs time to grow, what is the biblical solution? Look into the Word. The Word produces faith (Romans 10:17). My Bible doesn't say anything about miracles in that passage!

5. The hard-hearted are not changed by the miracles anyway.

The human mind is capable of the most incredible rationalizations. As with Pharaoh (Exodus 7:13), Jeroboam (1 Kings 13:4–6, 33), and the Nazi Goering,[1] we find a significant hardness of heart among the people of Jesus' day. After Jesus had raised Lazarus from the dead, the leaders of the Jews saw the truth; they did not deny the miracles. But they had no effect on them at all, except to accelerate their murderous hatred of Jesus:

> Then the chief priests and the Pharisees called a meeting of the Sanhedrin. "What are we accomplishing?" they asked. "Here is this man performing many miraculous signs. If we let him go on like this, everyone will believe in him, and then the Romans will come and take away both our place and our nation" (John 11:47–48).

Not all the leaders were this way, fortunately. Some, like Nicodemus (John 3:1ff, 7:51), had the integrity to acknowledge the truth when they saw it. But for the most part the Jewish people remained obstinate:

> Even after Jesus had done all these miraculous signs in their presence, they still would not believe in him (John 12:37).

The point: Miracles today would not make one whit of difference for people whose minds are already made up.

6. Jesus does not want to short-circuit our free will.

What would happen if, every time we were about to make a wrong decision, God himself appeared to us, coaxed us into doing what was right and then disappeared until our next moment of weakness? Personal responsibility and free will would go out the window! God respects our own decision-making ability, even if we misuse that faculty for selfish ends. That is why Jesus said,

"If anyone chooses to do God's will, he will find out whether my teaching comes from God or whether I speak on my own" (John 7:17).

Having experienced a miracle is not the fundamental requirement for finding out whether Jesus is the way, the truth, and the life. Nor is it having God work in your life in some mystical, uncanny way. The fundamental requirement is a willingness to follow the truth. That is the only way to decide correctly whether Christianity is true.[2]

Like the parable, which does not *force* its truth on the hearer, the ministry without miracles avoids the extremes of sensationalism, emotionalism and quick, but shallow, decisions. (Not to say miracles would be a hindrance—only that they are not as helpful as many would have us believe.)

7. Jesus wants us to base our faith on reason.

In the gospels we see Jesus calling people to reason again and again (Luke 20:17, 27–40, 41–44, etc.). We too must teach people to think. If Jesus granted every request for a sign, what would that teach the people? It would teach them to insist on a sign whenever faced with an important decision. It would teach them not to think for themselves, but to ask the Lord to give them the answer, and then give the praise (or the blame) to God. The charismatic approach sounds so spiritual, doesn't it? This would be the death of personal Bible study, for why put in the hours when God can speak the truth directly to your heart? This would be the death of Christianity!

Conclusion

Jesus discouraged the miracle-seeking mentality, and so should we. One of the most illuminating passages on the subject is Luke 11:29–32:

[29]As the crowds increased, Jesus said, "This is a wicked generation. It asks for a miraculous sign, but none will be given it except the sign of Jonah. [30]For as Jonah was a sign to the Ninevites, so also will the Son of Man be to this generation. [31]The Queen of the South will rise at the judgment with the men of this generation and condemn them; for she came from the ends of the earth to listen to Solomon's wisdom, and now one

greater than Solomon is here. [32]The men of Nineveh will stand up at the judgment with this generation and condemn it; for they repented at the preaching of Jonah, and now one greater than Jonah is here.

The Ninevites repented because Jonah preached the Word to them. They had no need of a miraculous sign—and yet how much it might have been appreciated: Jonah was a foreigner, he was all alone in his appeal, they had probably never heard of him, his religion was different from theirs. Jonah performed no miracle, and yet the entire city repented! (Jonah 3:5).

Over a century earlier, the Queen of the South (1 Kings 10:1–13) had responded favorably to Solomon, even though he performed no miracles at all for her. She listened to his wisdom and was moved to praise the God of Israel (1 Kings 10:9).

In both cases the response was not effected through or conditioned by miracles. Neither the people of Nineveh nor the Queen of Sheba received a miraculous sign—and yet they were moved by God's word. How little excuse Jesus' generation had compared with these believing foreigners!

And "the sign of Jonah?" The resurrection is a central miracle (1 Corinthians 15:12–19).[3] Does God re-enact the resurrection every time a non-Christian gets to the appropriate stage in his search for God? No, like everyone else, the one seeking God must read about the resurrection. And there is just as much reason to believe in Jesus because of the resurrection today as there was two thousand years ago—no more, no less.

For all intents and purposes, Jesus' response to his generation fits our own perfectly: No sign will be given!

_____ NOTES _____

1. The words of Goering are utterly haunting: "I have no conscience....The name of my conscience is Adolf Hitler. My job is not to practice justice; my job is to destroy and to exterminate, nothing more."

2. No, this is not a "Catch-22," since Jesus is not asking for blind faith, only for reasonableness. My challenge to non-Christians is never to "make believe" Christianity is true, but rather to be willing to follow the truth, wherever that may lead.

3. I agree with C. S. Lewis that the _greatest_ miracle of all is the Incarnation.

22. Of Angels and Men
Questions About 'Tongues'

It is very well to say that miracles fulfilled their historical purpose (Chapters 17, 18 and 20) and thus are not necessary today. And yet many persons do point to experiences which they claim are authentic in order to prove their position. One of the most common charismatic "miracles" is tongue-speaking. Tongues is, in fact, the spiritual gift most often claimed by those in the Charismatic Movement. The next two chapters focus substantially on this phenomenon. In this chapter we find answers to ten basic questions about tongue-speaking. In the next chapter we will explore 1 Corinthians 12-14 in depth.

Babbling

When I was an eight-year-old, our school class was blessed by the arrival of a student from Germany, Alexander Elschnig. Alex and I lived on the same street and often played together. As I had no experience of a foreign language, I tried to imitate what I heard. Without language classes, however, the best I could do was really only a rough-sounding approximation of the real thing. Alex and I would "talk" back and forth, laughing and babbling rapidly, pretending we could understand each other—to the consternation of our friends. So when I first heard "tongue-speaking," I could not help but inwardly chuckle. It was a throwback to the third grade! I found the mimicking of language so natural for me that I refused to try to speak in tongues, despite the pressure that was put on me to do so. I knew I could "do" it—and still can—yet what I heard in our prayer meetings felt childish to me. Matthew 6:7, where Jesus condemns "babbling," comes to mind.

1. What is "glossolalia"?

Glossolalia is the technical term for tongue-speaking.[1] It may refer to a wide range of psychological phenomena as well as to genuine biblical tongues. In this book we confine ourselves to the simpler "tongue-speaking."

Tongue-speaking, or glossolalia, requires "interpretation" to become intelligible. The same segments of tape-recorded glossolalia have elicited widely different "interpretations," depending on who was asked to interpret. The interpretation tends to be as subjective as the tongues. Once I was listening to a "message" in tongues and its "interpretation." The meaning given to the tongues was far longer than the original "message" itself. I pointed this out to the interpreter, who admitted that she had taken liberties with her interpretation—suspecting that I might have the true gift of interpretation!

2. *Is tongue-speaking really psychological?*

It is my conclusion that tongue-speaking is purely a psychological phenomenon. It is common among people who internalize their problems instead of bringing them out into the open and dealing with them.[2] Thus, persons with unresolved tension (due to sin, lack of prayer, lack of evangelism, or relationship conflict) are prime candidates. But other people also have this experience.

Tongue-speaking has been analyzed in the laboratory as well as on site in many church settings and has *consistently* been found to be linguistically meaningless. Upon analysis, it has been shown to resemble infantile speech and to comprise syllables and sounds predominantly from the tongue-speaker's own language or language group. A Chinese tongue-speaker will sound entirely different from a German tonguespeaker!

Occasionally a "sentence" in tongues may incorporate a foreign phrase, either by accident or through a phenomenon called "cryptomnesia," where the speaker has unconsciously recalled words in another language which he has heard at some point in his past. Although this is rare, it has been proven to occur, especially among people who at some time have lived in a linguistically plural environment.

One would think that the many claims of tongue-speakers, especially those who believed they were speaking in actual foreign languages, would have been submitted to experts in the linguistic field for analysis. And so they have! Some years ago I made my own study of the subject, reading a mountain of books and scholarly articles on *glossolalia*, most of which were authored by psychologists interested in studying the phenomenon for other than religious reasons. One such article concluded:

- Tongue-speaking is not foreign language.
- It is acquired behavior, and perfected with practice.
- It can be simulated, and tongue-speakers cannot discern this from charismatic tongue-speaking.
- It has characteristics of infantile speech.[3]

If you want to learn more, I recommend that you avail yourself of the Psychology of Religion section of any university library, where you will probably find more literature on the subject than you will be able to read.

3. Is tongue-speaking strictly a Christian phenomenon?

No, tongue-speaking is a religious phenomenon worldwide. Most relevant for our understanding of tongues in the New Testament is the glossolalia of the various Greek religions of the Mediterranean world in the first century. (For further information, see Chapter 19.)

4. What are tongues in the Bible?

The Greek word glossa, like its English counterpart, means "tongue or language." Glossa carries no more connotation of a mysterious language than the English word tongue. Yet much confusion has been caused by translation from Greek into English. The translators of the King James Version (KJV)[4] inserted the italicized word unknown before tongue in 1 Corinthians 14:2, 4, 13, 14, 19, and 27. This word is not actually part of the Greek text. They were only trying to be helpful, but ended up lending credence to the charismatic interpretation of "tongue" as something otherworldly.

Normally a book written nearly four centuries ago has minimal influence on the present generation, but the KJV's enduring popularity makes the "tongues" issue a continuing debate.[5] Many other English versions, particularly free translations and paraphrases, commit similar errors.[6]

Why should we even call tongues "tongues" when the original word means "languages"? To most English speakers it suggests the organ of the mouth more than a language. (Yes, glossa can mean "tongue," too.) An important principle of translation is to select a common word in the translation language to represent a common word in the original language and to choose a rare word in the translation language to represent a rare word in the original. This is the only way to keep a translation fresh, understandable and relevant. Glossa was a common word in first-century Koine Greek; "tongue" is quite rarely used in the sense of "language" in today's English. Sectarian bias sometimes prefers not to update a translation, in fear that a pet doctrine may be compromised.

When we turn to the Bible, we find no evidence at all that glossa is anything but actual human language. The glossai spoken at Pentecost were actual languages: Latin, Arabic, Cretan, Parthian, etc. (Acts 2:6–11). In fact glossa is used interchangeably with dialektos in Acts 2:6. Dialektos simply means a "regional language," a "dialect."[7] There is no hint here of a "mystery" language! Luke introduces Christian baptism to us in Acts 2, and as a result, it is safe to assume that whenever someone is baptized, Acts 2:38 describes his or her conversion. In the same way, Luke introduces tongues in Acts 2, and there is no reason to believe that it has a new meaning in later chapters. Once again, glossai in Acts and in the rest of the New Testament are actual foreign languages. It is also clear from Paul's first letter to the Corinthians that tongues are languages:

> Undoubtedly there are all sorts of languages in the world, yet none of them is without meaning. If then I do not grasp the meaning of what someone is saying, I am a foreigner to the speaker, and he is a foreigner to me (I Corinthians 14:10–11).

Actual languages are what Paul has in mind—"foreign" languages. Any language is a foreign language to someone who does not speak it. For example, to the vast majority of us Mongolian is a "foreign" language. (But not to a Mongolian!)

These tongues, or languages, were miraculously acquired foreign languages. The tongue-speaker never studied them. With translation (interpretation) they became intelligible, as with any foreign language today. I am confident that all of us are fully able to understand Swahili, Icelandic and Korean (with a translator, if necessary!).

5. What about "angel languages"?

Common sense would lead us to postulate that if angels, being nonphysical beings, communicate in languages, they would not consist of the sounds and sound waves human languages are made of. You might as well ask what language God speaks! Some, however, feel strongly that there is a heavenly language. I am reminded of fundamentalist Muslims I have met who insist, as the Koran teaches, that God's native tongue is Arabic. Anyway, there is only one passage that could lead to the impression that angels have languages which humans might speak, and that is 1 Corinthians 13:1:

> If I speak in the tongues of men and of angels, but have not love, I am only a resounding gong or a clanging cymbal.

The passage says, "If I speak in the tongues of...angels," not that there necessarily are angel languages. But even if we could speak in the angelic language, that would be worthless without love—a point often missed by tongue-speakers. More will be said about this in my analysis of 1 Corinthians 13 in Chapter 23.

6. What was the purpose of biblical tongues?

a.) A common Neopentecostal view is that tongues are evidence of salvation. That is not biblical; Chapter 24 takes up the subject at length. Neopentecostals also claim tongues as a private language of prayer. Most charismatics hold that speaking in tongues is the gateway to greater power and service in the kingdom. If you can just receive this gift, they argue, you can really begin to experience the blessings of the Christian life. And until you receive it, you will flounder around in mediocrity. This "shortcut to power" inevitably short-circuits the will of God.

b.) Tongues are also claimed to have been for missionary work. They were given, many argue, so that missionaries would not have to study the languages of the peoples they evangelized. Although this particular interpretation did not arise until the third century, it is certainly possible. (But you would think that such a use of tongues would have been mentioned in the book of Acts!) Perhaps tongues were being used to reach people who could not understand the speaker, and we have no record of the fact. In Acts 2 the audience, despite having their own national languages, spoke the same language as Peter. Further, the actual sermon Peter preached was not delivered "in tongues." Moreover, as a result of the efforts of Alexander the Great (356-323 BC) to forge a world culture, Koine Greek became the common language of the entire Mediterranean world. Thus it is unlikely that the early Christian missionaries were unable to find translators among the people they evangelized.

c.) In 1 Corinthians 12:7, 14:5, 26, we see that tongues were given for ed-ification. Edification of the church was possible only with translation. While one could conceivably dazzle a congregation with his linguistic prowess, it is unlikely he could truly edify them, since they would be taking away with them no more than a feeling, rather than "solid food."

d.) In 1 Corinthians 14:22 we read that tongues were a sign for the unbeliev-ers, a negative sign, a sign of rejection by God. This fact is appreciated by few.

e.) Finally, tongues were for confirmation of the gospel message, according to Mark 16:17, 20.

7. Were tongues a prayer language?

I imagine that certain Corinthians were using their gift of tongues at home for their personal devotions, but it is not my opinion that there would have been anything wrong with this. This may in fact have been edifying (1 Corinthians 14:4). (There was a time when I thought I might join a mission team and go to South America. In preparation I began having my prayer times in Spanish. I read my Spanish Bible and attempted to pray to the Lord in my "tongue." That was different, edifying!)

Exactly why is the gift of tongues considered by charismatics to be a private, personal language of ecstasy and praise? Partly it is because of their interpretation of 1 Corinthians 13:1. But there are other verses in 1 Corinthians 12-14 which seem to support their view. 1 Corinthians 14: 2 provides two lines of reasoning for the charismatic:

> For anyone who speaks in a tongue does not speak to men but to God. Indeed, no one understands him; he utters mysteries with his spirit.

It is claimed that the language of praise is private and not meant to be interpreted. Yet the rest of the chapter assumes that untranslated tongues are useless! There is no support for the idea that some tongues are foreign languages and that others are heavenly languages incapable of translation. The same claim is made on the basis of the word "mysteries." But a mystery ceases to be so when it is unraveled; likewise a tongue ceases to be unintelligible once it has been interpreted. The presence of the word "mysteries" does not prove the Neopentecostal position. Another passage used to promote the charismatic position is 1 Corinthians 14: 14, "For if I pray in a tongue, my spirit prays, but my mind is unfruitful."

It is argued that Paul is *advocating* such prayer. As we will see in the commentary (Chapter 23), this is not likely and certainly cannot be proved. The unspoken assumption is that it is somehow desirable to have an unfruitful mind. (Remember the advice to put your brain in a box and shoot it to the moon?) Finally, 1 Corinthians 14:28 can be interpreted as teaching that we ought to pray in tongues in our personal prayers:

> If there is no interpreter, the speaker should keep quiet in the church and speak to himself and God.

Certainly Paul is not forbidding private prayer in tongues. He is saying they are out of place in the assembly. Yet whether or not one might pray in tongues depended wholly on whether one possessed the genuine gift of tongues! That is the real issue. My position is that tongues are no longer present.

8. What should I do if someone starts speaking in tongues?

Listen and learn. There is really very little mystery in *glossolalia* once you have heard it a few times. Keeping an even keel can help you better to love and help your friends who believe they have this supernatural ability.

In the early '80s I was making friends with Mohan, a fellow postgraduate student at the University of London. He lived upstairs from me in my dormitory and was the churchgoing type but was somewhat confused about discipleship and rebirth. He spoke five languages fluently—but also glossolalia! Mohan was sincere, and quite knowledgeable of the Bible, and once he began to understand God's plan that God's children must be disciples ("really walk the walk"), he wanted answers! My friends Douglas Arthur, Douglas Blough and I studied the Scriptures with Mohan. The "three Dougs" tried hard to persuade Mohan to make a consistent decision for the truth, but after a dozen hours of intensive discussion, he still remained unconvinced. One day he walked into my room and asked me if I would like to hear him speak in tongues.

"Sure," I said, "go ahead."

Mohan used his prayer "language," hoping to convince me. "Is that supposed to prove to me you're saved?" I asked.

"Oh, you're just not listening!" a frustrated Mohan said.

"Now it's my turn! Do you want to hear me speak in tongues?" I asked.

"You can? Yes, go ahead," replied Mohan.

"*Korobka dvyer karandashkuya, boomega okno,*" I faked a few words of Russian.

"Wow, was that really tongues?" he said.

"Yeah—more than yours was!" I replied.

Was this the turning point? No! Hours of discussion did not do the trick—nor did impugning his tongue-speaking ability. What made all the difference? Going back and laying out what the word of God says about following Jesus is what changed Mohan's life. Two days later he was baptized into Christ.

Today Mohan is an evangelist serving powerfully in London, England. I am convinced that there are thousands of sincere men and women out there like Mohan. Reach out to them; help them to understand the will of God; and keep an even keel as they share their experiences—even if they begin to speak in tongues!

9. Did biblical tongues ever die out?

Yes, the gift certainly appears to have died out, at least after a century or two. Paul's prophecy (1 Corinthians 13:8) was not proved wrong. It is interesting that the miracles of the New Testament seem to be confined to the time of the life of Jesus and to the earlier years of Acts and the letters. Evidence for miraculous languages after the 50s is wholly absent. There seem to be two second-century references to tongue-speaking. One is by Irenaeus (c.180 AD). The other is in connection with the Montanist heresy (c. 157). And while there are occasional mentions of miraculous languages in the second and third centuries, it seems they are passing away. As Origen commented (c.228 AD):

The Holy Spirit gave signs of his presence at the beginning of Christ's ministry. And after his ascension, he gave still more. But since that time, these signs have diminished, although there are still traces of his presence in a few who have had their souls purified by the gospel, and their actions regulated by its influence.[8]

Eusebius, a fourth-century church historian at the court of Constantine (306-337), writes:

A certain recent convert to the faith named Montanus...gave the adversary a passage into his heart; and...moved by the spirit he suddenly fell into a state of possession, as it were, and abnormal ecstasy, insomuch that he became frenzied and began to babble and utter strange sounds, that is to say, prophesying contrary to the manner which the church had received from generation to generation by tradition from the beginning.[9]

Three observations are to be made:

- "This charismatic revival," which sounds remarkably like Neopentecostalism today, was rejected because of the disorderly manner in which the "Spirit" was taking control.
- It would appear there had been no supernatural activity for quite some time.
- The babbling of strange sounds was rejected; it was not considered to be genuine speaking in tongues.

John Chrysostom of Constantinople, writing late in the fourth century, seems to have been the first to refer to the cessation of the gift of tongues. He is discussing 1 Corinthians 12–14:

This whole passage is very obscure; but the obscurity is produced by our ignorance of the facts referred to and by their cessation, since they used to take place then but now no longer occur.

Finally, the words of Augustine (354-430 AD) sum up the perspective of the medieval church:

In the earliest times the Holy Spirit fell on those who believed, and they spoke in languages which they had not learned, as the Spirit enabled them. These were signs adapted to the time, for there had to be that sign of the Holy Spirit in all languages, to show that the gospel of God was to spread in all languages throughout the whole world. That was done as a sign, and it passed away.

Thus the greatest churchmen of the east (Chrysostom) and the west (Augustine) are skeptical about claims of miraculous speech. Yet this can hardly be because of an antisupernatural bias, since miracles are recorded in every century of church history.

Tongue-speaking recurred in the Middle Ages, during the Reformation and in every century since. The beginnings of the modern Charismatic Movement are usually traced to Topeka, Kansas, where an outbreak of tongue-speaking occurred in 1900, spreading to the West Coast soon after.[10] After World War II the rise of Neopentecostalism brought the Charismatic Movement into almost every denomination.

So, to answer the question, "Did tongues ever die out?" we must reply "yes and no." Yes, the genuine gift of tongues seems to have finally passed away. (None of the cases of "tongues" to which I have been exposed have been convincing, though I would be fascinated to hear true language—not glossolalia.) At any rate, there have always been individuals and sects who have practiced "tongue-speaking."

10. Is it "sin" to speak in tongues?

No, tongue-speaking is not sin per se. Those who practice it do so in ignorance; yet glossolalia should be seen for what it is: a psychological phenomenon, not of the Holy Spirit. However, it is absolutely certain that untranslated "tongues" in an assembly of Christians is forbidden by God's word.

Some say tongue-speaking is from Satan. Although no doubt Satan uses this practice to deceive and to divide, there is no proof that tongue-speaking is caused by evil spirits! Satan uses many things that are not intrinsically sinful to dividebelievers and give people false hope of salvation. The practice of tongue-speaking becomes sinful when it leads to division in the body of Christ—as it has in every generation in which men have insisted on following their feelings rather than the word of God.

Conclusion

As we have seen, biblical languages and modern glossolalia are worlds apart. In the upcoming chapter we approach the modern phenomena of tongues and prophecy from the vantage point of a legitimate New Testament "charismatic" church. On to Corinth!

NOTES

1. The word is simply compounded from the Greek words *glossa* (tongue, language) and *lalia* (speech). Not to be confused with glossalgia (endless chattering)!

2. Sometimes very intelligent people experience *glossolalia*. "The drawing power of the glossolalia movement among present day intellectual types is the unconscious need all people have to solve their personality conflicts, to shed their feelings of inadequacy and guilt" (Stuart Bergsma, *Speaking with Tongues*, Grand Rapids: Baker Book House, 1965).

3. E. Mansell Pattison, "Behavioral Science Research on the Nature of Glossolalia," Journal of the *American Scientific Affiliation* 20:3:74 (September, 1968).

4. Translated from 1605 to 1611.

5. Many Christians believe the KJV is the only "authorized" English Bible. Their attitude: "If it was good enough for Jesus and the apostles, it's good enough for me!" In our own time, many Bible readers have developed the same attitude toward the NIV. It is interesting to see history repeat itself.

6. Some versions overinterpret *glossa* and so depart from sound translation: "language of ecstasy" (NEB), "strange tongues" (TEV).

7. By the way, do not try to impress people with your knowledge of Greek unless you have studied it for many years at an academic level. Nearly every argument advanced in this book can be made with an English Bible alone. It is not fair to "snow" people with arguments from the Greek when they are not in a position to respond. (And for most of us, if the person we were trying to impress happened to be a Greek scholar, we would be paralyzed if he did—isn't that right?)

8. Origen, in *The Ante-Nicene Faithers*, 4.614.

9. Eusebius, *History of the Church*, V. 16.6ff. Eusebius (260-339 AD) was a prolific writer and historian. His *History of the Church* is our primary source for the history of the church down to c. 300. He records the activities of the charismatic sect of the Montanists in great detail.

10. The woman who spoke in "tongues"—the "sign" of the outpouring expected and prayed for at the start of the twentieth century—was Agnes Ozman. The "gifts" had spread to Azusa Street (Los Angeles) by 1906.

23. Correction, Not Direction
Exposition of 1 Corinthians 12-14

This chapter is an exposition of 1 Corinthians 12, 13 and 14, with a view to the work of the Holy Spirit. As we shall see, the chapters are hardly written to direct Christians toward greater spiritual experience. Rather, they were produced to correct the confusion the Corinthians had about the Spirit, to correct the serious dysfunction damaging the fellowship.

The Mother Lode

There is more material on the miraculous gifts of the Spirit in these chapters than in all other passages of the Bible on the subject put together. Although we must at times strain to understand what Paul is saying, this is indeed the "mother lode" of corrective teaching on the Holy Spirit in the New Testament. Eventually every one of us will have to tackle difficult questions from 1 Corinthians. These are not chapters to be avoided, but to be digested.

At the outset, let me say that I firmly believe the church at Corinth was a "charismatic" church. Not "charismatic" in the Neopentecostal sense, but in the sense of truly possessing the *charismata*. The Greek *charisma* (plural *charismata*) means "gift." (It derives from *charis*, "grace.") So we see that "charismatic" means pertaining to the gifts of the Spirit. God is the giver, men the recipients. I have been using the term loosely to refer to the gifts as seen in the New Testament, as well as to the broad range of religious phenomena resembling the charismata.

Welcome to Corinth!

By way of introduction, let us examine 1 Corinthians 1:4–7:

> [4]I always thank God for you because of his grace given you in Christ Jesus. [5]For in him you have been enriched in every way—in all your speaking and in all your knowledge—[6]because our testimony about Christ was confirmed in you. [7]Therefore you do not lack any spiritual gift as you eagerly wait for our Lord Jesus Christ to be revealed.

God's grace (charis) had been given to the Corinthians, and not just grace in justification (Titus 3:7), but the grace of the gifts (charismata) of the Spirit.

They were enriched in the area of speaking (tongues, prophecy), as well as in the area of knowledge (wisdom, knowledge, discerning spirits). Notice Paul says they do not lack any spiritual gift. Why? Because the testimony Paul gave was confirmed (Chapter 17). Confirmed how? Through miraculous gifts. And when did they receive these gifts? The strong implication is that they received them (the supernatural ones) while Paul was in Corinth (Acts 18), a visit of eighteen months—more than enough time for Paul to impart the gifts to many members of the Corinthian congregation. Paul alludes to this in 1 Corinthians 2:4-5.

Not only the Corinthian congregation, but most of the early Christian churches possessed miraculous gifts. (Galatians 3:5, Ephesians 1:17, 1 Thessalonians 5:19, 2 Timothy 1:6); and others would as soon as an apostle could visit them (Romans 1:11). It is certainly possible that there were some within the Corinthian community who counterfeited the real gift of tongues, as many do today, but that in no way means the genuine gifts of the Spirit were not present in Corinth!

1 Corinthians 12

The commentary that follows on 1 Corinthians 12 is not intended to be exhaustive or academic. But it will prove helpful as a corrective for temporary confusion, as well as for the clarification of principles that can bring greater reverence and order to our worship.

> ¹Now about spiritual gifts, brothers, I do not want you to be ignorant. ²You know that when you were pagans, somehow or other you were influenced and led astray to mute idols. ³Therefore I tell you that no one who is speaking by the Spirit of God says, "Jesus be cursed," and no one can say, "Jesus is Lord," except by the Holy Spirit.

Verse 1: "I do not want you to be ignorant": The implication is that they are ignorant. For even though the Corinthians have been spiritually enriched (1:4–7), Paul cannot commend them as a spiritual congregation. In 3:1 he says, "Brothers, I could not address you as spiritual but as worldly—mere infants in Christ." In many of their practices and notions, they were still infantile. The gifts were present in Corinth, but they were used egotistically and chaotically. This was the result of a lack of rationality, orderliness and above all, love.

Verse 2: Here is a clear allusion to the pagan background of the Corinthians. In Corinth, as in all the cities of the Roman world, there were many charismatic cults, and these cults had practices seemingly within the repertoire of the

Corinthian church. (We have discussed these cults at some length in Chapter 19.) As for the rationality of pagan religion, Plato wrote, "It is through mania that the greatest blessings come to us" (*Phaedrus*), and "No one in possession of his rational mind has reached divine and true exaltation" (*Timaeus*). Paul is reminding the Corinthians of their pre-Christian experience, when they surrendered their rationality, and even their wills, to the emotional subjectivism of the Greek religious cults.

That Paul doubts the genuineness of the Corinthians' pre-Christian experience is implied in his phrases "somehow or other" and "led astray." We must remember, however, that the supernatural gifts of the Spirit were present in Corinth, and Paul is chiding them, not for their enthusiasm, but rather for their misplaced emphases.

Yes, Paul dismisses the experiences of their heathen days and with them the central superstitious fallacy: that spirituality is *feeling* the divine, rather than *obeying* it. In the past, they had been "led"—led astray! Now it would seem the same psychological mechanism had carried over into their Christianity. Similarly, today in Neopentecostal circles being "led by the Spirit" has taken on a sense wholly alien to the biblical sense. To be led by the Spirit is not surrendering our intelligence to our emotions, but aligning our mind and life with the will of God as expressed in the Scriptures. Can any of us afford *not* to be led by the Spirit? (See Chapter 9.)

Verse 3: For many this is a confusing passage, and so it is not surprising that there have been several suggestions as to its meaning. One is that the Corinthians were under extreme persecution (7:26), pressured to renounce Christ. In the early second century (112 AD) Pliny, Roman governor of Bithynia, wrote back to the emperor Trajan (98-117 AD) about the Christians in his province,

> "Some who were or had been Christians...invoked the [pagan] gods and cursed Christ...which...it is said genuine Christians cannot be compelled to do" (Epistles 10.96).

It is assumed that in times of duress, the Holy Spirit comes to believers to give them words to speak—miraculously. That is inherent in Paul's phrase "speaking by the Spirit of God" (v. 3). To be sure, Jesus did make such promises in Luke 21:15 and Matthew 10:19-20, but to apply this to Christians generally would be to wrest those passages from their contexts, as they apply primarily to the apostles. (Still, there is something in there for us, isn't there?)

A second proposal is that this is a reference to the "good confession" (1

Timothy 6:12, Romans 10:9). In fact, most scholars consider this to be the earliest baptismal confession. However, the suggestion that we can make the confession only by the power of the Spirit can also be ruled out, since one could not speak by the Spirit (i.e. through a miraculous gift, since this is what Paul is discussing in verse 3) without first possessing the Spirit, which is received only when one obeys Christ and becomes a Christian (Acts 5:32). Since the confession is a prerequisite for salvation, the time sequence is violated if the good confession is what Paul has in mind.

A third possibility is that Paul is countering the teachings of a heretical Christian sect. For example, much later there arose the Gnostic Ophites, whose members were asked to curse Jesus![1] Obviously they were not even Christians if this was the case. But why would Paul find this relevant to the Corinthians?

A fourth possibility—that Paul means anyone who parrots the words "Jesus is Lord" must be saved—is clearly to be eliminated (Matthew 7:21, Luke 6:46). What do we make of this passage, then?

Here Paul is providing a criterion for determining whether one is speaking by God's Spirit: the content of what is said. If the content contradicts Scripture or does violence to the rules of logic, we can safely dismiss the "message." (1 Corinthians 14:29 and 1 Thessalonians 5:19–22 urged first-century listeners to examine the content of prophetic messages.) Imagine the scene: One of the Corinthians stands up in the middle of the service and begins to prophesy. He raises his voice and says something in contradiction to the word of God. Regardless of how animated or convincing he may be, the prophecy is not from God if it contradicts God's word. The lesson of verse 3 concerns true prophecy: Does it lift up Jesus as Lord? Does it point to our need to obey him as Lord?

4There are different kinds of gifts, but the same Spirit. 5There are different kinds of service, but the same Lord. 6There are different kinds of working, but the same God works all of them in all men.

7Now to each one the manifestation of the Spirit is given for the common good. 8To one there is given through the Spirit the message of wisdom, to another the message of knowledge by means of the same Spirit, 9to another faith by the same Spirit, to another gifts of healing by that one Spirit, 10to another miraculous powers, to another prophecy, to another distinguishing between spirits, to another speaking in different kinds of tongues, and to still another the interpretation of tongues. 11All these are the work of one and the same Spirit, and he gives them to each one, just as he determines.

Verses 4-6: The disunity of the congregation over the issue of the gifts is apparent. (See the approximate parallel in Ephesians 4:4-6.) Paul is attempting to show that since there is but one God behind the manifestations of the Spirit, he cannot be the one responsible for the divisive practices—for the chaos and lack of love—that were turning the gifts into a curse in Corinth.

Verse 7: The gifts were given for the common good, not for personal edification. The Corinthians had lost sight of this fact, though doubtless Paul had stressed it often during his eighteen-month sojourn in Corinth (Acts 18:11). Paul had confirmed his testimony by distributing miraculous gifts of the Holy Spirit to various members (1 Corinthians 1:4-7, 2:4-5, 2 Corinthians 12:12). This was probably effected by the laying on of his hands, as we saw in Chapter 20.

Paul is saying that when he imparted the miraculous gifts to the Corinthians, he had not intended to drive a wedge into the congregation, between those who had them and those who did not, or between those who had the more sensational gifts and those who had the less noticeable ones. Paul had intended that all the gifts be appreciated and used to the glory of God, the edification of the community and the conviction of unsaved men. But what a travesty it turned out to be!

Note that Paul said "to each one" a manifestation of the Spirit was given. He assumes that all disciples have gifts—as we saw in Chapter 7.

Verse 8-10: It is beyond the scope of this chapter to define each gift, though it seems that most of them here are miraculous. Again, Paul stresses that the "same Spirit" orchestrates all these gifts in a harmonious fashion.

Verse 11: The gifts were distributed according to God's will (Hebrews 2:4). One could not simply decide which gift he would receive and then receive it; God gave men the gifts in accordance with his wisdom, not their whims.

¹²The body is a unit, though it is made up of many parts; and though all its parts are many, they form one body. So it is with Christ. ¹³For we were all baptized by one Spirit into one body—whether Jews or Greeks, slave or free—and we were all given the one Spirit to drink.

¹⁴Now the body is not made up of one part but of many. ¹⁵If the foot should say, "Because I am not a hand, I do not belong to the body," it would not for that reason cease to be part of the body. ¹⁶And if the ear should say, "Because I am not an eye, I do not belong to the body," it would not for that reason cease to be part of the body. ¹⁷If the whole body were an eye, where would the sense of hearing be? If the whole body were an ear, where would the sense of smell be? ¹⁸But in fact

God has arranged the parts in the body, every one of them, just as he wanted them to be. [19]If they were all one part, where would the body be? [20]As it is, there are many parts, but one body.

[21]The eye cannot say to the hand, "I don't need you!" And the head cannot say to the feet, "I don't need you!" [22]On the contrary, those parts of the body that seem to be weaker are indispensable, [23]and the parts that we think are less honorable we treat with special honor. And the parts that are unpresentable are treated with special modesty, [24]while our presentable parts need no special treatment. But God has combined the members of the body and has given greater honor to the parts that lacked it, [25]so that there should be no division in the body, but that its parts should have equal concern for each other. [26]If one part suffers, every part suffers with it; if one part is honored, every part rejoices with it.

[27]Now you are the body of Christ, and each one of you is a part of it.

Verses 12–27: Of particular interest is verse 13. This is a reference to the baptism in the Holy Spirit. The English versions are quite right in commenting in a footnote that the Greek preposition may be rendered "with" or "in" just as easily as "by" (as in Mark 5:2). Regardless of how this one word is translated, Paul's point is that all the Corinthians received the same Spirit and therefore should be unified. They have all been added to the same body and so should exhibit mutual concern (see also vv. 25-26 and Romans 12:5). The reference is to their conversion, not some supplementary experience. The Spirit baptism is what made them fellow members in the body of Christ. Being "given the one Spirit to drink" may be a reference to (1) tasting of the Holy Spirit in Christ (see Hebrews 6:4–5), or (2) being given the indwelling of the Holy Spirit (Acts 2:38, Galatians 3:26–27, 4:6). It is clear that relationships in the Corinthian church were fragmented (1:10ff); whereas, in light of the unifying force of the Spirit, there should have been a high degree of interdependence.

[28]And in the church God has appointed first of all apostles, second prophets, third teachers, then workers of miracles, also those having gifts of healing, those able to help others, those with gifts of administration, and those speaking in different kinds of tongues. [29]Are all apostles? Are all prophets? Are all teachers? Do all work miracles? [30]Do all have gifts of healing? Do all speak in tongues? Do all interpret? [31]But eagerly desire the greater gifts.

And now I will show you the most excellent way.

Verse 28: Paul clearly places a much higher premium on the teaching gifts than on the more visible gifts, e.g. tongues and healing. For parallels see Ephesians 4:11. Paul's emphasis in this catalogue is the opposite of the Corinthians'. Notice where tongues is placed: last.

Verses 29–30: The answer to each one of these rhetorical questions is an emphatic "No!" Yet there are many groups today who insist that speaking in tongues is evidence of salvation and even more who believe that every Christian must speak in tongues initially, at the moment of conversion.

Interestingly enough, in the Arndt-Gingrich Greek Lexicon, the first meaning of the word translated "interpret" in most versions is "translate"—which would eliminate a lot of "charismatic chaos."[2] Still, "interpret" is technically correct and need not cause any problems, as long as we hold to a biblical definition of tongues.

Verses 31: Are we to understand that the "greater gifts" are the most excellent way? Are the "greater gifts" those of apostleship, prophecy and teaching, or are they faith, hope and love? From a look at 14:1, it seems the greater gifts are those gifts which involve teaching, and therefore "the most excellent way" is "the way of love."

Summary: Chapter 12

- The Corinthian church was legitimately charismatic. Paul had imparted miraculous gifts to them during his stay in Corinth.
- The Corinthians were allowing their pagan charismatic background to influence their lives as Christians. In their subjective religious past, they had been taught to surrender their rationality—a dangerous trend if unleashed in the church.
- The spiritual gifts were not for personal edification, but were given for the common good.
- The Corinthians were using their gifts selfishly, resulting in disunity and one-upmanship.
- The teaching gifts were of far more value than the more visible gifts.
- Tongues was the *most overvalued yet least valuable* gift.
- The Corinthians were creating a spiritual elite within the congregation, based on their charismatic experiences.

"The most excellent way" is "the way of love." This way of love, as we shall see in our analysis of 1 Corinthians 13, has nothing to do with the more sensational gifts. But what exactly is this way of love? And why does Paul place his eulogy of love in the middle of his discussion on the spiritual gifts?

1 Corinthians 13

This is one of the most well known chapters in the entire Bible, particularly the "Ode to Love." One of the most challenging tests we can give to ourselves is to remove the word "love" everywhere it occurs in verses 4-8, replace it with our name and see whether the eulogy still makes any sense. I have done this several times; it's always convicting![3]

> [1]If I speak in the tongues of men and of angels, but have not love, I am only a resounding gong or a clanging cymbal. [2]If have the gift of prophecy and can fathom all mysteries and all knowledge, and if I have a faith that can move mountains, but have not love, I am nothing. [3]If I give all I possess to the poor and surrender my body to the flames, but have not love, I gain nothing.

Verses 1-3: Paul discusses the possibility of speaking in the tongues of men and of angels. Some of the more modern versions give "languages" as an alternative translation for the Greek word *glossa*, commonly rendered "tongue" in the older versions, such as the KJV. "Languages" is a common English word for what was a common word in Greek and therefore a better translation of the original word. We must remember that when the first English translations were being made (starting in the 900s AD), "tongue" meant "language." Today, as it has for the most part gone out of use, it tends to be shrouded in mystery. Some translations preserve the word "tongue" out of a liturgical respect for tradition, or as a deliberate archaism in order not to offend those favoring the Neopentecostal interpretation.

Charismatics and others base their belief in angel languages on this lone scripture. The pseudepigraphal *Testament of Job* says Job's daughters spoke in the languages of angels,[4] so the idea that humans can speak in angelic tongues is nothing new. But are there angel languages? "If I speak in the languages...of angels" does not necessarily prove they exist, any more than "If I go up to the heavens" (Psalm 139:8) proves the psalmist was an astronaut. It is mere hypothesis and in this case turns out to be a good example of hyperbole (exaggeration for effect), which must not be taken literally. Perhaps some of the Corinthians claimed, in their attempts to outdo one another, to be speaking in angelic languages.

Veneration of angels was not unknown in the Pauline churches (Colossians 2:18).

Verse 2-3: Paul gives another exaggeration for effect; who can fathom all mysteries and all knowledge? No one! Similarly, which mountains have been literally moved by men of faith since Jesus uttered Mark 11: 23? None! Verse 3 is also hyperbolic. In essence Paul is saying, "Even if you could speak in angel languages, or fathom every mystery, or move mountains by your faith—wonderful as these things might be—they would be worthless indeed if you did not have love." And that is precisely where the Corinthians fell short. In all their enthusiasm for the gifts, they were failing to exercise Christian *agape* (self-denying love) in their relationships with one another. That is why Paul had to pen 1 Corinthians 13.

Without love, the gifts were nothing, regardless of how spectacular they might have been. The heart of true religion is practical (see James 1:26–27): love of man and love of neighbor, not the peripheral manifestations of God's Spirit or the experiential aspects of faith.

> ⁴Love is patient, love is kind. It does not envy, it does not boast, it is not proud. ⁵It is not rude, it is not self-seeking, it is not easily angered, it keeps no record of wrongs. ₆Love does not delight in evil but rejoices with the truth. ⁷It always protects, always trusts, always hopes, always perseveres.
>
> ⁸Love never fails.

Verses 4-8a: These verses are a beautiful poem, and sound extremely harmonious in the original tongue. In their relationships, many Corinthians apparently were failing to exhibit love in its various forms because they had become so puffed up over their spiritual gifts. The verb *physioo* appears here in "it is not proud," as in Colossians 2:18, and also in 1 Corinthians 8:1, where knowledge is said to puff up. *Physioo* means "puff up, inflate, 'get a big head.'" It is the same today: Many are keen to relate their "experiences" of the Holy Spirit and their speculations about God and his plans, yet these same persons have never really taken the biblical step of repentance.

The Corinthians had lost sight of the goal: "faith expressing itself through love" (Galatians 5:6). They had stopped living a life of love (Ephesians 5:1-2). The same will happen to us whenever we allow ourselves to get sidetracked from the central path of Christianity: love for God, love for his people, love for the lost. Let us learn the lesson from the Corinthians.

8bBut where there are prophecies, they will cease; where there are tongues, they will be stilled; where there is knowledge, it will pass away. 9For we know in part and we prophesy in part, 10but when perfection comes, the imperfect disappears. 11When I was a child, I talked like a child, I thought like a child, I reasoned like a child. When I became a man, I put childish ways behind me. 12Now we see but a poor reflection as in a mirror; then we shall see face to face. Now I know in part; then I shall know fully, even as I am fully known.

Verse 8b: Prophecies, tongues and knowledge, Paul says, will pass away. The Old Testament also seems to have prophesied the cessation of miraculous gifts.[5] Yes, miraculous gifts were to come to an end. But love will never come to an end! As Paul says, *"Hē agápē oudépote píptei!"* ("Love never fails/falls.") Of course, the debate centers on when the miraculous gifts end—whether at the end of time or at some point before Jesus comes again.

Verse 9: To put it another way, it may be that we prophesy in part because we do not know in full. Our understanding of God's will comes through knowledge plus prophecy. What may not have been known (i.e., via Scripture) could be known through inspiration operating in the lives of individuals in the Corinthian community. But was this always to be the situation?

Verse 10: The key term is "perfection" *(to teleion)*. *To teleion* means "that which is perfect, perfection; that which is mature, maturity; that which is complete, completion." (Note that the TNIV renders the word as completeness.) When perfection comes, the imperfect (literally, the partial) disappears. Love is already here. So is "the perfect" to be equated with heaven? With the Second Coming? With the church? With love itself? All of these have been suggested as possibilities.

Many have tried, through conjecture based on the gender of the Greek *to teleion*, to determine what the phrase means.[6] Such attempts, I believe, are destined to fail for lack of evidence. For example, if "the perfect" means "the perfect gift," then any one of those suggestions is possible. If "perfection" is a state resulting from something else (the thing whose gender scholars gingerly try to determine), then the underlying noun could be just about anything!

It is certainly possible that the "perfection" or "maturity" Paul envisions pertains to the passage of the church from its infant stage (from inception to the destruction of Jerusalem) to "adulthood" after the apostolic guardians had all died. Though difficult to "prove" this argument, let me present it in short anyway. This is the interpretation I sustain through the rest of this brief commentary.

Teleios is used seventeen times in the New Testament, but never of heaven, apart from Hebrews 9:11; cf. 9:24. And as perfection/completion is the subject of these verses, the complete (perfect) Scriptures, i.e. the Old Testament and the New Testament, seem the best option. After the apostles had died, and their writings were collected and disseminated, strictly speaking there would be no more need for knowledge to be gathered through the medium of prophecy. Perfection would then be perfection of quantity more than perfection of quality. Playing on the ambivalence of the word, Paul slides into another, more immediately relevant, meaning of the word: maturity. He is speaking in terms of spiritual maturity. Not so much personal maturity (lest 14:18 show Paul to be a spiritual toddler!) as collective maturity—the maturity of the early church. The apostles are like guardians, and as soon as the church is able to stand on its own two feet, they disappear from the scene.

Whichever meaning of *to teleion* makes best sense to you is the one you should hold on to. It is doubtful we are all going to agree on this one. But some things we can and should agree on. For example, we no longer need apostles to-day. Apostles set up the process of discipleship, which is self-perpetuating. They also taught authoritatively and infallibly, insofar as we have their writings in the New Testament. In addition, they were eyewitnesses of Jesus' resurrection, establishing it beyond dispute (1 Corinthians 9:1, Acts 1:21–22). Finally, the apostles confirmed the apostolic message with apostolic miracles, as we have seen.

Verse 12: The "poor reflection" is literally "through a mirror in a riddle." This does not necessarily show inaccuracy of revelation, as though our Bibles were insufficient to tell us truly about God. Seeing things through a mirror is only indirect, like using a periscope. The process of receiving, hearing, assessing and interpreting a prophetic message just isn't the same as reading a passage of Scripture and making the direct application.[7]

Seeing "face to face," a common metaphor in Greek, need not mean that Jesus' face is what is beheld. It implies rather a greater directness of revelation. Knowing "fully" probably does not refer to heaven, since we can know fully through the Scriptures (2 Timothy 3:17, Jude 3). Our understanding of this passage is improved considerably by a consideration of Numbers 12:6b–8a. The normal way God spoke to the prophets was indirect. It was an indirect method because a prophet's spiritual perception was limited to the vision (dream) he had received from God. Like a periscope, it was a roundabout way of discerning God's will. But with Moses God spoke "face to face," not "in riddles." (See also Exodus 33:11, Deuteronomy 34:10.) The literary similarity to 1 Corinthians 13:12 is more than coincidence!

When the perfect came, men no longer required the indirect methods of prophesying to ascertain God's will. Now men were able to look into God's perfect word themselves, without having to rely on what others said, without getting bogged down in the interpretation of prophetic messages (1 Corinthians 14:29, 1 Thessalonians 5:19-22, 1 John 4:1).

"Knowing fully" meant that there would be no more need for prophecy, and that is why prophecy passed away with the coming of the completed New Testament. "Knowing fully" cannot be taken to mean knowing everything about everything, since that is only for God, and there is no promise in all of Scripture that we will be omniscient in heaven.

¹³And now these three remain: faith, hope and love. But the greatest of these is love.

Verse 13: These three outlast the spiritual gifts. But when do the gifts vanish? With the Second Coming? No! There is no faith in heaven (2 Corinthians 5:7), nor hope (Romans 8:24), though love *will* be found there. Therefore any interpretation making "perfection" (v. 10) the perfection at the end of time would seem untenable. "Perfection" rather applies to the maturity of the early church (Ephesians 4:11-16), along with the completion of the New Testament canon. These two really should not be viewed separately, however, since one depends on the other.

Summary: Chapter 13

- Love is primary. It does not matter how impressive our spiritual achievements are if we do not have the love of God in our hearts.
- There is no biblical basis for the claim that certain humans can speak in "angel languages."
- The ugliness of ego had not only made a mockery of God and his gifts, but it had also infected and stressed the church.
- It is difficult to be dogmatic about the precise meaning of *to teleion*. The Neopentecostal claim that all the supernatural gifts are with us until Jesus comes, however, is completely indefensible.
- At the time Paul wrote to the Corinthians, Christians' knowledge of God's will was partial and required supplementing through the miraculous gift of prophecy.
- The Corinthians needed to stop being so childish in their worship and immature in their spirituality.

1 Corinthians 14

This chapter is the richest array of teaching on the gifts of prophecy and tongues in the Bible. Much misunderstanding has been caused by a lack of familiarity with the biblical concepts of prophecy and languages, especially the Old Testament background. Before we can begin to mine this incredibly rich source of teaching material, we must understand the basic meaning of the terms.

Prophecy, from the Greek words *pro* (before/for) + *phemi* (speak), means "to speak before" (in advance of the event predicted), or, more commonly, "to speak for" (God). And, as we saw in Chapter 22, tongues (*glossai*) are literally "languages," and so are intelligible only if the hearer understands the language spoken, or if the language is translated into a tongue known to the hearer. Although modern tongue-speaking is gibberish, biblical tongues were actual languages!

> [1]Follow the way of love and eagerly desire spiritual gifts, especially the gift of prophecy. [2]For anyone who speaks in a tongue does not speak to men but to God. Indeed, no one understands him; he utters mysteries with his spirit. [3]But everyone who prophesies speaks to men for their strengthening, encouragement and comfort. [4]He who speaks in a tongue edifies himself, but he who prophesies edifies the church. [5]I would like every one of you to speak in tongues, but I would rather have you prophesy. He who prophesies is greater than one who speaks in tongues, unless he interprets, so that the church may be edified.

Verse 1: The prophetic, or teaching, gifts are placed on a plane far above tongues (see 12:28). The verb could be rendered "be eager for," and so the second clause of the verse could be translated "and especially be eager to prophesy" (i.e. those who have this sort of gift should be eager to exercise it—to "excel" [v. 12]).

Verses 2-4: Untranslated tongues benefit no one. They are "mysteries" because no one else knows what is being said. Naturally, God understands, since he is Master of every tongue, but no one is edified. Edification is possible only when there is an intelligible message—the same as with a sermon.

Are we to believe that Paul actively encouraged Corinthian disciples to sit at home and pray in various languages? Who would benefit from it? Only the one who exercised the gift. It is like someone with a teaching gift studying and organizing his material into lectures which he prepared only for himself. Or someone with the gift of encouragement being warm and encouraging to himself but not to others. Or like someone blessed by God with money spending it all on himself! Our gifts are not to be lavished on ourselves, but on others.

Verse 5: Even though Paul expresses his wish that all speak in tongues, this is hypothetical and surely not possible (12:10–11, 30). Prophecy is clearly given preference over tongues. The exception of course is tongues with translation. From this we derive the simple equation: *tongues + translation = prophecy*. Keep this important principle in mind as you study the following paragraphs.

❖

⁶Now, brothers, if I come to you and speak in tongues, what good will I be to you, unless I bring you some revelation or knowledge or prophecy or word of instruction? ⁷Even in the case of lifeless things that make sounds, such as the flute or harp, how will anyone know what tune is being played unless there is a distinction in the notes? ⁸Again, if the trumpet does not sound a clear call, who will get ready for battle? ⁹So it is with you. Unless you speak intelligible words with your tongue, how will anyone know what you are saying? You will just be speaking into the air. ¹⁰Undoubtedly there are all sorts of languages in the world, yet none of them is without meaning. ¹¹If then I do not grasp the meaning of what someone is saying, I am a foreigner to the speaker, and he is a foreigner to me. ¹²So it is with you. Since you are eager to have spiritual gifts, try to excel in gifts that build up the church. ¹³For this reason anyone who speaks in a tongue should pray that he may interpret what he says.

Verses 6–9: Evidently some Corinthians were spouting off in "tongues" in the assemblies of the church. Paul insists, however, that tongues are utterly useless if not translated!

When I was a little boy, I had a blue toy piano. I banged away on it, not knowing what I was playing and not particularly caring, either. When a young child does such things, we smile and may chuckle. But when a grown man does the same thing, we pity him; no one would give a penny to hear him banging randomly on a piano. Paul is saying that that is precisely what the Corinthians were doing by irrational use of their gift of tongues. The so-called language is not just self-serving—it is chaotic, useless.

Just "speaking into the air" helps no one. When I was in high school in New Jersey, there was one girl in the neighborhood I would often phone. She loved to talk. Sometimes she would start talking, and for some reason I would leave the room, quietly setting the phone down. I would return a few minutes later, lift up the phone and say "Uh huh," and rejoin the conversation. She never knew I had left it! She was in her own world. So it is with those who come to church to babble into the air.

Verses 10–11: Tongues are actual foreign languages. The two passages in the Bible shedding conclusive light on the nature of tongues are Acts 2 and 1 Corinthians 14. The tongues of Pentecost are actual languages, as no reader can fail to notice. Similarly, the reference here is to actual languages, as is that in verse 21. The word foreigner (*barbaros*) also translates "barbarian," the term Greeks used of people who did not speak Greek. It is the word one would normally use to describe someone who spoke a foreign language. The point? The analogy implies that tongues are actual languages. More important, it shows that tongues make us *barbaroi*, "strangers" to one another. Fellowship is meant to be unifying, not alienating!

Verses 12–13: Note Paul's emphasis on edification. Paul unequivocally states that tongue-speaking does *not* edify the church.

¹⁴For if I pray in a tongue, my spirit prays, but my mind is unfruitful. ¹⁵So what shall I do? I will pray with my spirit, but I will also pray with my mind; I will sing with my spirit, but I will also sing with my mind. ¹⁶If you are praising God with your spirit, how can one who finds himself among those who do not understand say "Amen" to your thanksgiving, since he does not know what you are saying? ¹⁷You may be giving thanks well enough, but the other man is not edified.

¹⁸I thank God that I speak in tongues more than all of you. ¹⁹But in the church I would rather speak five intelligible words to instruct others than ten thousand words in a tongue.

²⁰Brothers, stop thinking like children. In regard to evil be infants, but in your thinking be adults. ²¹In the Law it is written:

"Through men of strange tongues
and through the lips of foreigners
I will speak to this people,
but even then they will not listen to me,"
says the Lord.

²²Tongues, then, are a sign, not for believers but for unbelievers; prophecy, however, is for believers, not for unbelievers.

Verses 14–17: Is "unfruitful" good? No—it means unproductive (Titus 3:14, Mark 4:19). God wants us to be productive (fruitful) in everything (Colossians 1:10), so why put yourself in a compromising position? We should pray with our spirit (enthusiastically and earnestly) but also with our mind (i.e. with understanding). That is also the way we should sing (vv. 15–16). Praying in the spirit (Ephesians 6:18) therefore cannot mean praying in tongues.

Many readers automatically assume that tongue-speakers in the Bible had no idea what they were saying unless someone translated their tongue. But why should we assume that? Because normally babbling would require a miracle in order to become intelligible! But tongues were not babbling; they were languages. For tongues to be fruitful, or productive, they had to be understood by the hearers. Someone needed to give the translation—whether the speaker or someone else who could concentrate on the message while offering a good translation.

Verses 18-19: Paul not only spoke Greek, Aramaic, Hebrew and possibly Latin, but also possessed the miraculous gift of speaking in some languages he had never studied. It is possible (though unsupported by the record) that his command of languages could have been tremendously helpful on his missionary journeys, but not in the church. Paul is emphatic that five intelligible words are worth a whole sermon in tongues!

Verse 20: The central fallacy of the superstitious approach to Christianity is that spirituality means *feeling* the divine. The Corinthian tongue-speakers were behaving childishly, flaunting their gifts in the assembly and trying to outdo one another. True religion is sensational, yes, but never sensationalist. In their approach the Corinthians were childish and selfish, turning the worship of the church into a funfair. Paul continues his instruction on the use and abuse of the gifts of the Spirit and now turns to the Old Testament to shed light on the subject.

Verses 21-22: Paul gives an example of tongues: Assyrian (technically, Akkadian), an actual language. Yes, the language of the cruel Assyrians—study Isaiah and you will see "tongues" for the Israelites were a sign of divine judgment. Numerous Old Testament examples of tongues show that they were a bewildering sign of judgment on unbelievers (Isaiah 18:2, 28:11, Deuteronomy 28:49, Jeremiah 5:15). The "men of strange tongues" are Assyrians, sent by God to punish Israel. The unbelievers in this case are therefore the Jews: unfaithful people! When they heard the sound of foreign tongues, it would not be very edifying! It would signify that their end had come.

Imagine waking up one morning, tuning in the radio, and hearing nothing but foreign tongues being spoken. You go outside and, much to your dismay, enemy troops are everywhere. Your homeland has been invaded. The "tongue" is the enemy's language. Not very edifying, is it? Because of our cultural and temporal separation from the events of the Old Testament, we can easily fail to appreciate the biblical significance of "tongues": judgment from God via invasion!

Incidentally, the *glossolalia* at Pentecost would have signified not only that all nations would take over the inheritance of the Jews, but also that the Jewish nation stood under the judgment of God for rejecting the Christ. (The prophecy of

Joel 2:28ff, which Peter cites in Acts 2, occurs in the context of divine judgment.) Jesus prophesied the destruction of Jerusalem (Matthew 24, Mark 13, Luke 17, 19, 21), a prophecy fulfilled forty years after Pentecost (70 AD). Many see in this a sort of "grace period" or last chance to repent, in which case the forty-year period would parallel the forty years of wandering in the desert. Thus the Pentecostal *glossolalia* heralded imminent doom for the Jewish people.

²³So if the whole church comes together and everyone speaks in tongues, and some who do not understand or some unbelievers come in, will they not say that you are out of your mind? ²⁴But if an unbeliever or someone who does not understand comes in while everybody is prophesying, he will be convinced by all that he is a sinner and will be judged by all, ²⁵and the secrets of his heart will be laid bare. So he will fall down and worship God, exclaiming, "God is really among you!"

Verses 23–25: Since tongues are a sign of judgment, a frightening and bewildering sign, it is not the sort of thing you want to be heard by visitors to the church services (particularly if everyone is doing it at once). It could well drive them away, convinced that you are mad! But prophecy (because of its preaching quality) will convict the sinner and effect repentance. Paul is continuing to urge the Corinthians to use their gifts in moderation and with sensitivity, and once more he plays down the role of tongues. Why? Because Christians have been given the commission to bring sinners to repentance, not to dazzle them with their gifts. After all, the Word is what brings people to faith, not miracles (Luke 16:31).

²⁶What then shall we say, brothers? When you come together, everyone has a hymn, or a word of instruction, a revelation, a tongue or an interpretation. All of these must be done for the strengthening of the church. ²⁷If anyone speaks in a tongue, two—or at the most three—should speak, one at a time, and someone must interpret. ²⁸If there is no interpreter, the speaker should keep quiet in the church and speak to himself and God.
        ²⁹Two or three prophets should speak, and the others should weigh carefully what is said. ³⁰And if a revelation comes to someone who is sitting down, the first speaker should stop. ³¹For you can all prophesy in turn so that everyone may be instructed and encouraged. ³²The spirits of prophets are subject to the control of prophets. ³³For God is not a God of disorder but of peace.

As in all the congregations of the saints, [34]women should remain silent in the churches. They are not allowed to speak, but must be in submission, as the Law says. [35]If they want to inquire about something, they should ask their own husbands at home; for it is disgraceful for a woman to speak in the church.

Verses 26–27: Paul now returns to his discussion of the exercise of tongues in the assembly of the church. He lays down certain procedural regulations:

- There should be a maximum of two or three tongue-speakers.
- Speakers must speak consecutively, not simultaneously.
- Tongues must be accompanied by interpretation.

Evidently the Corinthians were being disorderly in their services. There were numerous persons who tried to speak in tongues during a single service. Often the speakers used their gifts at the same time, causing confusion and cacophony! And the tongues were not translated, so no one benefited.

It is interesting to observe similar confusion today in groups that covet the Corinthian experience. I remember when the Charismatic Movement hit the youth group of my old church, and all the kids were busy trying to discover the "gifts" they had. When a time of prayer in the service morphed into a time of tongue-speaking, everyone starting singing in tongues ("singing in the Spirit"). It made my spine tingle, but I knew this wasn't right, so I interrupted the group, asked the leader to turn to 1 Corinthians 14 and showed him what the Bible said about having only one speaker at a time. Several in the group agreed with me. But within seconds, the entire room had returned to its "singing in the Spirit." Oh well!

Verse 28: If an interpretation just "came" to someone in the assembly, then this warning would be unnecessary. But in fact certain individuals had the gift of translating certain languages. One could know whether the translator was present, and hence whether a message in a foreign language might be beneficial (translated). All this underlines the fact that these "tongues" were actual languages. Paul does not discourage private tongue-speaking, which may have been quite edifying at a personal level.

That of course assumes that the tongue-speaker was able to understand his own tongue—and thus get some fruit from it.

Verses 29–36: Just as there were ground rules for the congregational exercise of the miraculous gift of languages, there are also procedural regulations for prophesying in the church:

- There should be a maximum of two or three prophets speaking. This rule is stricter than the Old Testament, which often allowed group prophecy (1 Samuel 19:20).
- The prophetic messages must be weighed, or tested, by the listeners, not just superficially or automatically accepted. It was no offence to God to wrestle with the message until the meaning (or validity) was clear. (See 1 Thessalonians 5:19–22.)
- The speaker should not let himself be carried away with his prophecy. A spiritual gift is not something that just takes control of you. You control it! Discipline must be exercised.

Compare Paul's wisdom to the teaching of the heretical Montanus who claimed "Man is like a lyre and I [the Spirit] rush upon it like a plectrum." Another Montanist leader claimed, "The Lord...has compelled me, willingly or unwillingly, to learn the knowledge of God."[8]

It is shocking how little respect or regard the Charismatic Movement has paid to Paul's clear instructions, which he delivered through the authority of the Holy Spirit (v. 37).

Paul adds one more caveat: Women are not to participate in the testing of the prophecies, since that would put them in the position of challenging men's authority (see also 1 Timothy 2:11ff).

36Did the word of God originate with you? Or are you the only people it has reached? 37If anybody thinks he is a prophet or spiri- tually gifted, let him acknowledge that what I am writing to you is the Lord's command. 38If he ignores this, he himself will be ignored.

39Therefore, my brothers, be eager to prophesy, and do not forbid speaking in tongues. 40But everything should be done in a fitting and orderly way.

Verses 36-40: After issuing a warning to those who might challenge his apostolic authority (vv. 37-38), Paul concludes (vv. 39-40). Paul's emphasis is clear: Although (translated) tongues may be of benefit, prophecy (preaching) is of paramount importance. Moreover, services must be conducted with propriety and order.

Summary: Chapter 14

- The teaching gifts are far more valuable than the more showy gifts of languages or prophecy.

- Untranslated languages were a mystery to those who did not understand them. Speaking in this kind of tongues was forbidden in the corporate setting.
- Translated tongues were the functional equivalent of prophecy.
- We are discouraged from "letting go" and disengaging our minds.
- Tongues are alienating and will have a negative effect on unbelievers.
- Languages and prophecy were regulated by strict guidelines: (1) no more than two or three of each per service and (2) no simultaneous speaking, only consecutive.
- Church services are to be warm and alive, and at the same time, conducted with dignity, propriety and order. (Is there a challenge here for us?)

Imitating the Corinthians?

Although many Neopentecostal groups exclaim, "We want to be just like the Corinthian church!" they do not realize how far off the mark that church had gone. The Corinthian church attached priority to the fairly insignificant gift of languages and seriously underrated the most important gifts, the teaching gifts.

They exalted the ego and made it grow big with "spiritual" experiences, while the heart was starved for the word of God (prophecy) and starved for fellowship (as each member was doing his own thing). Moreover, they had let their pagan backgrounds get the better of them—and many Corinthians came from such a background—and surrendered their minds to an experience. They were always trying to outdo one another, lacking the love that is so central to the true Spirit of Christ. They were disorderly! No wonder Paul called them back to the cross (1 Corinthians 1:18–2:5).

And this is the congregation charismatics look to for an example? Rather than view 1 Corinthians 12–14 as a set of *directions* for a spiritual congregation that needed to make use of its gifts, see it for what it is: a set of *corrections* for an unspiritual congregation that was misusing its gifts.

_____ NOTES _____

1. Origen, *Contra* Celsum 5:1:28.

2. See John MacArthur's helpful book *Charismatic Chaos* (Grand Rapids: Zondervan, 1992), as well as the counter response by Rich Nathan, "A Response to Charismatic Chaos," Vineyard Position Paper #5 (Anaheim: Vineyard, 1993).

3. Of course, this exercise really works only in verses 4-7. It can get you in trouble in v. 13. Just ask some who jumped into this publicly.

4. T. Job. 48-50.

5. Daniel 9:24 indicates that after the destruction of Jerusalem by the Romans, which occurred in 70 AD, "vision and prophecy" would be sealed up.

6. To teleion is neuter, whereas "heaven" (ho ouranos) is masculine, as is "Jesus" (ho Iesous). "Bible or little book" (to biblion) is neuter, as is "body" (to soma). "Church" (he ekklesia) is feminine. So which is the implied antecedent of to teleion? Good question! Many commentators presume that the phrase for maturity, to teleion, can only refer to a neuter noun. This is quite an assumption, however! Why is it that nonspecialists in Greek language "know" the meaning of a Greek word, while experts who have devoted decades of their lives to serious study feel constrained to leave their options open? If most preachers would stay away from "the Greek," I believe we would all be a lot less mystified! A helpful, and at times eye-opening, book on biblical exegesis is D. A. Carson, *Exegetical Fallacies, Second Edition* (Grand Rapids: Baker, 1996).

7. Incidentally, people often insist that mirrors in antiquity were of poor quality, and thus would yield a poor image. New Testament archeology indicates the opposite, especially for Corinth, which was renowned for its mirrors of fine quality.

8. Epiphanius Haer. 48:4.1, 13.1.

24. The 'Warm, Fuzzy Feeling'
Baptism with the Holy Spirit

In 1976, after my "conversion experience,"[1] I began attending charismatic prayer meetings. I continued to go because there were lots of food, nice girls and a high degree of spiritual novelty (for me). Our group was comprised of people from all sorts of backgrounds, including Protestants, Catholics and Jews. A typical meeting began with an hour of song and praise, in English as well as in "tongues," followed by another hour of "testimonies" or a lesson. The next two hours we would spend talking, eating or singing around the piano—I was the designated player! It was quite a social affair. I still attended my noncharismatic church. When anyone asked me what my faith was, I gave the answer most Neopentecostals give: "Christian."

After attending the prayer meetings for a few months, I was invited to a Pentecostal church service. This was more high-powered than anything I had ever attended! Voices—and hands—were raised. A note of near panic was in the air. Many spoke in "tongues." The preacher was asking for testimonies, for people to share how God had been working in their lives. A woman across the aisle from me was called on; she stood up, then fainted from the pressure! Then the preacher pointed his finger at me! I was off my guard; adrenaline flowed, it seemed, in a torrent. Standing up, I recounted a close brush I once had with death and how I thought perhaps it was God who had saved me. There were many "Hallelujahs" and "Amens." Whew! I felt fortunate to be able to think on my feet.

A few moments later the woman who was sitting next to me, the leader of our group, asked me, "Have you received it? Have you received the baptism of the Holy Spirit?" When I replied that I wasn't sure, she prayed for me. Nothing happened. I was missing something: that "higher dosage" of the Spirit everyone was talking about.

Defining Terms

What is meant by "the baptism of the Holy Spirit"?[2] You are probably aware that there are several opposing views on the matter. This chapter is an effort to (1) clarify the biblical doctrine of the baptism with the Holy Spirit and (2) to explain the subjective, modern interpretation of this baptism promoted in Neopentecostal circles.

We will begin our study with a look at the popular teaching of "Holy Spirit baptism," followed by a consideration of what might be called the "limited view." Afterwards, I will present my personal view. But first, the "charismatic" teaching.

'A Warm, Fuzzy Feeling'

In the Neopentecostal view, the baptism of the Holy Spirit is a sensational blessing available to all Christians. The broad Charismatic Movement teaches that "Holy Spirit baptism" is an experience supplementary to conversion, bestowing power for witnessing, for the initial manifestation of speaking in tongues and sometimes for an additional miraculous gift of the Holy Spirit.[3] This experience is sometimes called the "second blessing," and we are all urged to seek it, although it is not always preached as necessary for salvation. It is an extra. I, for my part, am convinced that the experience is fully explicable and nonmiraculous. My friend Charles recounts his story:

> The church leaders asked me, "Have you received the extra measure of the Holy Spirit?" I said no, and they invited me to a special prayer service taking place a few nights later.
>
> That night there were about twenty of us who were being prayed for. We were all "new converts" and hadn't yet received the baptism of the Holy Spirit. The leaders began to pray for us, and their voices got louder and louder. When they started screaming, I was thinking to myself, "What is this?"
>
> Five men surrounded me, laid their hands on me, and prayed for me to receive the Spirit baptism. I felt reluctant, a bit skeptical. But soon I felt a warm, fuzzy feeling in me. Their prayers in normal language changed to tongues, and before I knew it I was speaking in tongues, too. I was yelling at the top of my voice. They praised God, and told me that I was filled with the Holy Ghost. Just minutes later, I was helping them pray for others who still hadn't received this experience. Wow, it was amazing! Soon I got involved in the healing ministry of the church. I was the main person appointed to pray for others to be healed.
>
> But when I studied the Bible for myself and found out the truth, I was scared stiff. I knew I was lost, and then I thought I might be demon-possessed!

Tremendous pressure is placed on the individual to achieve "Spirit baptism," and in many circles, pressure is continually brought to bear until the person gets "zapped"—or fakes the experience. Without this "baptism," it is taught, you just do not have the complete power you need to be a disciple. You have not accepted the "full gospel."

My friend Tom Jones lived in a US city where the headquarters for a Pentecostal church was located. A daughter of a top church official came to his ministry seeking spiritual help. This woman was desperate. She had never been able to speak in tongues, in spite of numerous attempts to "instruct" her to do so. She was bringing shame on her father, and she was unwelcome in her denomination because she had never received the "baptism of the Spirit." The pressure placed on individuals to conform is considerable.[4] The belief, however, that miraculous experience is an essential part of the "full gospel," is unfounded.

The Neopentecostal View

In the Neopentecostal view, the hundred and twenty knew the Lord before Acts 2:4, but their lives were powerless. They were missing out on the power of the Christian life; but after they were "baptized in the Spirit" and received the gift of "tongues," God was able to use them in a powerful way. The Holy Spirit truly does bring us into a dynamic new dimension of Christian life, but biblical baptism with the Holy Spirit has nothing to do with any "warm fuzzy feeling." The Bible, in fact, places no emphasis on the feeling of the Spirit.

Evaluation

As we assess the Neopentecostal view, we find numerous deficiencies:

1. It seems clear from the book of Acts that outpourings of the Holy Spirit reported there—with the visible miraculous manifestations—are special cases, not the norm.[5]

Support for the necessity of a "second blessing" (something beyond conversion), taken almost entirely from the book of Acts, interprets critical moments in the history of the early church as personal experiences all believers should strive for. In each of the passages, however, individuals had a special experience only because God was revealing his historical purpose to his people. (We have expounded this point at length in Chapter 18.)

2. The apostles performed miracles—some fairly impressive ones!—long before Pentecost (Luke 9:2, Matthew 10:8).

In each situation in Acts it is claimed the ability to perform miracles is contingent upon receiving the "baptism of the Holy Spirit." Yet if you will allow a little "tongue-in-cheek" humor, what about Balaam's donkey? It spoke in tongues! (Numbers 22:28). It was a language it had never studied (Hebrew); it spoke the language miraculously; and it was empowered to be a better "witness" (to Balaam). Should we infer the donkey was "Spirit baptized"? Neopentecostalism equates being "filled with the Spirit" with Spirit baptism. But many were filled with the Spirit before Pentecost: John the Baptist (Luke 1:15), Elizabeth (Luke 1:41) and Zechariah (Luke 1:67), to name a few.

3. Insufficient attention is paid to the unique role of the apostles in the early church.
The apostles appear to be the speakers in Acts 2, as they all have Galilean accents (Acts 2:7). Neopentecostalism creates two types of Christians: those filled with the Spirit and those not. While there may be degrees of this filling (Acts 6:3), the New Testament teaches only one life for the child of God: life in the Spirit (Romans 8:14), which is possessed by all Christians (1 John 3:24). Life in the flesh is the alternative! Therefore there is no excuse for lukewarmness; we cannot just sit around doing nothing, and say, "If God wants to use me, he will." Paul says in Ephesians 1:3 that God "has blessed us...with every spiritual blessing in Christ." If that is so, why do charismatics encourage us to seek a "second blessing?" As Peter puts it, "His divine power has given us everything we need for life and godliness" (2 Peter 1:3). All blessings are ours! We received them when we were immersed into Christ. We are not lacking anything. There is nothing God is holding back from us. So what else can there be to receive if we have already received every spiritual blessing?

4. There is no evidence at all for the position that tongue-speaking is the initial sign of sanctification.
1 Corinthians 12:10 and 12:30 show that not all Christians had the gift of tongues.

5. The experience of the Samaritans in Acts 8 is never called "baptism of the Holy Spirit."
Apart from possible tongue-speaking, there are few similarities between Acts 2 and Acts 8. In Acts 2 the Spirit comes directly from heaven; in Acts 8 it is mediated by the laying on of apostolic hands. In Acts 2 it happens to the apostles; in Acts 8 it happens to Samaritans who were already Christians. In Acts 2 there were tongues of fire and a mighty wind; in Acts 8 there were no such signs.

6. The Caesareans were not saved by the interruption of the outpoured Spirit.
Peter had just begun to bring Cornelius, along with his "friends and family" (Acts 10:24), the message through which they would be saved (Acts 11:15).

7. Acts 10 is certainly not normative for Christians then or today.

Peter has to think all the way back to Pentecost for a similar event (Acts 10:47, 11:1–17)—some eight years previous!

8. A common misconception of the Neopentecostal view is that the recipients of Spirit baptism were Christians before Pentecost.

It is correct that the recipients of the Spirit were in a right relationship with God under the Old Covenant, but the analogy between their lives before Pentecost and ours today falls down on one rather significant point: The Spirit was not given before Jesus was glorified (John 7:39) and had ascended (John 16:7). Romans 8:9 shows that possessing the indwelling Spirit is the *sine qua non* of being a Christian.[6]

9. The Ephesian disciples (Acts 19) were not Christians, but disciples of John the Baptist.

Paul was not concerned with whether John the Baptist's disciples had received a second blessing of the Spirit; he was concerned with whether they had received the indwelling of the Spirit at all. When he found they had not, he realized they were not saved (Romans 8:9, Acts 5:32), and therefore he baptized them. And once again, the Spirit coming on them was not normative; an apostle was present to lay his hands on them. The Spirit is the decisive difference between the Christian ministry and that of John. John's baptism conferred the forgiveness of sins, but not the Holy Spirit (Mark 1:4). Many Neopentecostals teach that we receive the Spirit, in many cases, some time after conversion. But the New Testament says we receive the Spirit because we have become God's sons (Galatians 4:6), not the other way around. We hear the gospel and respond to it in faith, and then we receive the Spirit as a deposit.

In light of the above truths, the Pentecostal view must be ruled completely out of court.[7] Before I present my understanding of Spirit baptism, we need to examine one popular alternative to the Pentecostal view.

The Limited View

With "the limited view" (one many of my readers will be familiar with), the Holy Spirit baptism occurs only once or twice in the New Testament and does not occur today, since there is only one baptism (Ephesians 4:5). This baptism occurred in fulfillment of prophecy and served an historical purpose: the establishment of the kingdom on earth. It was for the apostles, empowering them with infallibility and authority. Many proponents maintain that the outpouring of Acts 10 (on the Gentiles) was complementary to that of Acts 2 (on the Jews). Since the historical purpose of the outpouring was accomplished, the "experience" is not available today.[8] It was limited to the historical occasion(s) which effected God's will in the first half of the first century. The similarities between Acts 2 and Acts 10 are stressed, and on this basis it is concluded that the two events are both baptism with the Holy Spirit. Statements true of both outpourings include:

1. It came suddenly.	Acts 2:2/10:44
2. There was no laying on of hands.	Acts 2:4/10:44
3. Miraculous languages were spoken.	Acts 2:4/10:46
4. The prophecy of Joel was (half) fulfilled.	Acts 2:16 (Jews)/10:1, 10:24, 44 (Gentiles)
5. The baptism was promised, not commanded.	Acts 1:5, 8/11:15-16
6. It ushered in the church.	Acts 2:6, 41/10:48, 11:18,15:7-8
7. It did not forgive sins.	Acts 2:38/10:43, 48 (baptism in name of Jesus)

Evaluation

While the view makes many helpful observations, parts of it are nonetheless artificially constructed. The similarities are looked for; the differences are ignored; and the two are viewed as the same. Yet of course they are going to appear the same—we are guaranteed that they would be! Granted, there are similarities. But the differences must be taken into account, too:

1. In Acts 2 the baptism in the Spirit establishes the church, but in Acts 10 the church is already established. Many of the Gentiles had already been converted (and not just the Samaritans). The Gentile mission actually began with the persecution of Acts 8—see Acts 11:20-21. An intentional mission to the Gentiles, however, begins only in Acts 13.

2. There was no mighty wind in Acts 10, unlike Acts 2.

3. And what about the tongues of fire? They too are missing in Acts 10.

4. As for infallibility, in Acts 2 the apostles received the promise of the Holy Spirit to guide their minds and enable them to teach doctrine infallibly (John 14:26, 16:13); yet there is no evidence the Gentiles "devoted themselves to the Caesareans' teaching."

5. Acts 2 fulfilled the promise of Acts 1:5, but Acts 10 did not.

6. This position does not allow for the Apostle Paul to be baptized in the Spirit. If he did not receive the Holy Spirit baptism at Pentecost (Acts 2), and was not present at Caesarea (Acts 10), then the man who was arguably the greatest apostle missed out on the gift received by all the others.

7. While the Pentecostal outpouring does establish the church of Christ in history, as the kingdom comes powerfully in Jerusalem, the perspective that the primary purpose of the Holy Spirit baptism was to advance the kingdom of God is too restricted. It is that, but it is more and certainly has application for us today.

What about these differences? For example, let's say there are two mystery people. They both have two ears, dark hair and a facial wart. They are both over six feet tall (never mind that one weighs 150 pounds, the other 230, or that one is only twenty years old, the other fifty). They are both male, phlegmatic with a touch of choleric and unmarried. They both tend to move suddenly, speak the same tongue and are ushers in the church. Eureka—they are identical twins! Not necessarily. In the same way, the alleged Holy Spirit baptism examples in Acts 2 and Acts 10 are not necessarily twins.

Furthermore, this view does not square fully with the promise of John the Baptist (Matthew 3:11, Mark 1:8, Luke 3:16, John 1:33). It is maintained that the baptism with the Spirit applies to the apostles, whereas the baptism with fire applies to judgment. The natural reading of John's promise is that all disciples would have been baptized in the Spirit, not just a few. This possibility will be elaborated shortly. Saying the apostles only were baptized in the Spirit is highly problematic.

Imagine a group of twelve men won the lottery, took the money and spent it. Would it make any sense for a reporter to write, "Last week the entire nation won the jackpot. Yes sir, although only twelve persons shared the purse, we are all so happy they could partake of it as our representatives."[9] This will not do! Although the "apostles-only view" and "two-times view" (Acts 2 and 10) have much to commend them, insofar as they attempt to tie up the loose ends and produce a unified theory of the action of the Spirit, they minimize the promise of John the Baptist, whose message was neither complex nor confusing.

Under cross-examination, the limited view's weaknesses have come to light (Proverbs 18:17). And the apostles-only view, like the Acts 2/Acts 10 view, raises as many questions as it answers.

Spirit and Fire

We read the words of John the Baptist early in Mark, considered by most scholars to be the oldest of the gospels. John's promise to the Israelites is emphatic about a "baptism with the Holy Spirit."

> [5]The whole Judean countryside and all the people of Jerusalem went out to him. Confessing their sins, they were baptized by him in the Jordan River… [7]And this was his message: "After me will come one more powerful than I, the thongs of whose sandals I am not worthy to stoop down and untie. [8]I baptize you with water, but he will baptize you with the Holy Spirit" (Mark 1:5, 7–8).

To whom does the "you" of verse 8 refer? Is it only Judeans and Jerusalemites to whom this baptism is promised? If so, why do we read in Paul's letter to the Corinthians that we were all baptized "by one Spirit"? Look at the verse, and decide what you think is the most natural reading—and the correct one!

> [13]For we were all baptized by one Spirit into one body—whether Jews or Greeks, slave or free—and we were all given the one Spirit to drink (1 Corinthians 12:13).

The text states that *all* disciples have been baptized by one Spirit. There appear to be no exceptions. The promised outpouring and baptism of the Spirit was to be universal, in keeping with John's prophecy. Jesus himself reiterated the promise in the forty-day instruction period before the Ascension:

> [4]On one occasion, while he was eating with them, he gave them this command: "Do not leave Jerusalem, but wait for the gift my Father promised, which you have heard me speak about. [5]For John baptized with water, but in a few days you will be baptized with the Holy Spirit" (Acts 1:4–5).

Unless Jesus was mistaken, something was to happen in May of 30 AD which was entirely new. This was a radical departure from God's normal way of being with his people in Old Covenant times. The position taken in this chapter is that *all Christians have been baptized with the Spirit*.[10]

Water and Spirit

The new birth has two elements: water and Spirit. Since we are born again of water and Spirit, is it not simple, symmetrical and biblically accurate to say we are baptized of water and Spirit? Weigh carefully the passage in John's gospel:

> [3]In reply Jesus declared, "I tell you the truth, no one can see the kingdom of God unless he is born again."
>
> [4]"How can a man be born when he is old?" Nicodemus asked. "Surely he cannot enter a second time into his mother's womb to be born!"
>
> [5]Jesus answered, "I tell you the truth, no one can enter the kingdom of God unless he is born of water and the Spirit. [6]Flesh gives birth to flesh, but the Spirit gives birth to spirit. [7]You should not be surprised at my saying, 'You must be born again'" (John 3:3-7).

Many exegetes contend that all Christians are born of water, but only the apostles were born, or baptized, of Spirit. They say the apostles represented the Jews, and Cornelius and company, the Gentiles, and thus that "all flesh" received the outpouring. But why separate water from Spirit? Besides, nowhere does the Bible say one person can be baptized (representatively) for another. (And about baptism in Spirit and fire: If only a few men were to receive the baptism in the Spirit, are only a few sent to hell, representing the rest of us?) Surely this is an overreaction to Neopentecostalism.

Let's take a closer look at the logic of John 3.

Born of water   => Baptized in water
John 3:5[11]   Acts 8:36, 38, 1 Peter 3:21

Born of Spirit   => Baptized in Spirit
John 3:3, 3:8[12]   1 Corinthians 12:13, Mark 1:8

We understand that we are born of water and Spirit. We understand that water and spirit are two elements of one birth. We understand that birth of water refers to baptism in water. Isn't it odd that we should not see that birth of the Spirit refers to baptism in the Spirit? Understanding that we are all baptized in the Spirit when we are baptized into Christ is not only the most natural and consistent reading of all the passages on Spirit baptism; it is also the easiest view to defend.

> [4]But when the kindness and love of God our Savior appeared, [5]he saved us, not because of righteous things we had done, but because of his

mercy. He saved us through the washing of rebirth and renewal by the Holy Spirit, ⁶whom he poured out on us generously through Jesus Christ our Savior (Titus 3:4-6).

Paul's letter to Titus reminds us that the Spirit was poured out on us when we became Christians. In baptism, the water is available (it has already been "poured out," and is present in the baptistery, lake, river…), and yet it floods over us, immersing us, only when we come personally into contact with the it. Similarly, the Spirit was poured out at Pentecost, yet it "immerses" us and is poured into our hearts (Titus 3:6, Romans 5:5) only *when* we are baptized in Spirit. What 1 Corinthians 12:13 and John 3:5 do is to tie water and Spirit together in one event: baptism.

Further Considerations

1. "How can the Spirit, poured out nearly two millennia ago, still be appropriated today?"

The Bible does not limit the effects of past events to the past; historical events may have continuing and present effects. Jesus died in the first century AD, yet that death becomes real and practical for us only when we become Christians. Once we are baptized into Christ (Romans 6:3, Galatians 3:27)—and not earlier than that time—we too "die." Our "old self was crucified with him" (Romans 6:6, 6:1-4). We "died" (Colossians 3:3, 1:22, 2:12, 3:5). We were "crucified *with* Christ" (Galatians 2:20, emphasis added), "crucified to the world" (Galatians 6:14, 5:24). But, once again, we "die" only when we are baptized into Christ. The Holy Spirit baptism is parallel to this: The Spirit was poured out, yet only when we are immersed into Christ does it become ours. The historical becomes personal and practical. We thus are baptized with the Spirit, just as we die with Christ—provided we appropriate those blessings in receiving the gospel.

2. It is objected, "Ephesians 4:5 allows for only one baptism. If there is Spirit baptism and water baptism, there were two baptisms, at least at the time Paul wrote Ephesians."

This is a weak argument. As we read, John 3:5 says there are two components to the one baptism! The New Testament teaches there are three "persons" to the one God. The kingdom of God and the kingdom of heaven are one and the same, not two. We must read more carefully.

3. "If all of us have been baptized in the Spirit, then" it might be objected, "all

of us should have the miraculous gifts or be able to work miracles."

Such a statement manifests a fundamental confusion about the gifts of the Spirit. Jesus and Jesus alone baptized in the Spirit. But he does not confer the gifts. The Spirit is the one who gives us gifts and power (1 Corinthians 12:11). Besides, as we have already argued, the apostles performed miracles long before the outpouring of the Spirit (Luke 9:2). The miraculous phenomena were indeed primarily for the apostles; this is not a point of dispute. But where does the Bible say that Spirit baptism confers miraculous powers? (That is the Neopentecostal interpretation!) Moreover, John the Baptist never said miraculous signs would accompany Spirit baptism.

4. "Isn't the Holy Spirit baptism only for the apostles, according to Acts 1 and John 14 and 16?"[13]

If we assume that John 14:26 and 16:13 are fulfilled for the apostles at Pentecost when they are baptized in the Spirit (assuming John 20:22 is a piece of prophetic drama), and if we assume the Caesareans had the identical experience, it is difficult to see why the promises of Jesus in John do not also apply to Cornelius. I do not deny Acts 2 and Acts 10 are nonrepeatable, historically unique events. Nor do I deny that Acts 2 and Acts 10 are linked in some way, and that the term "baptism in the Holy Spirit" is used in connection with both of them. But there are serious problems with maintaining that these two events completely sum up the meaning of "the baptism in the Holy Spirit."

5. Returning to Luke 3, either the Spirit and the fire[14] apply to the apostles and the apostles only, or to all believers.

Let's be consistent! Take another look at Luke 3:16:

> John answered them all, "I baptize you with water. But one more powerful than I will come, the thongs of whose sandals I am not worthy to untie. He will baptize you with the Holy Spirit and with fire."

The most natural understanding of the Baptist's promise is that it applies to all believers.[15] Again, if the promise of Acts 1:5 refers only to the apostles, it cannot include Cornelius. This puts some strain on the Acts 2/Acts 10 view, unless we widen the application of Acts 1:5 to include all mankind. If that is the case, then all of us have been baptized in the Spirit, not in an experience supplementary to conversion, but *as a result* of the Pentecostal outpouring, and *through* the new birth.

Outpouring and the Old Testament

The baptism in the Holy Spirit, as described in Matthew 3, Mark 1, Luke 3, John 1 and Acts 1 is possible because of the historic outpouring of the Holy Spirit. This view makes sense of the Old Testament prophets.

Joel prophesied, "And afterwards, I will pour out my Spirit on all people" (Joel 2:28). Joel's prophecy informs us that all people are to benefit from the outpoured Spirit. Now this no more means God pours the Spirit on unbelievers, than "therefore all died" (2 Corinthians 5:14) means that every person has been saved by sharing in Christ's death through baptism. Our response is the deciding factor.

Isaiah (eighth century BC) also looked forward to the age of the Spirit (Isaiah 32:15, 44:3):

> "Till the Spirit is poured upon us from on high,
>   and the desert becomes a fertile field,
>   and the fertile field seems like a forest....
> For I will pour out water on the thirsty land,
>   and streams on the dry ground,
> I will pour out my Spirit on your offspring,
>   and my blessing on your descendants."

Then Ezekiel (sixth century) had a similar vision (Ezekiel 39:29):

> "I will no longer hide my face from them, for I will pour out my Spirit on the house of Israel," declares the Sovereign LORD.

In the late sixth century, Zechariah offered the same message of hope (Zechariah 12:10, 13:1, 14:8):

> "And I will pour out on the house of David and the inhabitants of Jerusalem a Spirit of grace and supplication. They will look on me, the one they have pierced, and they will mourn for him as one mourns for an only child....
>
> "On that day a fountain will be opened to the house of David and the inhabitants of Jerusalem, to cleanse them from sin and im- purity....
>
> "On that day living water will flow out from Jerusalem."

Finally John, the last of the prophets of the Old Testament, prophesied the same thing (Mark 1:8): "I baptize you with water, but he will baptize you with the Holy Spirit." The Old Testament prophets anticipated the age of the new covenant, the age of the Spirit in which we are blessed to live (Matthew 11:11). Peter says in Acts 2:16, "This is what was spoken by the prophet Joel." Pentecost is the fulfillment of the promised outpouring of the Spirit (Acts 2:33).

Pouring and Immersing

Are "baptism" and "outpouring" identical? No, but they do describe the same event from two different viewpoints. From the perspective of heaven, the Spirit was poured out; from the perspective of the earth, there was a baptism in the Spirit. Pouring is the event from Jesus' viewpoint. Baptizing is the event from the recipient's viewpoint.

To cite an often quoted illustration, a coin placed in a glass is immersed after water is poured upon it. The pouring is not the immersion; it is the water leaving the source. The immersion is not the pouring; it is the result, the covering of the coin. So it is here in this case.

The Spirit is available for all who are willing to drink (1 Corinthians 12:13). But Pentecost can never be repeated; it was a once-for-all event.[16]

Summary

As we have seen, the "warm, fuzzy feeling" so prized today in Neopentecostal circles is ninety-five percent fantasy and five percent Scripture. The baptism in the Spirit is a result of the outpouring prophesied by Joel (Acts 2:16–17, Joel 2:28–32), rooted firmly in God's historical purposes. Perhaps it would be helpful to list what it was not:

1. a second measure of the Spirit intended to equip the saints for greater service.
2. to confer miraculous abilities. The apostles worked miracles even before they received the Spirit (Luke 9:2).
3. administered by man. In the New Testament it was not received through special services or crusades.
4. the means whereby Christians received the gift of tongues. Not everybody in the first century spoke in tongues (1 Corinthians 12:10, 30).
5. the only means whereby one is filled with the Spirit. Peter was filled with the Spirit in Acts 2:4, and subsequently in Acts 4:8. Paul was filled with the Spirit initially in Acts 9:17, and subsequently, in Acts 13:9.
6. an experience creating a second order of Christians. There is only life in the Spirit and life in the flesh (Romans 7–8).

Because of that unique event—the historic outpouring of the Spirit on the day of Pentecost in Jerusalem—all mankind may receive the baptism in the Spirit. The experience of the apostles in Acts 2 results from that outpouring, as does the experience of the three thousand, who received the now-available gift of the indwelling Spirit. The supernatural spiritual gifts the church received for its edification are also a consequence of the outpouring of the Spirit at Pentecost. Cornelius and the other early Gentile Christians received the Spirit first externally (outpouring), then inwardly (indwelling) in Christian baptism.

Finally, the Spirit continues to be "poured out" as we are baptized in the Spirit at conversion (Titus 3:6) and as we pray for God to fill us and work through us as his people (Acts 4:23, 31).

Quite simply, all disciples were baptized in the Spirit by virtue of their baptism in water.

NOTES

1. I put it in quotation marks because I do not consider it to have been a true conversion.

2. Some parts of this section are somewhat controversial. Views presented are those of the author, not necessarily of the publisher.

3. The largest Neopentecostal denomination in the world, the Assemblies of God, affirms this tenet in its Statement of Fundamental Truths: "The baptism of believers in the Holy Ghost is witnessed by the initial physical sign of speaking with other tongues" (§ 8).

4. And well illuminated in Hank Hanegraaff's *Counterfeit Revival: Looking for God in All the Wrong Places* (Dallas: Word Publishing, 1997).

5. Ironically, Pentecostal theology fails to grasp the historical significance of Pentecost: the commencement of the new covenant.

6. It is also erroneously assumed that Saul became a Christian before he was baptized. This is wrong (Acts 22:16). Furthermore, Ananias laid hands on him not to baptize him in the Spirit but to restore his sight (9:12, 17).

7. Accounts of "warm, fuzzy feelings" are common in the history of Christianity. Consider the following conversion account from the journal of John Wesley.

> What occurred on Wednesday the 24th, I think best to relate at large, after premissing what may make it the better understood. Let him that cannot receive it ask of the Father of lights that He would give more light both to him and me. I think it was about five this morning, that I opened my Testament on those words, 'There are given unto us exceeding great and precious promises even that ye should be partakers of the divine nature' (2 Peter i.4). Just as I went out, I opened it again on those words, 'Thou art not far from the kingdom

of God.' In the afternoon I was asked to go to St. Paul's. The anthem was, 'Out of the deep have I called unto Thee, O Lord: Lord, hear my voice. O let Thine ears consider well the voice of my complaint. If thou, Lord, wilt be extreme to mark what is done amiss, O Lord, who may abide it? But there is mercy with Thee; therefore thou shalt be feared. O Israel, trust in the Lord; for with the Lord there is mercy, and with Him is plenteous redemption. And he shall redeem Israel from all his sins.

In the evening I went very unwillingly to a society in Aldersgate Street, where one was reading Luther's Preface to the Epistle to the Romans.

About a quarter before nine, while he was describing the change which God works in the heart through faith in Christ, I felt my heart strangely warmed. I felt I did trust in Christ, Christ alone for salvation; and an assurancy was given me that He had taken away my sins, even mine, and saved me from the law of sin and death" (*John Wesley's Journal*, Wednesday May 24th, 1738).

8. Most who hold this view go on to say that although Acts 1:5 indicates that the experience was for the apostles, Acts 11:15–17 implies that Cornelius, his relatives and close friends also shared in this historical experience, thus fulfilling Joel's prophecy that the Holy Spirit baptism would come on "all flesh," both Jews and Gentiles, representatively (Joel 2:28, Acts 2:17).

9. Incidentally, although I would not dispute that the apostles received their doctrinal gift at the Holy Spirit baptism, this was not their first promise of inspiration; see Matthew 10:20.

10. This is the same position I took in my 1987 book *The Powerful Delusion*, and though I have sharpened the view, it has not substantially changed. Douglas Jacoby, *The Powerful Delusion* (London: C.L.C.C., 1987). For a nearly identical view, see Gordon Ferguson's *Prepared to Answer* (Billerica, Mass.: Illumination Publishers 2008) pp. 143-148.

11. See also Ephesians 5:26, Hebrews 10:22.

12. See also Galatians 4:29, 1 John 5:4–6.

13. If so, it wasn't only Matthias who was missing something; even the apostle Paul would have missed out on the promise. And Cornelius wouldn't have stood a chance! Luke 3:15-17 shows that the Holy Spirit baptism was for more than just the Twelve.

14. Some ask whether the baptism in fire might not refer to the tongues of fire in Acts 2. Yes, that is possible, if we are willing to allow sprinkling or pouring instead of immersion! Since the apostles were never immersed in fire, this is an unlikely suggestion.

15. Some believe this refers to the universal day of judgment, others the destruction of Jerusalem in 70 AD (Luke says that the axe is already at the root of the trees, implying an imminent judgment. Moreover, Malachi 3 and 4 show that the winnowing and the burning are to happen to the Jewish nation. John comes first ("Elijah"—Matthew 11:14) and then Jesus (Malachi 3:1) before the great and dreadful day of the Lord (Malachi 4:5).

16. That the outpouring of the Spirit was a once-for-all event, not to be repeated (e.g. Acts 10), is supported by a study of the verb "has poured out" (Acts 2:33) in the original language. The verb is in the aorist aspect. What that means is that the outpouring as an action occurred at one specific point in time. It is hard to see how the prophets could even have imagined separate outpourings for Jews and Gentiles, especially as their visions often included the Gentiles anyway (e.g. Isaiah 26:18, 42:6, 45:22, 49:6, 66:19-21).

25. The Unforgivable Sin?
'Who Then Can Be Saved?'

Feeling challenged after some of the things in this book (especially in Part One)? Wondering whether you have the Holy Spirit at all? Alas, the Spirit does remind us "we all stumble in many ways" (James 3:2, John 16:8)—just to keep us humble! Sometimes when you realize the commitment the Lord expects, you may look at your life and gasp, as did the disciples, "Who then can be saved?" (Mark 10:26). If so, chances are slim you have committed the unforgivable sin, the subject of this short chapter.

The Blasphemy

One of my all-time favorite movies is *Indiana Jones and the Last Crusade*. I viewed this action-packed Harrison Ford classic in a cinema full of Christians. In the movie, father and son are searching for the "Holy Grail," the cup from which Jesus supposedly drank wine at the Last Supper. One scene was particularly enjoyable: Indiana Jones (the son) takes the Lord's name in vain, and his father (played by Sean Connery), a more reverent man, reacts strongly. He slaps his son's face, exclaiming, "That's the blasphemy!" (Yes, the theater broke into spontaneous applause!)

What is the blasphemy of the Spirit? Is it violating the third commandment? What is God trying to teach us through the scriptures that mention it?

The Point of No Return

God is a God of grace, and yet the Bible clearly teaches that there is a "point of no return." In the Old Testament we read, "A man who remains stiff-necked after many rebukes will suddenly be destroyed—without remedy" (Proverbs 29:1). In the New Testament there are several passages on the subject. Consider the epistle to the Hebrews, for example:

> [26]If we deliberately keep on sinning after we have received the knowledge of the truth, no sacrifice for sins is left, [27]but only a fear- ful expectation of judgment and of raging fire that will consume the enemies of God. [28]Anyone who rejected the law of Moses died without mercy on the testimony of two or three witnesses. [29]How much more severely do you think a man deserves to be punished who has trampled the Son of

God under foot, who has treated as an unholy thing the blood of the covenant that sanctified him, and who has insulted the Spirit of grace? [30]For we know him who said, "It is mine to avenge; I will repay," and again, "The Lord will judge his people." [31]It is a dreadful thing to fall into the hands of the living God (Hebrews 10:26–31).

This passage is, unfortunately, often preached incorrectly. In the context of Hebrews, the sin in question is total apostasy—giving up on Jesus and returning to one's old religion (2:1-3, 3:14, 4:1-11, 6:4-12). The Spirit of grace has been insulted (Hebrews 10:29), not because someone told a lie or got drunk a number of times, but because someone has rejected the sacrifice of Jesus as necessary or sufficient for salvation. The truth (v. 26) has been rejected and the covenant has been repudiated (v. 29). This is a conscious, willful decision to turn one's back on Jesus—more than a "down time" spiritually or a temporary relapse.

The issue is not so much at what point one is "without remedy," but that there is such a point. It may be no more possible to pin down than the elusive "age of accountability" at which one is ready to repent and become a disciple of Jesus. The Scriptures do teach that one may reach a fatal hardness of heart.

The Context

In the passage below we see the hardness of heart of the Pharisees, who could not see the truth in front of their eyes. Attributing the work of God to Satan was not the thing for which Jesus said that they stood condemned and without hope of forgiveness. Nor was it their bad logic, in attributing to Satan something that would have undermined Satan. It was, rather, irremediable hardness of heart that prompted Jesus to say they could not be forgiven.

[22]Then they brought him a demon-possessed man who was blind and mute, and Jesus healed him, so that he could both talk and see. [23]All the people were astonished and said, "Could this be the Son of David?"

[24]But when the Pharisees heard this, they said, "It is only by Beelzebub, the prince of demons, that this fellow drives out demons." [25]Jesus knew their thoughts and said to them, "Every kingdom divided against itself will be ruined, and every city or household divided against itself will not stand. [26]If Satan drives out Satan, he is divided against himself. How then can his kingdom stand? [27]And if I drive out demons by Beelzebub, by whom do your people drive them out? So then, they will be your judges. [28]But if I drive out demons by the Spirit of God, then the kingdom of God has come upon you.

²⁹"Or again, how can anyone enter a strong man's house and carry off his possessions unless he first ties up the strong man? Then he can rob his house.
³⁰ "He who is not with me is against me, and he who does not gather with me scatters. ³¹And so I tell you, every sin and blasphemy will be forgiven men, but the blasphemy against the Spirit will not be forgiven. ³²Anyone who speaks a word against the Son of Man will be forgiven, but anyone who speaks against the Holy Spirit will not be forgiven, either in this age or in the age to come" (Matthew 12:22–32).

Jesus remarks that speaking against him (the Son of Man) is less serious than speaking against (blaspheming) the Spirit. What? Is one member of the trinity more touchy than another? Such cannot be the case. Jesus must be saying that not all enemies of the truth are beyond recovery. Some, however, have crossed the line and God's Spirit cannot work in their hearts; they are broken beyond repair.

Interestingly, the apostle Paul discloses that before his baptism he was a blasphemer (1 Timothy 1:13). He spoke against Jesus and attempted to force others to do the same. Still, he did so with great zeal and good conscience (Galatians 1:13–14, Acts 23:1). He did not go beyond "the point of no return." Yet the other apostles, initially at least, seemed to have thought his situation was hopeless (Acts 9:26). How many people do you know who are worse than (pre-Christian) Paul?

So if you find yourself wondering whether you have committed the unforgivable sin, it is virtually certain you haven't. You are still walking with God, coming to church, sharing your faith, caring for the needy. (People like this usually have pretty good hearts. Please, let's not harshly judge motives—1 Corinthians 4:3–5.)

All things considered, we must conclude that the sin against the Spirit is not an action but a state of heart. Once again, and for the record, feeling guilty or having a low time spiritually is not the sin against the Spirit.

'But Sometimes I Feel So Guilty!'

You may say, "But sometimes I feel so guilty." So do I. We may feel guilty because of sin. Once we have confessed it and "renounced it" (Proverbs 28:13), we can once again "sing and be glad" (Proverbs 29:6). Guilt feelings are God's way of letting us know something is not right. (The sin against the Spirit is much more than this.) Moreover, feeling guilty isn't the same as being guilty. Many are guilty without feeling any remorse, and there are many troubled souls that feel burdened although they have done little to warrant it. Sometimes we have been conditioned to feel certain ways. In time, as we mature spiritually, we can learn to grow out of this kind of false guilt.

The First Day of the Rest of Your Life

Good news: Jesus makes sure our sins are forgiven, even when we as Christians "should know better" (1 John 2:1–2). Here's more good news: You have the rest of your life to let the Spirit transform you, root out the sin and smooth out every wrinkle!

26. Everything You Always Wanted to Know, 1
Difficult Questions About the Spirit

Some of the questions answered below review material covered elsewhere in the book. This chapter is intended first as a refresher and second as a springboard for those who want to dive deeper into our subject. Hopefully between this chapter and the next, most of everything you wanted to know, you will know!

1. What is the 'Holy Ghost'?

Sounds spooky! Why "ghost"? "Ghost" was the Elizabethan[1] term for the "spirit"; and "spirit" was the word we would use nowadays for "ghost." Thus, in the King James Version when the disciples saw Jesus walking on water, they cried out in terror, "It is a spirit!" And before his ascension he instructed that people be baptized in the name of the Father, Son and Holy Ghost. Since in our English the meanings of the terms are reversed, it is better to say "Holy Spirit" than "Holy Ghost."

In the Greek of the New Testament, as well as in the Hebrew of the Old Testament, the word translated "spirit" also means "breath or wind." (Hebrew *ruach*, Greek *pneuma*.) The exact translation must be determined by the context.

2. *He, She* or *It*?

Good question! It is often noted that the pronouns in the New Testament used to refer to the Spirit are consistently masculine, although the word pneuma is neuter. This is deliberate, and so in some sense it is fair to say that the Spirit is a "he." Also, God is referred to as "he"—not that God is sexual, but the male-female analogy correctly defines the God-human relationship. (We are "the bride of Christ." God protects and "provides" for us. We "have the children"—bear fruit—for him.) If you feel more comfortable calling the Spirit "it," I think that is fine.[2]

The Holy Spirit has mind, will and affections (Romans 8:27, 1 Corinthians 12:11, Romans 15:30). He speaks, teaches and leads (1 Timothy 4:1, John 14:26, Acts 16:6-10). He can even be resisted, grieved, blasphemed or lied to (Acts 7:51, Ephesians 4:30, Matthew 12:31, Acts 5:3). None of these things would be possible if the Spirit were not personal. Moreover, the Spirit is omniscient, omnipresent and eternal (1 Corinthians 2:10, Psalm 139:7–10, Hebrews 9:14)—in short, divine. He is more than just an influence, or an impersonal force like gravity or magnetism; he is a Divine Person and a member of the trinity (see Question 7).

3. What does it mean to be "filled with the Spirit"?

It means to be a thoroughly spiritual person; also it means to receive power from the Spirit in response to a specific need or request. The filling extends to every nook and cranny of our lives (see Chapter 1).

In Acts 6:3, Stephen and Philip were Spirit-filled before they received miraculous abilities. John the Baptist was Spirit-filled before birth (Luke 1:15), yet he never performed a miracle (John 10:41). The Neopentecostal claim that being filled with the Spirit is miraculous must be dismissed.

4. Do miracles prove that someone is saved?

Not at all! See Deuteronomy 13:1–5, 1 Samuel 19:18–24, Matthew 7:21–23, Mark 13:22, Acts 19:13, 2 Thessalonians 2:9–11, Revelation 13:13. Even unsaved people may work, or appear to work, miracles.

5. What does it mean to be "led by the Spirit"?

It actually has next to nothing to do with divining God's will. It is not "reading your feelings" (Proverbs 14:12, Jeremiah 17:9). Rather it is triumphing over the flesh by the Spirit (Galatians 5:16-26, Romans 8:1–16)—a learning process—and there are no shortcuts (Psalm 143:10, Ezekiel 36:27). Someone who falls into sin over and over again needs to submit to the leading of the Spirit. (For more, see Chapter 9.)

6. What is the primary purpose of biblical miracles?

Miracles were for bringing people the word of God. See Exodus 4:5, 1 Kings 17:24, Mark 16:20, Acts 14:3, Hebrews 2:4. Nearly every biblical miracle happened in one of the three bursts of miraculous activity in biblical history: at the giving of the law (Moses), at the rise of the prophetic movement (Elijah) and at the proclamation of the gospel (Jesus). Miracles never confirmed the written word, only the spoken word (a.k.a. new revelation).

There is no new revelation today, as the Bible is completed and canonized.[3] (See Chapter 19.)

7. Can you feel the Spirit in you?

Aren't there some days when we feel spiritually stronger than on others?

Is this not the working of the Spirit in our hearts? (Ephesians 3:16). To deny that we can feel God's Spirit in our hearts—or the effects of it—is to overreact to the superstitious view. This is not to encourage the "warm, fuzzy feeling" mentality, only to offer an explanation for the everyday reality of the feeling of spiritual strength or weakness (compare Psalm 32 and 38 with Psalm 18:28–50). However, there is no biblical evidence for the claim that the Spirit gives us personal direction(s) through our feelings.

8. Can you ever lose the Spirit?

No passage of scripture says the "deposit" (2 Corinthians 1:22, 5:5) is withdrawn if we lose our faith. We may live in a state of grieving the Spirit (Ephesians 4:30), and we can quench the Spirit's fire within us (1 Thessalonians 5:19), but no one needs to receive the Spirit over again. When Simon's heart became evil, he was not told to consider a second baptism, only to pray to God for forgiveness (Acts 8:22).

9. Are our spirits reincarnated?

Hebrews 9:27 is enough to answer that question: "Man is destined to die once and after that to face judgment." See also Job 7:9–10.

Teachers like Edgar Cayce say Jesus taught reincarnation when he identified John the Baptist with Elijah. Yet John denied being Elijah (John 1), and Jesus said he was the one coming "in the spirit of" Elijah (Luke 1). In other words, he was spiritually like Elijah. For if he actually were Elijah, how do you explain Jesus' "summit" meeting with him and Moses atop the Mount of Transfiguration? You can't! There is no evidence at all for reincarnation. And we have not even begun to discuss the mathematical problems involved with the recycling of so many souls in light of present world population!

10. What is the "indwelling"?

Many passages testify to the fact that the Spirit lives in our hearts (Romans 8:9, 1 Corinthians 6:19, 2 Timothy 1:14). God lives in us by the gift of the Spirit received at baptism (Acts 2:38–39). This living in our hearts on the part of the Spirit is called "the indwelling," since the Spirit dwells in us.

11. Does the Spirit live and work in us only through the Word?

There is a school of thought that claims the Spirit works in us only through his representative, the Word. It is denied that the Spirit lives "personally" in our hearts.

Without a doubt there is a link of the most intimate kind between the Spirit and the Word. For example, many things normally attributed in the Bible to the Spirit are also attributed to the Word:

- The Word quickens ["preserves my life" in NIV] us (Psalm 119:50).
- The Word strengthens us (Psalm 119:28).
- The Word sanctifies us (John 17:17).
- The Word gives us wisdom (2 Timothy 3:14–15).
- The Word enlightens us (Psalm 119:130).
- The Word allows us to share in the divine nature (2 Peter 1:4).

However, there is not sufficient grounds to say that the Spirit works only through the Word, or the sword of the Spirit (Ephesians 6:17). If this were the case Acts 2:38 would need to be reworded, in principle at least, to read, "Repent and be baptized, every one of you, in the name of Jesus Christ so that your sins will be forgiven. And you will receive the word of God." This is certainly not the natural reading, as even advocates of the view will admit. Acts 2 refers to the promised Holy Spirit several times (vv. 17, 33, 38, 39). Furthermore, the natural reading of such verses as Acts 5:32, 1 John 3:24, and John 14:16–23 is not that God has given us his representative but his actual presence.

It would seem accurate to say that the Spirit in our hearts does his work through the Word or that God is able to work in us to the extent that we surrender to his Word. In closing, the fact that we can only know the Holy Spirit as he reveals himself through the Word is accepted, but it has no bearing on how the Spirit dwells in the Christian.

12. Is it wrong to ask God for an "open door"?

Asking God to open a door is not the same thing as "fleecing." The difference is this: If you try to "put out a fleece," you are free to do whatever you wish regardless of the outcome, since the fleece is not directly related to the course of action you are considering. If God does not open a door, however, you are not free to do what you please, since your decision hinges on God's changing the situation by opening the door. (You can walk through an open door, but not through a fleece!) There is nothing wrong with asking God for an open door (Colossians 4:3).

13. What about prophecy in the Old Testament?

Old Testament prophecy was normally *preaching based on visions!*

Moses was the exception to the rule. Think about Numbers 12:6b–8a:

> "When a prophet of the LORD is among you,
>> I reveal myself to him in visions,
>> I speak to him in dreams.
> But this is not true of my servant Moses;
>> he is faithful in all my house.
> With him I speak face to face,
>> clearly and not in riddles;
>> he sees the form of the LORD."

Normally, a prophet would have a vision of God (Hosea 12:10, Joel 2:28, Micah 3:6), usually in a dream while he slept (Deuteronomy 13:1, 1 Samuel 3:1,16, 1 Kings 3:5–15, 1 Chronicles 17:3, and the otherwise enigmatic Jeremiah 31:26). Based on that vision he would preach to the needs of the people. The prophet had time to reflect on the meaning of the vision before preaching, and he was in full control of his prophetic presentation (1 Corinthians 14:32).

Moses was exceptional. With him God did not speak indirectly, through visions; with Moses he spoke directly, face to face.[4] Let's now turn our attention to Exodus 7:1:

> Then the LORD said to Moses, "See, I have made you like God to Pharaoh, and your brother Aaron will be your prophet."

Moses is like God, and Aaron is Moses' "prophet"; in other words, Aaron is really only a channel for Moses' message. *God speaks to men through men* (not a bad definition of prophecy).

It is true that prophecy often had a predictive element. Many religious leaders are well known for their predictions, most of which either are too vague to test or fail to come true. (On a random hit-or-miss basis, a certain percentage of predictions are bound to be accurate.) In the Old Testament any "prophet" whose "prophecy" came to naught was to be executed! (Deuteronomy 18:20–22). That is how seriously God takes false prophecy. But overall, prophecy in the Bible is more a matter of preaching than of prediction, as is clear from Ezra 6:14a:

> So the elders of the Jews continued to build and prosper under the preaching of Haggai the prophet and Zechariah, a descendant of Iddo.

Haggai and Zechariah (coworkers active around 520 BC) were prophets. What did that mean? It meant they were preachers. They spoke to people's needs. They spoke to contemporaries. Rather than writing for a generation yet unborn (which they unwittingly did on occasion), prophets addressed the present generation. Amos 7:15-16 is also relevant:

> But the LORD took me from tending the flock and said to me, "Go, prophesy to my people Israel." Now then, hear the word of the LORD. You say,
>
> "Do not prophesy against Israel,
>   and stop preaching against the house of Isaac" (Amos 7:15–16).

In typical poetic parallelism, prophecy and preaching are synonymous. Prophetic messages were nearly always challenging. How different to the ethereal "prophecies" one hears in some churches today!

In closing, it should be said that the Old Testament scriptures are collectively "prophetic," in the broadest sense, according to Jesus (Matthew 11:13). How much the genealogies and a few other types of literature in the Old Testament contribute to the overall prophetic effect is debatable. The point stands: Old Testament prophecy was normally preaching based on visions.

14. What is "the laying on of hands"?

In Neopentecostal circles, "the laying on of hands" normally accompanies attempts to heal or to induce the experience of "Holy Spirit baptism." Understanding the Old Testament background is helpful:

    a. Genesis 48:14 (blessing)
    b. Leviticus 1:4 (sacrifice)
    c. Leviticus 14:18 (in connection with atonement)
    d. Numbers 8:10 (ordination)
    e. Numbers 27:18/Deuteronomy 34:9 (commissioning)
    f. 2 Kings 4:34 (healing)

In the New Testament, all types are found except b and c (Matthew 19:15, Acts 13:3, Mark 16:18). If we were to add to the list, purpose (g) would be for the transmission of a supernatural gift of the Spirit.

    g. Acts 8:18 (apostolic laying on of hands)

15. What's the difference between soul and spirit?

In Hebrews 4:12, spirit refers to the human spirit. The sword penetrates the heart, dividing (human) soul from (human) spirit. Is this a poetic way of describing the state of being unprepared at Judgment Day, or is something deeper indicated? That is hard to say.

We moderns may be tempted to impose our own categories of thought on biblical concepts and terminology. When I was a small child, I believed that when one died, his soul left his body. Yet in the Old Testament, *nephesh* includes the body. Even in older English usage, one might say "all souls lost" (as in a shipwreck). Yet nowadays such phraseology is rare. You may also remember that in the older English versions of the parable of the rich fool (Luke 12), the materialistic fool speaks to himself, "Soul, you have plenty of good things." In mainstream biblical thought, it must be emphasized that soul is not a part of the person; it is the person.

The spirit, on the other hand, is not the person, but something interior and immaterial. (Recall that spirit in the biblical languages also can mean breath.) Spirit was not conceived as something imaginary or intangible, but rather something very real, even if hidden from sight. Spirit is nothing else than the gift of God to every human, which inclines toward doing what is right—in contrast to the flesh, which inclines toward doing what is wrong.

This means that the soul has free will. It must choose between spirit and flesh. "The spirit is willing, but the flesh is weak" (Mark 14:38).

To divide soul and spirit, then (Hebrews 4:12), would mean to distinguish the spiritual aspect of a person (spirit) from the decision-making soul.

In 1 Thessalonians 5:23 spirit, soul, and body are not three separate parts of a person. Rather, they refer to the person in three different aspects: the spiritual person, the entire person, and the physical person. There Paul is asking for thorough sanctification for the Thessalonians.

16. Are miracles necessary today?

No, miracles are not essential. Luke 16:19–31 and John 20:30–31 make this crystal clear! By the way, this should not be taken as a statement that God *cannot* do miracles, for he certainly can (Psalm 115:3), nor that he does not on occasion answer prayers miraculously. Today we can read of the previous miracles (John 20:30-31) and believe, especially the miracle of the Resurrection (Luke 16:19–31).[5]

17. What are "tongues"?

"Tongues" are actual languages miraculously acquired (Acts 2:3–12, 1 Corinthians 14:10). "Tongue" is a more common, early Modern English word for "language," appearing in the KJV.[6] Today's *glossolalia* is an easily produced psychological phenomenon, common to many man-made religions around the world. In the New Testament, tongues had to be translated if spoken in the assembly (church). In the confused Corinthian fellowship, tongue-speaking was the most highly valued and yet least valuable gift (1 Corinthians 12:30–31). The Bible nowhere says we can speak in the languages of angels (1 Corinthians 13:1), and more than that, that we can move mountains (literally) or possess all knowledge! (The "if" of 1 Corinthians 13:1 proves nothing about the actual existence of angel languages—any more than Obadiah 4 proves some people make their nest in the stars.) And even if we could, without love we would be nothing!

18. What is "quenching the Spirit"?

The reference (1 Thessalonians 5:19 KJV) concerns how prophetic messages were treated. In context (vv. 19–23), they are instructed to show respect (not contempt) and to assess the messages, clearly separating gold from dross.

19. How were the miraculous spiritual gifts received?

Mainly through the laying on of the apostles' hands. See Acts 6:6, 6:8, 8:6, 8:14ff, 8:18, Romans 1:11, 1 Corinthians 1:7 and 2 Timothy 1:6. In the early church, the recorded miracles were done almost exclusively *by* or *in the presence of an apostle* (Acts 2:43). Church history records a decline and an eventual end to the miracles. Thus after one full generation, during which the New Testament was written and disseminated, the miraculous gifts came to an end.[7]

20. Are you charismatic?

Insofar as *charismatikos* (Greek) means "gifted," yes, you are. First, most of the gifts of the Spirit are still present today. Second, the Spirit is moving powerfully as the kingdom of God advances: The gospel is preached, lives change, souls are saved, the church is growing, the poor are helped, God is glorified.

_____ NOTES _____

1. Elizabethan (Shakespearean) English was spoken in the sixteenth and seventeenth centuries. Sometimes this is mistakenly called "Old English." In fact, Old English (*Beowulf*) was phased out and replaced by Middle English (Chaucer) in the eleventh century,

which in turn gave way to Modern English by the year 1500. Despite the alien feel of King James English, it is still technically classified as "modern"!

2. Interestingly, early Syriac manuscripts use the feminine personal pronoun for the Spirit! See George Anton Kiraz, *Comparative Edition of the Syriac Gospels, Aligning the Sinaiticus, Curetonianus, Peshitta and Harklean Version, Vol. I* (Leiden: Brill, 1996), reviewed in Novum Testamentum, Vol. XXXIX, Fasc. 4 (October 1997), 405-412.

3. In the Old Testament, far less had been revealed about the nature of God's Spirit. According to Michael Ramsay, hundredth Archbishop of Canterbury, "'Spirit' in the writings of the Old Testament is not a person or a definable object or substance. It is a mode of describing how the holy God is active in the world he created, and especially in persons in whom his purpose is fulfilled." *Holy Spirit* (Grand Rapids, MI: Eerdmans, 1977), 10.

He continues: "In the church of the early centuries it was the tendency to continue the terminology found in the New Testament writings. The Greek and Latin Fathers, when they wrote of the activity of God in nature or pagan philosophy, would use the term Logos rather than Spirit. Such was the concentration of the Church upon the sphere of redemption and often upon hostility to the world, that a Christian concern about the presence of God in nature was often far to seek" (123).

4. This distinction also helps to clarify 1 Corinthians 13:10. Interestingly, the TNIV says "when completeness comes, what is in part disappears." This is an improvement over the NIV's "perfection."

5. Incidentally, John 14:12 cannot mean that we should expect to do miracles, for who has done "greater" miracles than Jesus? Who do you know who has walked on water or healed the blind? The "greater things" seems to apply to the scope and extent of the Great Commission. Whereas Jesus reached only a few in his lifetime, through the church (Ephesians 3:20–21) we can reach the whole world!

6. To return to the developing English language, there are three periods in its development: Old English, roughly up to 1100 AD; Middle English, 1100-1400; Modern English, 1400-present. The KJV, written in Elizabethan English (the language of Shakespeare), is now 400 years out of date!

7. But the nonmiraculous gifts (which outnumber the miraculous ones) continued.

27. Everything You Always Wanted to Know, 2
Problematic Bible Passages

This chapter covers twenty difficult passages on the Spirit. The material following is somewhat more technical than that found in Chapter 26.

1. Genesis 1:2 (The "Spirit of God" and the Holy Spirit)

"The Spirit of God" is translated "a mighty wind" in some versions. The phrase "spirit of God" cannot be equated with the Holy Spirit in every instance the phrase occurs, for there is a point of translation to consider. In Hebrew, the construction X-God can be translated "the X of God," but it can equally well be translated "a great X." For example, in Genesis 23:6 we find "mighty prince" instead of "a prince of God." Similarly, in 1 Samuel 14:15, we read of "a terrible panic" although it can also be rendered "a panic of/from God." Jonah 3:3 should clinch the argument, for there we find "an exceedingly great city," whereas the Hebrew says "a great city of God": If that were true, there would have been no need for Jonah to go and preach to it!

Thus there are six possible translations for *ruach 'elohim* in Genesis 1:2: "Spirit of God," "mighty spirit," "breath of God," "mighty breath," "wind of God" and "mighty wind." That is why "the Spirit of God" in Genesis 1:2 is only provisionally identified with the Holy Spirit.

2. 1 Samuel 16:23 (the evil spirit from God)

Two observations should be made. First, the fact that something is attributed to God does not necessarily mean God is the direct cause of it, for God allows many things to happen, which are thus part of God's sovereign will. Yet such wording is all the more appropriate in this instance, where it is because Saul has fallen from favor with God that God has allowed the spirit to come.

Second, very little is revealed about Satan in the Old Testament. In fact, except for the book of Job and Genesis 3, which doesn't even explicitly identify the serpent with Satan (that identification is made only in Revelation 12:9), there is no revelation about Satan until the Persian period (539-333 BC, during which 1 Chronicles, Zechariah, etc. were written). Interestingly, whereas in 2 Samuel 24:1 David's ordering of the census is attributed to God's anger, in the later book of 1 Chronicles the cause is attributed to Satan (1 Chronicles 21:1). Both accounts are correct, since God was indirectly responsible in 2 Samuel 24 and Satan is responsible in 1 Chronicles 21. To sum up, Saul's evil spirit was allowed by God, but God no more personally dispatched it from his presence than God created Satan as an evil being.

3. 2 Chronicles 16:12 (relying on physicians)

Asa, sixth King of Judah, wavered in his faith near the end of his life. Although his disease was severe—he should have turned to God (2 Corinthians 1:9)—he put his trust in men. The phrase "only from the physicians" does not mean that it is a sin to accept medical care, as some "faith healers" claim, only that it is unspiritual to rely on doctors without any thought of God.

There are three ways God heals: "natural healing," when the body repairs itself, healing through medical expertise, and miraculous healing. From a biblical point of view, all three are equally divine and wonderful, and all three are true "healing."

4. Isaiah 30:21 (the guiding voice)

Some consider this passage to prophesy the direct leading of the Spirit, or "inner voice," in the age of the Spirit. An examination of the context, however, proves otherwise. The "teachers" of Isaiah 30:20 are the spiritual teachers or true prophets, hidden from the time of the wicked Ahaz, fourteenth king of Judah. In saying they "will be hidden no more" Isaiah is prophesying the return of actual human teachers—not the whispering voice of the Spirit. The "voice" of verse 21 is the voice of the prophets (see Nehemiah 9:20, 30). In the Old Testament, "turning neither to the right nor the left" means obeying God's commands, as opposed to some internal personal guidance mechanism (Deuteronomy 28:14). The "voice" behind them is the true prophet's voice, leading to repentance (Isaiah 30:22; see also Lamentations 2:14), as opposed to the subjective message and religion of the false prophets (Jeremiah 23:26). Furthermore, the Neopentecostal interpretation is overliteral, as a reading of Isaiah 30:26 shows, since in the age of the Spirit the luminosity of the sun and moon is unchanged!

5. Mark 9:38-40 (the man driving out demons in Jesus' name)

The disciples wanted to stop the man from his activity. Jesus' reply, "Whoever is not against us is for us," may mean that the man is saved, or at least saved under Judaism, but it need not be taken that way, insofar as it is possible for a non-Christian to promote the work of Christ. Consider the seven sons of Sceva

(Acts 19:13–16). These Jews tried to drive out demons in Jesus' name but were unsuccessful. The fact that this exorcism attempt came after the abolition of the Jewish legal system must be taken into account, as must the possibility that their efforts sprang from less than pure motives. When all is said and done, Mark 9:38 is too fragmentary an account from which to draw any sweeping theological conclusions.

6. Mark 16:19-20[1] (Should all believers speak in tongues?)

On first inspection, "whoever believes" (Mark 16:16) and "these signs will accompany those who believe" (v. 17) seem permanently linked. Why would verse 17 be less important than verse 15 or verse 16? However, it does not prove that the miraculous promises still apply today, for a number of reasons:

a. Those signs *did* accompany those who believed in the first century. In the book of Acts all except the drinking of poison happened—and we know that this sign happened too, because Jesus said it would.

b. The purpose of the signs was the confirmation of the Word, as we have already discussed. The Word has been confirmed and does not require reconfirmation, so the primary need for the miracles has passed away.

c. If this is a universal promise, why is it that "faith healers" do not take it at face value? Few indeed have the courage to handle snakes, and I have not yet heard of anyone who attempted to drink poison (except the unfortunate cultists of Jonestown, Guyana). In other words, Neopentecostals pick and choose.

d. Verse 20 is written in the *past tense*. Although this is not a strong argument against the Neopentecostal interpretation, it is worth taking into account. A similar passage which looks back on confirmatory miraculous activity is Hebrews 2:4.

e. In Matthew 28 Jesus explicitly said he would be with his disciples until the very end. In Mark 16 he does not explicitly promise that the gifts would be with us until the end. It is quite possible that the confirming signs were never intended for more than the first generation.

7. Luke 11:13 (the Father giving the Spirit to those who ask him)

Some use this verse to support the innovative conversion doctrine of "pray Jesus into your heart," and a number of Neopentecostals claim the passage says we should ask God for a "Holy Spirit baptism."

What does it mean? To begin with, even if the passage refers to conversion, it does not specify how one receives the Spirit, and so certainly is not in competition with clearer passages on how one becomes a Christian.

Second, we know that a simple request is not enough to acquire the Holy Spirit because Acts 5:32 says obedience is essential.

Third, it is possible that the passage, which is discussing God's willingness to bless us and answer our prayers, cites the Holy Spirit as an example of the greatest gift that God will give us. (This would be an *a fortiori* argument: If God is willing to give us the Spirit, then there is nothing that he will hold back from us if we ask in the right way.)

A comparison of this passage with the parallel in Matthew 7:11 shows that "good gifts" may be the best interpretation. The Greek phrase *pneuma hagion* ("holy spirit," as opposed to "the Holy Spirit"[2]) may suggest that it is not the Spirit himself that is referred to but rather some gift, aspect or manifestation of the Spirit. Some have suggested that "the Spirit" in this passage is "being filled with the Spirit," as in the sense of Acts 4:31. If this is the case, it would mean that God is more than willing to give us spiritual power (Ephesians 3:16) as we yield our lives to him.

8. Luke 21:15 (divine inspiration when brought to trial)

This passage seems to indicate that God will give us inspiration when we are "under the gun." Considering the passage in context, however, we see that Jesus is addressing apostles. They certainly had a guarantee of inspiration. There is therefore no weighty reason why the promise should be extended to all believers. However, there is another way of looking at it: Jesus may be promising that God will give any believer assistance when he or she is in dire straits, for example when forced to speak on trial.

9. John 3:8 (the wind blows where it pleases)

The analogy between the wind and the Spirit (recall that *pneuma*, "spirit," also means "wind") is taken by some to support the mysterious "leading" of the Spirit in the Neopentecostal sense. But when Jesus says, "So it is with everyone born of the Spirit," he is referring not to miraculous leading, but to the new birth, as even a cursory scanning of the passage makes clear. What Jesus means is that, just as you cannot understand the wind merely by looking at it (although you can certainly see its effects), so you cannot understand the nature or source of the new birth with human eyes alone. We are born "again" or "from above"—the Greek word means both.

10. John 6:63 (Jesus' words are spirit and life)

The word of God is powerful (Hebrews 4:12). The Bible is not just literature, but a penetrating sword with life-giving force. Here it does not seem like Jesus is equating the Word with the Spirit; he is only saying that the Word is spiritual—having effects in the spiritual realm. God communicates with us through his word (Hebrews 1:1-3), not through mysterious spiritual influences—a notion John 6:63 cannot be made to support.

11. John 14:12 (greater things than these)

Is Jesus saying that those who came after him would do greater miracles than he did? Certainly not, for even the miracles of Peter and Paul are less sensational than those of Jesus, and the most that can be said is that occasionally they are equally sensational. So how can we do "greater things"?[3]

The "greater things," then, is not referring to the miracles of John 14:11, but to the ministry potential of the church. Through Jesus' ministry actually only a very small number of men and women became committed believers. He was greatly restricted, since he had to return to the Father (John 14:12). The number of his disciples was very small indeed compared with the figures in the book of Acts (2:41, 4:4, etc.). The "greater things" are not miracles, as some claim, but rather the amazing ministry potential we enjoy—the opportunity to win millions to the cause of Christ, turning the world "upside down."

12. John 20:22 ("receive the Holy Spirit")

Jesus breathed on the disciples as he uttered these words, a prophetic illustration of the coming Pentecostal outpouring. Some, however, believe this was the time when the apostles received the Spirit. The passage is inconclusive. The word *labete* (receive) can equally well be translated "receive"! (imperative), you are receiving (present indicative progressive) or possibly you are going to receive (as in English we might say "I am going away for a few days," whether we leave today or not). I interpret this action of Jesus as a symbolic act, reminiscent of Genesis 2:7, Ezekiel 37:9, etc., though I realize that this act may also have been the means whereby the Eleven received the indwelling Spirit.

13. Acts 18:24-19:6 (Apollos and the Ephesian disciples)

What was going on here? How did a man with only the baptism of John speak so effectively? What was it about which he required "more adequate" explanation? Why is there confusion when the Christian movement is already some twenty years old? Is the story of the Ephesian disciples related by Luke as an analogous situation, or as a contrast?

The NIV notes an alternate translation for Acts 18:25: "He spoke with fervor in the Spirit." Could Apollos have received the Spirit without being baptized in Jesus' name? Why does Luke tell us the Ephesians received Christian baptism, without telling us whether Apollos was immersed again or not? There are certainly several possibilities here.[4]

a. Apollos taught accurately about the life of Jesus—but was uninformed about the apostolic teaching which was foundational for the Christian faith (Acts 2:42, Ephesians 2:20). He was a convert of the Baptist's movement, yet not saved under the new covenant. Like the Ephesian group in Acts 19, he was baptized again, in Jesus' name (Acts 19:5, 2:38).

b. Another option is that Apollos was different from the Ephesians. They are ignorant of the Spirit, whereas Apollos is better informed. His passion for Christ is, in this case, evidence of his true conversion. The Bible never says those baptized with John's baptism were immersed again at or after Pentecost. At most that would be an inference and not a necessary one. Apollos may have been saved as the apostles were. They had received John's baptism (John 1:35ff), been cleansed by the word of Jesus' teaching (John 15:3) and received the Spirit either in the upper room (John 20:22) or at Pentecost (Acts 2:4). Prisca and Aquila pull Apollos aside and explain to him that John's baptism may have worked fine for him—since he was immersed before Pentecost—but it is now defunct. The terms of the new covenant from Pentecost onward are very clear (Acts 2:38, 39).

This section of Acts seems to support either of the two interpretations we have considered.

14. Romans 8:16 (the Spirit bearing witness with our spirit)

Neopentecostals claim that the feeling of being saved is proof that we possess the Holy Spirit. This is not likely, in the light of other things Paul said (e.g. 1 Corinthians 4:4) and in the light of other parts of the New Testament (e.g. 1 John 2:3–6). A better possibility is that the Spirit testifies through the lives we live that we are Christians. Some have even suggested that "our spirit" is the corporate spirit of the church in worship, still another possibility that is hard to prove. All told, this may not be one of the clearest Pauline passages. All the same, the Neopentecostal interpretation finds no support here.

15. 2 Corinthians 12:2 (the third heaven)

Since Paul speaks of the man caught up to the third heaven in the third person, many do not realize that he is speaking of himself. Speaking of oneself in the third person is common in the Bible. For example, John refers to himself as merely "the disciple whom Jesus loved,"and Jesus speaks of himself with the third person appellation "Son of Man." Moreover, the context demands that the passage is referring to Paul since the "thorn in the flesh" (1 Corinthians 12:7) was given to prevent Paul from becoming conceited. Paul was the one who received "these surpassingly great revelations," of which he is so hesitant to speak (v. 4).

Just where, or what, is the third heaven? Many religions conceive of many levels of heaven and hell. The simplest model is that the first heaven is the sky (where birds fly), the second, space (where the stars are) and the third, heaven (where God is). In Jewish apocalyptic writings (written roughly between 200 BC and 100 AD), one sometimes finds a seven-level heaven motif in which the third heaven is the place of revelation from which one can see into the seventh heaven—the place of God.

Many have fancied themselves to have been caught up to heaven (à la Colossians 2:18!). One woman told me of blissful feelings she had after losing all track of time as she sat in her living room easy chair. Some two hours elapsed, and afterwards she felt so refreshed! Was she in heaven—or in deep sleep? God only knows! Experiences are too subjective and too hard to assess. Mystics and charismatics in many religions have claimed direct encounters with God. We would be well advised not to make too much of such experiences.

16. 1 Timothy 2:8 (the lifting up of hands)

Many groups practice the lifting of hands during prayer. This custom may be unsettling to some, but there is ample scriptural warrant for it. The practice is extremely common in the Old Testament. For example, consider the references in Psalms alone (28:2, 63:4, 77:2, 88:9, 134:2, 141:2, 143:6). The New Testament continues the lifting of hands in prayer, as we see in 1 Timothy 2:8. In later centuries men prayed with arms outstretched in the form of the cross—a very strenuous way to pray![5]

If it is argued that "men" (andres, "males") is not generic, but applies to males only, it could be counterargued that the injunction to modesty (1 Timothy 2:9) is not for women only. It is a universal principle. Therefore women (as well as men) ought to dress modestly, and similarly men (as well as women) ought to lift up holy hands in prayer.

On the other hand, there are prayers in the Bible where hands are not lifted (Matthew 19:13, 26:39, Jonah 2:1!), so it is certainly not essential to lift hands while praying. All things considered, the custom is biblical, though probably culturally conditioned and certainly not a matter to be dogmatic about.

17. Hebrews 6:2 (the laying on of hands)

Why would this be listed in a series of fundamentals, where the Hebrew writer places it? As we have seen, there are many varieties of the laying on of hands (Chapter 20). Perhaps to clarify the function of the apostolic imposition of hands, especially against the rich background of laying on of hands in the Jewish tradition, the Hebrew writer lists it here. The interpretation that it refers to the "baptism of the Holy Spirit" is implausible. After research on the text, I conclude that the passage is too obscure for a definitive interpretation at this time. Perhaps the Hebrew writer is discussing advancing Christians into leadership—a vital need if we are to evangelize the world in our time. In 1 Timothy 5:22 (see 3:6) Paul warned Timothy not to be too hasty in "the laying on of hands" (appointing leaders).

18. James 5:14-15 (anointing with oil)

Spiritual men accomplish great things through prayer. That the elders should be chosen for the honor of praying for a healing may be a mystery for us, until we realize the high qualifications for the eldership laid down in the New Testament. Elders were men who truly led the congregation, in character, hard work, love, evangelism, hospitality and so much more. They were not just a "board of directors."

But what about the anointing with oil? Was it merely medicinal? There is ample evidence from antiquity that olive oil was used in this way. The verb for "anoint" is not the usual *chrio* (as in *christos* ["Christ," "anointed one"]) used for the anointing of prophets, priests and kings—indicating a special calling or action of God—but the more general word *aleipho,* "to oil." Does this explain the passage? Was the oil used to promote healing or to call down God's healing power?

There is another way to look at the issue.[6] Consider the following passages on the use of oil: Ruth 3:3, 2 Samuel 14:2, Daniel 10:3, 2 Samuel 12:16, 20, Matthew 6:17, Isaiah 1:6, Ezekiel 16:9, Mark 6:13. It quickly becomes evident that the use of oil was a routine practice in biblical times. In fact, oil was used when one was in a *normal* state of health or disposition. It was not used when one was mourning, fasting or ill. Jesus told his followers to use oil when they fasted, lest people detect that something was abnormal and realize that they were fasting. (Surely he would not instruct them to do this if miraculous healing were smeared all over their faces!) Is it not likely that people were anointed with oil as an expression of faith that they would recover and rejoin the mainstream of life? The anointing has no connection, then, with the healing, but is done in anticipation of the healing. This interpretation does justice to the many passages on anointing in the Bible, and reveals sound principles for cultural sensitivity in biblical interpretation.[7]

19. 1 Peter 3:18-20 *(Jesus preaching to the spirits in prison)*

Did Jesus, at some time between his death and resurrection, preach to the lost souls in Hades? There is no indication in the Bible that people have a second chance to make peace with God. But there were ways to be saved before the new covenant. It is clear that Noah was justified, yet Christ is not said to have preached to him. Also, the Spirit of Christ was in the Old Testament prophets (1 Peter 1:11), and presumably Noah was no exception (2 Peter 2:5). Christ preached through Noah to those souls who refused to follow God—not thousands of years after their death, but in their generation. This is not the only interpretation of the passage—only my favorite.[8]

20. 1 John 4:1 *(test the spirits)*

Why does John urge us to test the spirits? "Because many false prophets have gone out into the world." The "spirits" are "prophetic messages." While the gift of prophecy was still present (which would seem to be the case when 1 John was written), there was a constant need to assess, to weigh, what the prophet said. This explains Paul's instructions in 1 Corinthians 14:29 and 1 Thessalonians 5:19-22, both of which deal exclusively with the testing of prophetic messages. Moreover, the term rendered "prophecy" in 2 Thessalonians 2:2 (NIV) is actually the Greek word *pneuma* ("spirit," which is retained in some translations). "Spirit," then (strange as it may seem), is a synonym for "prophecy" or "prophetic message." Testing the spirits in 1 John 4:1 means testing prophetic messages—the same advice given to the Corinthians and the Thessalonians.

_____ NOTES _____

1. Scholars have questions about the authenticity of Mark 16:9-20. The ending to Mark's gospel is not found in some manuscripts, most notably *Codex Sinaiticus* and *Codex Vaticanus* (both dating from the fourth century), and so it is considered to be spurious by a number of scholars, who prefer to include the passage in a footnote or dispense with it altogether. It is important to consider whether it belongs in the New Testament, because it is a crucial passage for Neopentecostal theology, especially vv. 17-20, which mention certain miraculous signs accompanying believers.

The easiest solution may be to deny that this section is a legitimate part of the gospel of Mark, but this does not seem wise. First, many other ancient manuscripts (MSS) do have this ending (Λ, C, D, W, Q, etc.). Second, it was not uncommon for ancient MSS to develop *lacunae* (gaps due to moths, rot, erasure), or to lose some of their leaves. Third, it is quoted from by several early Christian writers (e.g. Justin Martyr, writing in the mid-second century), and so was surely known at an early date. Fourth, even if someone other than Mark wrote the passage (and that is possible), that would not invalidate the passage as a legitimate portion of Scripture. Many books of the Bible are of compound authorship (e.g. Psalms and Proverbs). Fifth, with the possible exception of drinking poison, everything mentioned in this passage happens in the book of Acts, and so there is in no sense any "addition" to the word of God, even if the passage is not original. Summing up, it must be said that we cannot prove one way or the other whether Mark 16: 9-20 is authentic, but the weight of the evidence indicates that it does belong in our New Testaments.

2. It simply is not true that all Greek words without the definite article must be translated the same in English! Many, many words in the Greek New Testament are anarthrous despite an obvious definite sense. Similarly, nouns in the Latin language, which lacks the definite article entirely, are rendered definite or indefinite based on context.

3. Charles Spurgeon, the captivating preacher for London's Metropolitan Baptist Tabernacle, who regularly drew Sunday crowds of 6,000 in attendance over a century ago, commented, "It is true that we can work no miracles, yet...we can work spiritual miracles. Today, can we not stand at the grave of the dead sinner, and say, 'Lazarus, come forth'? And has not God often made the dead to rise at our word, by the power of His Holy Spirit?" (C.H. Spurgeon, New Park Street Pulpit, Vol. XVIII, 185).

4. In my earlier work, *The Powerful Delusion* I was less open to other possibilities. At that time confidence that I had found the correct interpretation of the Holy Spirit passages was high. Several issues in this book I see differently than I did twenty years ago!

5. Roberta Bondi, *To Pray and to Love: Conversations on Prayer with the Early Church* (Minneapolis: Fortress Press, 1991), 23.

6. I owe this insight to Jim McGuiggan, "Anointing with Oil," *The Living Word* (Tony Coffey, ed.), Dublin: DCC, 1985.

7. The answer is not completely clear-cut, however. Leviticus 14:18 (see LXX) seems neither medicinal, nor setting apart to a special service, nor an expression of faith. In this case the leper has already been cleansed and is anointed only after purification. Perhaps there is a connection with remission of sins, as in James 5:15-16. In the absence of a definitive explanation, let us avoid dogmatism (and also superstition).

8. For a longer exegesis of this passage, including other possible interpretations, see my *Life to the Full* (Spring, Texas.: Illumination Publishers, 2006), 85-88.

28. Everything You Always Wanted to Know, 3
The Trinity

No Simple Doctrine

This chapter attempts to explain the doctrine of the trinity. Maybe it's my high church past or my instinctive distrust of the abstractions of medieval theology, but something about the doctrine of the trinity just feels contrived—it's just too neat, too simple. (Or maybe it's too deep for my shallow mind!) Yet I know I must not shirk my authorial duty; moreover, it's good to push oneself. I like what C. S. Lewis said:

> If Christianity was something we were making up, of course we would make it easier. But it is not. We cannot compete, in simplicity, with people who are inventing religions. How could we? We are dealing with Fact. Of course anyone can be simple if he has no facts to bother about.[1]

We are indeed concerned with the facts, with sifting truth and error. The truth is, the trinity is not the sort of doctrine inventors of religions would concoct—which is one reason it has the ring of truth to it. And though I rarely use the term "trinity," in my opinion, as I shall attempt to show, the doctrine does give as good an explanation of the nature of the godhead as anything man has come up with.

What Is the Trinity?

The OED (Oxford English Dictionary) defines "trinity": "Being three; group of three. From Latin trinitas, 'triad.'" Surely, the persons of the trinity are not distinct persons like the Three Musketeers, the Three Stooges, the Three Tenors or the Three Little Pigs. On the other hand, we aren't simply dealing with one person in three roles, like a person who functions as mother, wife and professional. The first error to be avoided is tritheism, three separate gods; the second is modalism, where God "morphs" from one form to another according to the need of the hour.

Part of coming to terms with the doctrine is grasping what theologians mean when they discuss the "persons" of the trinity. In modern English "three persons" strongly implies a triad of gods. But the theological term "person" is from the Latin persona, which means "mask, part or character," as in the characters of a play. This of course does not mean that God is somehow "pretending," like an actor.[2]

In brief, the Holy Trinity is the three-in-one.

Biblical Basis

Often the Father, Son and Spirit are mentioned together in the New Testament (2 Corinthians 13:14, Matthew 28:19, John 14:17-23).[3] They are three in personality but one in nature or essence. Father, Son and Spirit are each God (in essence), but none can be identified with the other.

Again, we must guard ourselves against false understandings of trinity, or else we will drift into either the errors of "unitarianism" (which roundly rejects the trinity) or the errors of tritheism. (The Qur'an mistakes belief in the trinity for tritheism when it condemns "those who say Allah is three."[4])

In short, all three persons are divine. Obviously, our heavenly Father is God.[5] In addition, many verses state that Christ is divine (2 Peter 1:1, Titus 2:13, John 1:1, 14), not to mention the indirect proofs of his deity, such as his forgiveness of man's sins (Mark 2) and claiming as his own the name of God (John 8:58). But how can Christ have two natures simultaneously? An illustration may help. Orange juice is 100% wet, and yet it is also 100% citrus. It isn't somehow half wet and half citrus—it's wholly both at the same time. In the same way, Jesus is human and God.[6]

Finally, it is also clear from the Scriptures that the Spirit, the third person of the trinity, or the "Spirit of God," is divine. Let's check out the OED definition of the Spirit: "The active essence or essential power of the Deity, conceived as a creative, animating or inspiring influence." Now this may be an accurate definition, but how does it help us be closer to God? It makes a difference in our lives only when we sense and appreciate that God, through his Spirit, is living within us (John 14). The Spirit in nature is God;[7] All members of the trinity are equally divine.

Trinity in Church History

The earlier "ecumenical councils" strove to define and describe the relationships between the members of the godhead (Nicea in 325, Constantinople in 381 and Chalcedon in 451, to mention a few). Yes, many believers in the early Christian era spent generations exploring the doctrine of the trinity, investigating the intricacies of the Spirit. Even in the Middle Ages, interest in the trinity was strong. Aquinas produced the most thorough treatise on "The Blessed Trinity."[8]

In the Restoration movement, especially in the nineteenth century, there was a reaction against trinitarian language. The famous hymn "Holy, Holy, Holy" mentions "God in three persons, blessed Trinity!"[9] And yet in the overreaction to "traditional" doctrines, these words were changed to "God over all and blessed eternally." Was this really necessary? Is it not true that Father, Son and Spirit are all divine?

Analogies Good and Bad

While it is true that Father, Son and Spirit are all God, we cannot correctly say that the Father is the Son, or that Spirit and Son are interchangeable. Analogies therefore need to be carefully selected, lest we inadvertently support false doctrine through our attempts to refute it.

The analogy I most often use to explain the trinity is the analogy of the amorphous forms of H_2O. Ice – water; liquid water – water; and steam – water (in essence); but ice $\neq$ steam; ice $\neq$ liquid water; and liquid water $\neq$ steam. Though I like the water analogy, its shortcoming is that it implies the false doctrine of modalism, that God appears in one form now, another at another time.[10] I have heard worse analogies: time (past, present and future), even an egg (shell, white and yolk).

Opponents of trinity ask, how can 1 + 1 + 1 = 1? But the mathematics is all wrong. Really it's a case of 1^3: 1 x 1 x 1 = 1. Moving from simple math to geometry, the triangular illustration may better encapsulate the truth about the relations among the persons of the trinity.

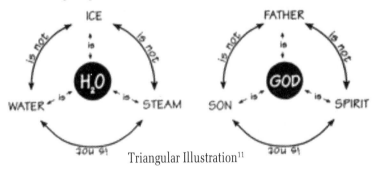

Triangular Illustration[11]

As someone put it more academically, "A better illustration based in human nature would be, as suggested earlier, the relation between our mind, its ideas and the expression of these ideas in words. There is obviously a unity among all three of these without there being an identity. In this sense, they illustrate the trinity."[12]

No single analogy captures the divine mystery, though the various pictures will be more convincing to different people.

Trinity and Our Walk with God

The doctrine of the trinity has been firmly established. Let me now suggest some ways in which understanding trinity illuminates our walk with the Lord:

1. Trinity brings us great assurance. The Father is God above us, the Son is God beside us, and the Spirit is God within us.

2. Trinity helps us to see that God is love. How could God have been (eternally) love if he had no one to love? But as Augustine commented, love always existed among the members of the trinity. This theme has often been elevated and discussed in our century by C. S. Lewis and Francis Schaeffer. The three-in-one God is a divine family, in which perfect love has always been exchanged.

3. Respect for the trinity deepens our humility, as we see God's transcendence. As Isaiah says (Isaiah 55:8-9), his ways are not our ways, and there is an unfathomable distance between his ways and wisdom and our own. (See also Romans 11:33-36.)

Summary

If the whole concept seems complicated, don't fret! If theologians struggled for centuries to put the divine mystery into words, and if you cannot manage it in half an hour, I wouldn't be too concerned! To wrap it all up, all this does not mean that:

- there are three gods (tritheism).
- we are normally to pray to Jesus or pray to the Spirit. In John 16:23–26 Jesus explains that we are to pray to the Father in his name, although occasionally in the New Testament prayer is also addressed to the Lord Jesus (e.g. Acts 7:59).
- God "morphs" from one person to another (modalism). The persons of the trinity always remain distinct.
- this chapter is the last word on the subject! God cannot be put in a box.

It does, however, mean that:

- Trinity is biblical. Whether or not the word itself appears in the New

Testament, it is valid. (Even the word "Bible" does not occur in the Bible, yet it is a completely functional and useful term.)

- God's nature is a mystery—and so we will always have to strive to our utmost to embrace and accept the nature of God in our lives.
- We need to dig deeper into the word of God if we are going to go higher in our walk with him.

Holy, Holy, Holy!

Despite my initial apprehension, my study has led me to accept the time-honored doctrine of the Holy Trinity. Returning to the corrections made to the old hymn, I do not mean to dispute the words "God over all and blessed eternally," for he is. Yet it is wholly unnecessary to distance ourselves from the original wording of the song. Its final verse spoke the truth perfectly well:

Holy, holy, holy! Lord God Almighty!
All thy works shall praise thy name,
in earth, and sky, and sea;
Holy, holy, holy! Merciful and mighty!
God in three persons, blessèd Trinity!

NOTES

1. C. S. Lewis, *Mere Christianity* (New York: The Macmillan Company, 1943), 145.

2. Remember theatergoers, think about the term *Dramatis personae.*

3. Several religions have "trinities." Hinduism has Shiva, Vishnu and Brahma. The Druids had Taranis, Esus and Teutates. The ancient Egyptians also had their trinity. Yet, unlike the Biblical trinity, these "trinities" are triads of gods, not one triune god.

4. Islamic accusations denied that God, Jesus and Mary were gods. This clearly reflects the exalted, and erroneous, position of Mary in the seventh century AD.

5. For further reading on the nature and divinity of God, see Edwin A. Abbot, *Flatland* (Oxford: Blackwell, 1875); J. I. Packer, *Knowing God* (Downers Grove: InterVarsity, 1975); Francis A. Schaeffer, *He Is There and He Is Not Silent* (Wheaton, Ill.: Tyndale House, 1972); and *The God Who Is There* (Downers Grove: InterVarsity Press, 1968).

6. For further reading on the nature and divinity of the Son of God, see William Barclay, *The Mind of Jesus* (New York: Harper & Row, 1961); Charles Edward Jefferson, *Jesus—the Same* (Billerica, Mass.: DPI, 1997; original edition 1908); *Jesus with the People,* ed. Toney Mulhollan (Spring, Texas: Illumination Publishers, 2017); and Philip Yancey, *The Jesus I Never Knew* (Grand Rapids: Zondervan, 1995).

7. For further reading on the nature and divinity of the Spirit, see Frederick Dale Bruner, *A Theology of the Holy Spirit* (London: Hodder & Stoughton, 1970); and John R. W. Stott, *Baptism and Fullness* (London: InterVarsity Press, 1975).

8. See Thomas Aquinas (1225-1274), *Summa Theologica.*

9. Bishop R. Heber, 1783-1826.

10. Worse, that the Father is "harder" than the Son, the Spirit more ethereal than both, and so forth!

11. In my understanding of trinity, the trinitarian triangle may not be totally equilateral!

12. Norman L. Geisler and Abdul Saleeb, *Answering Islam* (Grand Rapids: Baker, 1993), 269.

29. Ghostbusters!

The Spirit and the Occult

Halloween was just a few weeks away, and around the family dinner table we were having a talk about things that go bump in the night. The opportunity seemed too good to let go by. A little "hallowed" humor surely wouldn't hurt my (then) seven-year-old. I asked Emma, "Where do spiderwebs come from?"

"Spiders," she quickly answered.

"How about cobwebs? Where do you think they come from?" I asked in a spooky voice.

"I don't know," Emma replied.

"If spiderwebs come from spiders, then cobwebs come from…" I hesitated while she collected her thoughts. The answer was not long in coming. "From cobs!" said Emma, eyes widening like saucers. "What's a 'cob'?"

"You mean you've never seen a cob?" I asked.

Now my nine-year-old joined in on the fun. "Oh yes," James added, "they're in the house. You can hear them sometimes." At this point the fear was evident on Emma's face—at the same time we could see that she wanted to be spooked!

"Emma," I continued in a Karloff-like voice, "cobs are much bigger than spiders. They often move across the ceiling at night. I will tell you when I see one. You aren't afraid, are you?" By this time Emma was definitely looking spooked.

We all share some degree of fascination with the "dark side." We have all had spooky experiences, nightmares and brushes with the world beyond. Maybe you have even had the eerie experience of Eliphaz:

"A word was secretly brought to me,
    my ears caught a whisper of it.
Amid disquieting dreams in the night,
    when deep sleep falls on men,
fear and trembling seized me
    and made all my bones shake.
A spirit glided past my face,
    and the hair on my body stood on end.
It stopped,
    but I could not tell what it was.
A form stood before my eyes,
    and I heard a hushed voice" (Job 4:12–16).

What does the Spirit have to do with all this? Are ghosts real? Do Christians have some extra protection against the forces of evil? We will consider seven areas of interest.

1. Ghosts

My grandmother recalled seeing, when she was a little girl (during the 1890s), a ghost strolling in the graveyard. It was a woman who walked back and forth, her white gown shimmering in the moonlight. A good friend of mine lived in a house with a "cold room." No matter how warm the house, this room where the "ghost" lived was always frigid. And then there was the rapping at the door in the middle of the night! Another fellow told me about the sounds he "recorded" at the cemetery: "voices" emanating from the burial plots of the talkative dead. In Chinese culture, the Feast of the Hungry Ghosts is held annually to appease the spirits of the departed, and incense and paper offerings are routinely offered to one's ancestors. Is not the awareness of ghosts universal?

Yes it is, and there are many possible explanations which still harmonize with the Bible. One thing is certain: Satan exploits our fear of death and the unknown. Hebrews 2:15 describes us, outside of Christ, as being held in slavery by our fear of death. But Jesus came to liberate us; there is now no reason to fear. Whether "ghosts" are counterfeits or somehow real, we need stand no more in fear of them than we do of death itself!

Nowhere does the Bible say that the dead return as ghosts. The quotation from Job 4 (above) does not lend credence to this belief. According to biblical revelation, the dead await judgment. There is no "comeback."

2. Demon possession

Claims of demonic possession are by no means limited to Christendom, but have been reported worldwide. While some claims are frightening and difficult to explain away, most are unconvincing.[1] Consider the following report from Pittsburgh:

> According to doctors in Pittsburgh, Pennsylvania, in June 1997, Sherri Lynn Rossi was hit in the head more than 20 times with a blunt object and left covered in blood and in a coma on the side of a road. When she came out of the coma, she identified her attacker as her husband, Richard A. Rossi, Jr., pastor of the local, independent, charismatic First Love Church, telling police that Rev. Rossi had alighted from his own car, "started acting weird," taken the wheel of her car with her inside, driven to a rural area, and beat her.
>
> Rev. Rossi immediately denied the charge, insisting that the hijacker

must have been a man who looked like him and had a car like his, and that it was "very possible, oh, yes" that his wife's attacker was Satan in human form. In October, Sherri Lynn Rossi abruptly withdrew her accusation, said she was looking forward to resuming their family life, and concurred that her attacker might have been a demon in human form.[2]

As in the case of ghosts and demonic possession, the overwhelming majority of the sensational phenomena reported by occultists is sheer fabrication or gross distortion of the facts.

You may have noticed that demon possession is unheard of in the Old Testament, even though the neighbors of Israel widely believed in demons. Was God protecting his people, or were the beliefs of the Assyrians, Babylonians, Canaanites and others mere superstition? Even in the New Testament, almost all the references are in the gospels. There are occasional references in the second century,[3] but Christianity was recording fewer and fewer incidences of demon possession and exorcism. I have come across some anecdotal evidence that I am reluctant to explain away. Perhaps Satan and his demons became especially active around the time the gospel was preached, and then were "driven out." Why? A matter for speculation![4]

Was demon possession in the New Testament just mental illness? Although some cases of demon possession seem to have been rooted in actual physical illness, or vice versa (Matthew 17:14ff, Mark 9:14ff), accounts of demon possession cannot be rationalized as a supernatural explanation for physiological or psychological disorders. Psychological abnormalities do not normally drown two thousand pigs! (Mark 5:13).

There are good reasons for believing that demon possession cannot happen to a Christian. Being taken over by a demon would mean loss of one's free will, hence a diminishing of one's personal moral responsibility before God. In that case, the promise of 1 Corinthians 10:13—that God will not allow us to be tempted above our ability to resist—would seem to be null and void. Do not be intimidated by wild stories of exorcisms, unsubstantiated, usually coming from the other side of the globe. Anyway, even if demon possession is possible today, there are serious theological problems with the position that it can happen to true Christians. Stay with Jesus, and you will have nothing to fear!

As far as Neopentecostalism goes, the heavy emphasis on the demonic— and on the "spiritual"—has much in common with spiritism and even occultism. Be careful what you believe. Test everything (1 Thessalonians 5:21-22).

3. Astrology

Zodiacal systems are ancient indeed, and, like claims of ghosts, nearly universal. These nonsensical systems are based on the alleged influences of heavenly bodies on human beings, depending on the birth date of the individual.

The first serious error of this superstition is that the time at which we have a physical "mass" which can be subject to gravitational forces is surely the date of conception, not the date of birth. There is no evidence that a fetus develops according to different physical laws than those which will govern it once it is born.

The second serious error—somewhat understandable centuries before gravitational theory had been worked out by Newton—is that attractive forces between objects in the universe depend on the mass of the objects and their distance apart. The gravitational effect of the earth far, far outweighs the pull of the "heavenly" bodies. Jupiter's influence on you is so minimal, in fact, that it has less gravitational force on you than does this book out of which you are reading!

My opinion: Astrology is for the gullible, for the birds. So do I sin if I take a peek at the "Leo" report for the day? For purposes of entertainment—a good laugh at a ridiculous belief—perhaps not. Yet astrology is firmly rejected by Scripture (Ecclesiastes 7:14, 8:7, Isaiah 47:13).[5]

4. Séances

In 1 Samuel 28 we read of the Witch of Endor, who evidently called the prophet Samuel up from the dead. Necromancy—or consulting the dead— was forbidden under the Old Testament (Deuteronomy 18:11, Isaiah 8:19). In the Endor episode, apostate King Saul was consulting a medium after he had expelled all the mediums from the land. Was this a conjurer's trick? Was this illusion? When the witch saw the spirit rising, she was startled. Some have suggested that the witch of Endor was a fraud, yet in this case either God "played her game" or Satan took advantage of the situation to work a counterfeit miracle. The problem with the second interpretation is that "Samuel" (whoever he is) prophesies the truth. It does indeed appear, weighing up the evidence, that God has brought Samuel back from the dead to deliver his ominous testimony against Saul. Regardless, the people of God are forbidden from engaging in necromancy.

5. On Halloween

What about Halloween? Is this playing with fire? While it is freely admitted that the origins of Halloween are quite pagan, I do not believe there is any harm in children's having fun in their annual costume party. If it is argued that anything with pagan origins must be rejected, then what about the days of the week? When we say "Sunday" does that mean we worship the sun? Does "Saturday" mean we revere the planet/god Saturn? Is it only Thor worshipers who say "Thursday"? Should we as Christians invent new names for the days and months? Of course not! There is neither intent to worship idols nor veneration of evil spirits in the traditions and trappings of Halloween. Jesus said we are in the world, though not of it. It would be impossible to filter out everything pagan in origin! Only practices that are sinful per se should be rejected. The harmless celebration of Halloween is not, in my opinion, one of them. However, do not judge those whose opinion is different from your own (Romans 14:1).

6. About the principalities and the powers[6]

Do we live in a world haunted by many orders and levels of spiritual beings? Is the spiritual landscape sketched by Frank Perretti[7] accurate—are there demons in every shadow, breathing out sulfurous fumes as they sink their talons into our brains? It would seem unlikely. Ephesians 6 clearly paints a picture of the spiritual battle raging in the cosmos, yet the specifics of how this war is waged are never spelled out. All books and claims to the contrary, our best estimates of how the minions of Satan do their work will remain speculations. It is equally difficult to rank the evil spirits, although the Bible does make it clear that there are several different orders. This discussion is, alas, beyond the scope of this book.[8] Whether the powers are political forces (one view), malignant or neutral spiritual beings (another), or irrelevant because they have been vanquished by the cross (Colossians 2:15) requires further study. Why bring it up, then, if not to offer some definite answer? Because we all need to delve deeper into the Word, ensuring that our views are biblically informed, and not just following the currents of popular opinion.

7. Is just a little dabbling okay?

Is it wrong to dabble in the occult? Is there really anything wrong with "playing" with the dark forces of the cosmos, as long as we are careful? (Is there anything wrong with a little lying, as long as the general course of our life is on track?) Satanism claims millions of followers worldwide. Would it be wrong to attend some of their meetings, in order better to understand the enemy? (See Romans 16:19 if you are confused about the answer.)

The occult is roundly condemned in the Old Testament (Leviticus 19:31, 20:27, 1 Samuel 28) and in the New Testament as well (Acts 19:19, Galatians 5:20, Revelation 21:8). We are not to consult mediums (Isaiah 8:19). In the

Galatians "sin list," witchcraft and idolatry appear smack between the sexual sins and hatred. Yes, it could indeed be deadly to "dabble." Why should we desire to draw near to anything that put Jesus on the cross?

Conclusion

Satan is real; let's keep at a safe distance. On the other hand, there is no virtue in giving credence to silly superstitions and discredited medieval notions allegedly based on the Bible. Christians have all the power of the Spirit, every weapon in the arsenal, the "panoply" (full armor) of God to defeat the evil one. Disciples are the true "ghostbusters." Not that the "ghosts" have any true power—only what we give them when we are willing to let Satan shape our faith rather than molding it through careful Bible study. May the word of God be our light (Psalm 119:105) through the darkness of sin and error.

_____ **NOTES** _____

1. Other reports, like this one in the *St. Louis Star* (1925), are easier to dis- miss:

A large man industriously rubbing the head of a smaller man at Broadway and Market Street attracted the attention of Detective Sergeant Behnken.

"Do you feel relief?" asked the large man. The small man announced that he did not, and in addition demanded help, aid and succor.

"What is this?" inquired Behnken.

"Very simple," said the large man. "This poor fellow has demons. I am taking them out of him."

"Have you got demons?" asked Behnken.

"I have not," said the small man. "This bird grabbed me as I was walking down the street and began to rub my head."

Behnken settled the matter by giving the demon hunter a swift kick. Tim Healey, ed., *Strange But True* (London: Octopus Books, 1983).

2. *Pittsburgh Post-Gazette,* October 15, 1994.

3. E.g., Justin, *2nd Apology,* 6.

4. If you are interested in pursuing the subject, I advise you to obtain a copy of John Clayton's audio lesson "Demonology and Exorcism," available from *Does God Exist?* (17411 Battles Road, South Bend, Indiana 46614).

5. According to research undertaken by David P. Phillips and colleagues at the University of California at San Diego, there is some correlation between be- lief in astrology and health, though not in the way commonly supposed. 28,169 Chinese Americans were tracked against a control group of 412,632 who died in the years 1969-1990. For the group believing that those born under the "earth sign," which the culture

believes is most inauspicious, people died an average 1.6 years earlier than their less superstitious counterparts born under the same sign. In short, these persons expected to die earlier—and they did. (Reported in Birgitte Svennevig, "Tro på astrologi får manniskor att dö tidigare," *Illustrerad Vetenskap* Number 12, 1997 (28/10-10/11).

6. For an intriguing alternative interpretation, see Walter Wink's trilogy: *Naming the Powers: The Language of Power in the New Testament* (Philadelphia: Fortress Press, 1984); *Unmasking the Powers: The Invisible Forces That Determine Human Existence* (Philadelphia: Fortress Press, 1986); and *Engaging the Powers: Discernment and Resistance in a World of Domination* (Minneapolis: Fortress Press, 1992).

7. Frank E. Peretti, *This Present Darkness* (Wheaton, Illinois: Crossway Books, 1986) and *Piercing the Darkness* (Crossway Books: Westchester, Illinois, 1989). In my opinion, these overdone works easily lead Christians into superstition deeper than that which they seek to counter.

8. For one of the more helpful books on the subject, see Billy Graham, *Angels: God's Secret Agents* (London: Hodder and Stoughton, 1986).

Appendix
Where Do I Fit In?

Spiritual Gifts Worksheet

For by the grace given me I say to every one of you: Do not think of yourself more highly than you ought, but rather think of yourself with sober judgment, in accordance with the measure of faith God has given you (Romans 12:3).

(Check the appropriate columns opposite the corresponding gifts.)

Spiritual gift[1] (Top Twelve)	I'm certain that I have this gift. Others say so.	I might have this gift. It's a strength.	No! I probably don't have this one!
Administration			
Artistic Gifts			
Celibacy			
Contentment			
Contributing			
Encouragement			
Evangelist			
Hospitality			
Leadership			
Shepherding			
Showing mercy			
Teaching			
Other[2]			

_____ NOTES _____

1. As the miraculous spiritual gifts are no longer available today, these have been excluded from the list of Chapter 7. For example, no matter how badly you might want it, you cannot be one of the apostles or possess the first-century gift of healing. You can, however, become a missionary (apostles were inspired missionaries) or pray for a healing to take place. All Scripture references may be found in Chapter 7, "Gifts of the Spirit."

2. "Whatever gift" (1 Peter 4:10). The Bible does not rigidly categorize or define the spiritual gifts.

Selected Bibliography

Barclay, William, *Flesh and Spirit*. London: SCM Press, 1962.
————— , *The Promise of Spirit*. London: Epworth Press, 1960.
Beasley-Murray, George R., *Baptism in the New Testament*. Grand Rapids, Michigan: Eerdmans, 1962.
Berçot, David W., *Will the Real Heretics Please Stand Up: A New Look at Today's Evangelical Church in the Light of Early Christianity*. Tyler, Texas: Scroll, 1989.
Bruner, Frederick Dale, *A Theology of the Holy Spirit*. London: Hodder & Stoughton, 1970.
Budgen, Victor, *The Charismatics and the Word of God*. Welwyn, U.K.: Evangelical Press, 1985.
Campbell, Alexander, "Essays on the Work of the Holy Spirit," in *The Christian Messenger and Reformer* (I: 19-24, 50-55, 80-94, 181-188). London: Simpkin, Marshall & Co., 1838.
Carson, D. A., *Exegetical Fallacies, 2nd edition*. Grand Rapids, MI: Baker, 1996.
Chadwick, Henry, *The Early Church*. New York: Penguin, 1981.
Cho, Paul Yonggi, *The Fourth Dimension*. Plainfield, New Jersey: Logos International, 1979.
Clayton, John, *"Demonology and Exorcism,"* (audio lesson). South Bend, Indiana: Does God Exist?, 1978.
Cottrell, Jack. *Baptism: A Biblical Study*. Joplin, Missouri: College Press, 1989.
Dieter, Melvin E., *The Holiness Revival of the Nineteenth Century*. Lanham, Maryland: The Scarecrow Press, 1996.
Dodd, E.R., *The Greeks and the Irrational*. Boston: Bacon Press, 1957.
Dunn, James D. G., *Baptism in the Holy Spirit* (Studies in Biblical Theology, Second Series). London: S.C.M., 1970.
Eerdmans' Handbook to the World's Religions. Grand Rapids, MI: Eerdmans, 1982.
Foster, Scott A., *Speaking in Tongues: A Survey of Biblical Tongues and the Charismatic Movement*. Grove City, Pennsylvania: Covenant Ministries, 1985.
Fox, Robin Lane, *Pagans and Christians*. San Francisco: Harper Collins, 1986.
Friesen, Garry, *Decision Making and the Will of God: A Biblical Alternative to the Traditional View*. Portland, Oregon: Multnomah Press, 1980.
Graham, Billy, *Angels: God's Secret Agents*. London: Hodder and Stoughton, 1986.
————— , *The Holy Spirit*. Waco, Texas: Word Books, 1978.
Green, Michael, *I Believe in the Holy Spirit*. London: Hodder and Stoughton, 1975.
Grudem, Wayne A., *The Gift of Prophecy in 1 Corinthians*. Washington, D.C.: University Press of America, 1982.
Hagin, Kenneth, *You Can Be Led By the Spirit of God*. Tulsa, Oklahoma: Faith Library Publications, 1981.
Hanegraaff, Hank, *Counterfeit Revival: Looking for God in All the Wrong Places*. Dallas: Word Publishing, 1997.

Harrell, David Edwin, Jr., *All Things are Possible: The Healing and Charismatic Revivals in Modern America*. Bloomington: Indiana, University Press, 1975.

Hoekema, Anthony A., *Holy Spirit Baptism*. Exeter: Paternoster Press, 1972.

————— , *What About Tongue Speaking?* Exeter: Paternoster Press, 1966.

Horsley, Richard, *The Liberation of Christmas*. New York: Continuum, 1993.

Jackson, Ralph, *Doctors and Diseases in the Roman Empire*. London: British Museum Press, 1988.

Jefferson, Charles Edward, *Jesus the Same: The Compelling Christ, Yesterday, Today* and Forever. Woburn, Mass.: DPI, 1997. (Original edition 1908.)

Jividen, Jimmy, *Glossolalia: From God or Man?* Fort Worth, Texas: Star Bible Publications, 1971.

————— , *Miracles: From God or Man?* Abilene, Texas: ACU Press, 1987.

Jordan, Michael, *Encyclopedia of Gods: Over 2,500 Deities of the World*. New York: Facts on File, 1993.

Kee, Howard C., *Miracles in the Early Christian World.*, New York: The Edwin Mellon Press, 1984.

Kinnard, G. Steve, *Jesus and the Poor*. Spring, Texas: Illumination Publishers, 2017.

Lewis, C. S., *Miracles: A Preliminary Study*. New York: Macmillan, 1978.

————— , *The Four Loves*. London: HarperCollins, 1977.

MacArthur, John F. Jr., *Charismatic Chaos*. Grand Rapid, MI: Zondervan, 1992.

McGuiggan, Jim, *The Book of 1 Corinthians*. Forth Worth, Texas: Star Bible Publications, 1984.

Metaxas, Eric. *Miracles: What They Are, Why They Happen, and How They Can Change Your Life*. New York: Penguin, 2014.

Miller, Elliot and Kenneth. R. Samples. *The Cult of the Virgin: Catholic Mariology and the Apparitions of Mary*. Grand Rapids, Michigan: Baker Book House, 1992.

Nathan, Rich, "A Response to Charismatic Chaos" (Vineyard Position Paper #5). Anaheim: Vineyard, 1993.

Randi, James, *The Faith Healers*. Buffalo, New York: Prometheus Books, 1987.

Stott, John R. W., *Baptism and Fullness*. London: IVP, 1975.

Wuthnow, Robert, *Christianity in the 21st Century: Reflections on the Challenges Ahead*, New York: Oxford University Press, 1993

————— , *Poor Richard's Principle: Recovering the American Dream Through the Moral Dimension of Work, Business, & Money*. Princeton: Princeton University Press, 1996.

Warfield, Benjamin B., *Counterfeit Miracles*. New York: Charles Scribner's Sons, 1918.

Glossary

Anointing with Oil — A daily custom in biblical times, except in times of mourning or fasting. In connection with miraculous healing, performed in anticipation of a recovery to a state of full health (James 5:14-16).

Aphrodite — The Greek goddess of beauty (Roman: Venus). Her cult was one of many charismatic sects in the first-century Mediterranean world.

Apostle — In the strict sense, an apostle (Greek: apostolos, "sent one") was one of the closest disciples of Jesus (Mark 3:14), an eyewitness of his resurrection (Acts 1:22, 1 Corinthians 9:1), inspired to contribute to Scripture (John 14:26, 16:13) and miraculously empowered (2 Corinthians 12:12). The apostles' teaching has been authoritative ever since Pentecost (Acts 2:42), in fulfillment of Jesus' special promise to the Apostles that he would guide them into all truth. In the broad sense of the word, an apostle is any missionary (Romans 16:7).

Baptism — Transliteration of the Greek word for immersion (*baptisma*).

Blasphemy Against the Spirit — A state of such hardness of heart that one cannot repent and acknowledge the plain truth (Matthew 12:22-32). It is the point of no return.

Charismatic — (Greek: *charisma*, "gift") Exercising the gifts of the Spirit. In the broader sense of the word, "charismatics" seek miracles. They are found in most of the world's religions. In Christendom, it denotes one believing in the presence of the miraculous spiritual gifts. Charismatics are scattered among many denominations (Neopentecostalism), while some denominations are completely charismatic. The modern Charismatic Movement traces its roots to 1900 in Topeka, Kansas. The resurgent influence of the Charismatic Movement began in the US in the 1950s.

Chrysosandaliaimopotichthonia — A Greek divinity: "blood-sucking goddess of the underworld who wears golden sandals." One of the longer Greek words found in the ancient magical papyri!

Demon — A malignant supernatural being, subservient to Satan himself. Possibly a fallen angel.

Dionysus — A Greek nature god, worshiped through sensuality, especially drunkenness (Roman: Bacchus).

Ecstasy — (Greek: *ekstasis*, "being put out of place") Exalted state of feeling, rapture; trance; poetic frenzy. In ecstasy, one "loses himself," relying more on the emotional than on the intellectual faculties.

Exorcism — The expulsion of a demon (e.g. from a person) by the invocation of a holy name. Claims of exorcism have been made for thousands of years, most of which have no connection with Christendom.

Filled with the Spirit — Spiritual; controlled by the Spirit, especially with reference to boldness or evangelism; putting the word of God into one's life. It is possible to not be completely filled with the spirit and yet be saved—the implication of Acts 6:3. In

Neopentecostal lingo, it means having received "the baptism of the Holy Spirit," or being in tune with the "leading" of the Spirit.

Fleecing — Gideon put out a fleece, testing God's faithfulness (Judges 6:36ff). In charismatic terminology "fleecing" is asking God to use an event to point to his will in order to provide guidance for a decision, usually asking for a "yes" or "no" answer. The "fleece" is usually unrelated to the decision.

Glossolalia — (Greek *glossa,* "tongue" + *lalia,* "speech.") The technical term for speaking in tongues. With the exception of first-century biblical tongues, *glossolalia* is a psychological phenomenon, technically classified as gibberish.

Hermes — A Greek god whose worshipers constituted one of many charismatic sects in the Mediterranean world of the Roman Empire (Roman: Mercury).

Holy Ghost — The Holy Spirit, in the Elizabethan language of the King James Version (1611).

Holy Spirit — The active personal presence and agency of God; the third person of the trinity.

Indwelling — The presence of the Holy Spirit in our hearts; the internal reception of the Spirit.

Miracle — Marvelous event due to supernatural agency; a contravening of the laws of nature; anything that lies outside the normal sphere of cause and effect in the physical world, especially an action by God to give his approval to a message or the speaker of the message. Sometimes the Bible calls seemingly "natural" events "miracles" (Job 5:9-15).

Montanism — Mid-second-century (Phrygian) charismatic sect founded by Montanus; denounced by the church.

Mormonism — A nineteenth-century American religious sect, which believes *The Book of Mormon* (1827), the King James Bible, *The Doctrine and Covenants,* and *The Pearl of Great Price* to be inspired scripture. Mormonism practices prophesying and tonguespeaking, and even has "apostles," thus they are the most consistent "charismatic" group today.

Mystical — Esoteric, mysterious and awe-inspiring; believing that through contemplation or meditation one can obtain absorption into the Deity; affirming the spiritual apprehension of truths beyond rationality.

Neopentecostalism — Contemporary charismatic religion, Pentecostal in theology, prevalent in most denominations. The movement in which Pentecostal teachings and practices have spilled over into non-Pentecostal churches.

Objectivity — Understanding of actual facts without emotional or personal bias; ability to see issues in focus, from the viewpoint of others, or as they really are.

Pentecost — A Jewish festival, the fiftieth day after the second day of Passover (Leviticus 23:15-16), when the Spirit was poured out, the church began, the prophecy of Joel was fulfilled and the Christian age was inaugurated.

Praying in the Spirit — (Ephesians 6:18, Jude 20) Interpreted by Neopentecostals to be "praying in tongues." Biblically the phrase indicates powerful, specific, spiritual prayer in expectation of God's hearing the request.

Prophecy — (Greek: pro, "for" or "before" + phemi, "speak") Speaking on behalf of God, or speaking before (an event). Prophecy is almost always directed to the generation contemporary with the prophet. Not to be confused with prophesy, to exercise a prophetic gift. (Note: the verb is spelled with an 's,' the noun with a 'c.')

Prophet — One who speaks for God, sometimes in advance of an event.

Psychosomatic — Connecting mind and body; caused or aggravated by mental stress.

Scripture — The written word of God, as opposed to the spoken word.

Second Blessing — In charismatic terminology, the "baptism of the Holy Spirit," which brings additional gifts that do not come at conversion.

Shaman — A priest or witch doctor of class, claiming to have privileged contacts with the gods or spirits.

Shinto — The native religion of Japan. There is a charismatic element in Shinto.

Sign — A miraculous event whose meaning is to be found in that to which it points (e.g. Jesus did not perform miracles simply to impress; God worked signs through Jesus to point to his purposes and will and to accredit Jesus to the Jewish people and to the world—see Acts 2:22).

Singing in the Spirit — In charismatic lingo, "singing in tongues." Biblical singing in the Spirit is spiritual singing, or singing which focuses on or incorporates the word of God.

Slaying in the Spirit — In charismatic jargon, being knocked to the ground by the "power" of the Spirit. May be accompanied by miraculous healing.

Spirit — The animating or vital principle of man; the intelligent or immaterial part of man. "The Spirit" is the Holy Spirit. A prophetic message may also be referred to as a "spirit" (2 Thessalonians 2:2).

Sufis — Muslim charismatic mystics.

Testing the Spirits — Weighing prophetic messages. In charismatic thought, the supernatural ability to discern whether a person, message or event is from Satan or from God.

Vision — A glimpse, view, panorama or apprehension of spiritual truth or reality, or of a future state of events. Visions may come by day (in a trance) or by night (in a dream). "Vision" and "dream" are synonyms and are the standard means by which God communicated with the prophets (Numbers 12:6).

Witch Doctor — A tribal priest or magician.

www.ipibooks.com